COMPUTATIONAL INTELLIGENCE APPLICATIONS IN SMART GRIDS

Enabling Methodologies for Proactive and Self-Organizing Power Systems

COMPUTATIONAL INTELLIGENCE APPLICATIONS IN SMART GRIDS

Enabling Methodologies for Proactive and Self-Organizing Power Systems

Editors

Ahmed F Zobaa
Brunel University, UK

Alfredo Vaccaro
University of Sannio, Italy

ICP

Imperial College Press

Published by

Imperial College Press
57 Shelton Street
Covent Garden
London WC2H 9HE

Distributed by

World Scientific Publishing Co. Pte. Ltd.
5 Toh Tuck Link, Singapore 596224
USA office: 27 Warren Street, Suite 401-402, Hackensack, NJ 07601
UK office: 57 Shelton Street, Covent Garden, London WC2H 9HE

Library of Congress Cataloging-in-Publication Data
Zobaa, Ahmed F.
Computational intelligence applications in smart grids : enabling methodologies for proactive and self organizing power systems / Ahmed F Zobaa, Brunel University, UK, Alfredo Vaccaro, University of Sannio, Italy.
pages cm
Includes bibliographical references and index.
ISBN 978-1-78326-587-9 (hardcover : alk. paper)
1. Smart power grids. 2. Computational intelligence. I. Vaccaro, Alfredo. II. Title.
TK3105.Z63 2015
006.3--dc23

2014039079

British Library Cataloguing-in-Publication Data
A catalogue record for this book is available from the British Library.

Typeset by Stallion Press
Email: enquiries@stallionpress.com

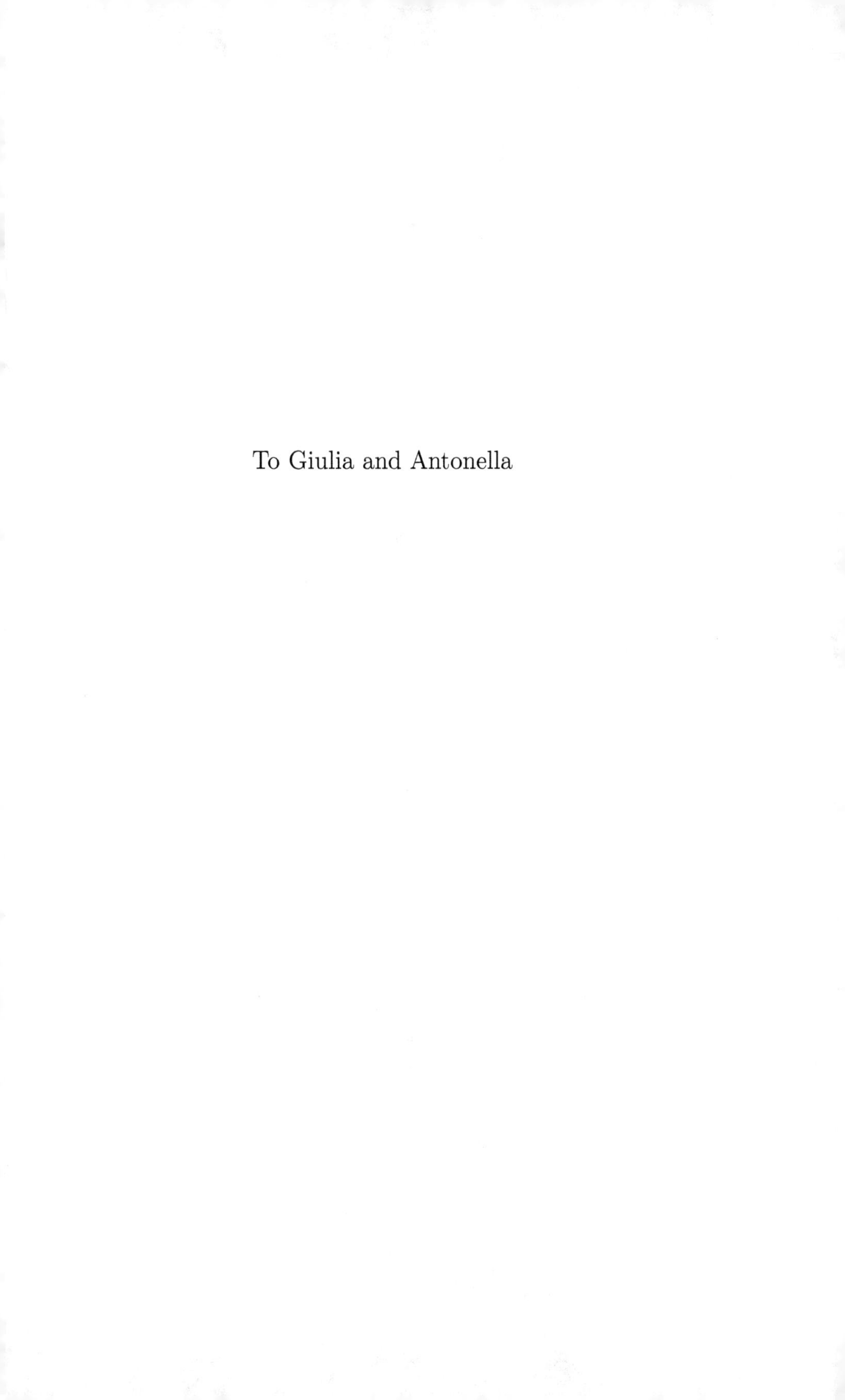

To Giulia and Antonella

Preface

The large-scale deployment of the smart grid (SG) paradigm could play a strategic role in supporting the evolution of conventional electrical grids toward active, flexible and self-healing web energy networks composed of distributed and cooperative energy resources. From a conceptual point of view, the SG is the convergence of information and operational technologies applied to the electric grid, providing sustainable options to customers and improved security. Advances in research on SGs could increase the efficiency of modern electrical power systems by: (i) supporting the massive penetration of small-scale distributed and dispersed generators; (ii) facilitating the integration of pervasive synchronized metering systems; (iii) improving the interaction and cooperation between the network components; and (iv) allowing the wider deployment of self-healing and proactive control/protection paradigms.

However, several studies have highlighted open problems and ongoing technological and methodological challenges that must be addressed for the full exploitation of these benefits to be possible.

SG technologies include advanced sensing systems, two-way high-speed communications, monitoring and enterprise analysis software and related services for collecting location-specific and real-time actionable data, in order to provide enhanced services for both system operators (i.e. distribution automation, asset management, advanced metering infrastructure) and end-users (i.e. demand side management, demand response). The cornerstone of these technologies is the ability for multiple entities (e.g. devices or software processes) to manage accurate and heterogeneous information. It follows that the development of reliable and flexible distributed measurement systems represents a crucial issue in both structuring and operating smart networks.

To address this complex issue, Chapter 1 analyzes the strategic role of wide-area monitoring, protection and control (WAMPAC). WAMPAC involves the use of system-wide information to avoid large disturbances and reduce the probability of catastrophic events by supporting the application of adaptive protection and control strategies aimed at increasing the network capacity and minimizing wide-area disturbances. The adoption of accurate phasor and frequency information from multiple synchronized devices installed at various power system locations allows WAMPAC to monitor power flows in interconnected areas and/or heavily loaded lines and offers the opportunity to reliably operate the SG closer to its stability limits. Additionally, these systems can monitor the dynamic behavior of the power system and identify inter-area oscillations in real-time. The ability to detect and reduce inter-area oscillations could allow the system operator to exploit transmission and generation capacity more efficiently. As a result, renewable power generators can be used more effectively, and the marginal cost of power generation can be reduced.

Effective WAMPAC operation requires intensive numerical analysis aimed at studying and improving power system security and reliability. To achieve this aim, the streams of data acquired by the field sensors, (i.e. phasor measurement units), should be effectively processed in order to provide SG operators with the necessary information for better understanding and reducing the impact of perturbations. For large-scale networks, this process requires massive data processing and complex and NP-hard problem solutions in computation times that should be fast enough for the information to be useful in a short-term operation horizon. In solving this challenging issue, the development of advanced computing paradigms based on metaheuristic and bio-inspired algorithms could play a strategic role in supporting rapid power systems analysis in a data-rich, but information-limited, environment.

Armed with such a vision, Chapter 2 proposes an advanced optimization algorithm integrating both soft and hard computing techniques for optimal network reconfiguration in smart distribution systems. The proposed computing paradigm can be easily integrated in conventional processing architectures since it is based on pieces of information usually available at a control center and relies on common actuators. For the same reason, it is expected to be easily implementable in the extended real-time framework of power system distribution operation. These features are particularly useful in SGs where the constant growth of interactive software processes (i.e. WAMPAC, energy management systems, distribution management systems, demand side managements systems) will raise the interdependency between distributed processing systems. For these systems, data heterogeneity, a non-issue in traditional electricity distribution systems, must be addressed since data growth over time is unlikely to scale with the same hardware and software base. Manageability also becomes of paramount importance, since SGs could integrate hundreds or even thousands of field sensors. Thus, even in the presence of fast models aimed at converting the data into information, the SG operator must face the challenge of not having a full understanding of the context of the information and, consequently, that the information content cannot be used with any degree of confidence.

To address this problem, Chapter 3 analyzes the important role of metaheuristic optimization for solving multi-objective programming problems in SG. Four different evolutionary algorithms have been proposed to solve a complex SG operation problem, namely the economic emission dispatch problem of thermal power generators by considering the simultaneous minimization of cost, NOx (mono-nitrogen oxide) emission and active losses. The main idea is to deploy a non-dominated sorting technique along with a crowded distance ranking to find and manage the Pareto optimal front. The obtained results show that, compared to traditional optimization methods, the adoption of evolutionary computing exhibits several intrinsic advantages making them an ideal candidate for solving complex optimization problems in SGs.

This conclusion has been confirmed in Chapter 4, where a case-based reasoning system for voltage security assessment and optimal load-shedding scheme is described. This is a complex issue in SG operation control, since voltage collapse can occur suddenly and there may not be sufficient time for analysis of system operating condition and operator actions to stabilize the system. In such emergencies, load shedding is the most effective and practical way to mitigate the voltage collapse. Therefore, after voltage security assessment, providing a real-time optimal load-shedding plan for insecure operating states can help the SG operators to avoid the voltage collapse. Solving this problem in near real-time is still a challenging task. In this context there is a need for fast detection of the potentially dangerous situations of voltage instability so that necessary corrective actions can be taken to avoid voltage collapse. To face this problem, the application of decision support systems based on artificial intelligence represents a very promising research direction.

Chapter 5 addresses another challenging task in SGs control and monitoring, namely the deployment of fast and reliable state estimation procedures. To solve this problem, iterative numerical algorithms based on iterative numerical techniques have traditionally been deployed. These solution paradigms usually work quite well in the presence of well-conditioned power system equations but they could become unstable or divergent in the presence of critical operating points. A manifestation of this numerical instability is an ill-conditioned set of linear equations that should be solved at each iteration. To try and overcome these limitations, this chapter conceptualizes two solution paradigms based on the dynamic systems theory. The challenging idea is to formulate the state estimation equations by a set of ordinary differential equations, whose equilibrium points represent the problem solutions. Starting from the Lyapunov theory it will be rigorously demonstrated that this artificial dynamic model can be designed to be asymptotically stable and exponentially converges to the state estimation solution.

The experimental deployment of the solution strategies discussed in these chapters requires the definition of advanced control architectures aimed at acquiring and processing all the power system measurements. A debate on the requirements of these architectures in the context of the modern SGs has been recently undertaken in the power systems research community. In particular, it is expected that the large-scale deployment of the SGs paradigm will massively increase the data exchange rate leading centralized control architectures to become rapidly saturated. Consequently, the streams of data acquired by distributed grid sensors may not provide system operators with the necessary information to act on in appropriate timeframes. To address this issue, SGs researchers are reviewing the design criteria and assumptions concerning the scalability, reliability, heterogeneity and manageability of SG control architectures. These research works conjecture that the hierarchical control paradigm would be not affordable in addressing the increasing network complexity and the massive pervasion of distributed generators characterizing modern SGs. In this context, the research for distributed multi-agent optimization paradigms has been identified as the most promising enabling technology. This is mainly due to the successful application of decentralized and cooperative agent networks in enhancing operational effectiveness of complex systems. Armed with such a vision, Chapter 6 outlines the important role played by multi-agent systems equipped with a novel fuzzy inference engine, named timed automata based fuzzy controller, in solving the optimal voltage regulation problem in the presence of a massive pervasion of distribution generation systems. As shown in the experiments, the proposed strategy results in an effective and suitable method for solving voltage regulation problem in SGs by improving the grid voltage profile and reducing power losses. It is expected that this multi-agent-based solution strategy will exhibit several advantages over traditional client server-based paradigms, including less network bandwidth use, less computation time, and ease of extension and reconfiguration.

The cornerstone of multi-agent frameworks is the ability for multiple entities (e.g. devices or software processes) to interact via communication networks. It follows that the development of a reliable and pervasive communication infrastructure represents a crucial issue in both structuring and operating the SG. A strategic requirement in supporting this process is the development of a reliable communications backbone, establishing robust data transport wide-area networks (WANs) to the distribution feeder and customer level. Existing electrical utility WANs are based on a hybrid mix of technologies including fiber optics, power line carrier systems, copper-wire line, and a variety of wireless technologies. They are designed to support a wide range of applications as far as SCADA/EMS (supervisory control and data acquisition/energy management system), generating plant automation, distribution feeder automation and physical security are concerned. As outlined in Chapter 7, these communication infrastructures should evolve toward nearly ubiquitous transport networks able to handle traditional utility power delivery applications along with vast amounts of new data from the SG. These networks should be scalable in order to support the new and future sets of functions characterizing the emerging SGs technological platform, and highly pervasive in order to support the deployment of last-mile communications (i.e. from a backbone node to the customer locations).

Table of Contents

Chapter 1

Wide-Area Monitoring, Protection and Control Needs, Applications, and Benefits

Vahid Madani[a], Damir Novosel[b] and Roger King[c]

[a]*Pacific Gas and Electric Company (PG&E), Oakland, USA*
[b]*Technology Division, Quanta Technology, Raleigh, USA*
[c]*Department of Electrical and Computer Engineering, Mississippi State University, Starkville, USA*

1.1 Introduction

Electrical grids are, in general, among the most reliable systems in the world. These large interconnected systems, however, are subject to a host of challenges: aging infrastructure, need for siting new generation near load centers, transmission expansion to meet growing demand, distributed resources, dynamic reactive compensation, congestion management, grid ownership versus system operation, reliability coordination, etc. Some of the major challenges facing the electric industry today include balancing resource adequacy, reliability, economics, environmental concerns, and other public purpose objectives to optimize transmission and distribution resources to meet the growing demand and avoid large power system blackouts.

Power system blackouts result in complete interruption of electricity supply to all consumers in a large area. While it may be possible to trace initiation of a blackout to a single incident (e.g. a transmission line sagging into a tree), cascading outages are the result of multiple low-probability events occurring in an unanticipated or unintended sequence. The likelihood of power system disturbances escalating into a large-scale cascading outage increases when the grid is already under stress due to certain preconditions, such as transmission system congestion, aging infrastructure, scheduled or uncoordinated maintenance, and sub-optimal operating practices, to name a few. In other words, blackouts are the result of how we manage the grid. Statistically, a sequence of low-probability contingencies with complex interactions causing a blackout may not happen often, but will eventually take place unless measures are taken to arrest the system. Presently, some of the grids around the world may be susceptible to large-scale blackouts with impacts as large as 30% of a nation (e.g. the 2012 Indian blackout that affected over 620 million people, the 2009 Brazil and Paraguay blackouts impacting 87 million) as aging and insufficient grid infrastructure may not be adequate to accommodate grid changes, such as renewable generation resources and load growth. Deployment of "Smart Grid" monitoring, control and protection devices, software tools, and telecommunication infrastructure helps better manage the grid, but does not replace investments in the infrastructure.

Wide-area monitoring, protection and control (WAMPAC) systems, including situational awareness tools and system integrity protection schemes (SIPS), are important for meeting the challenges of the electrical grid in the 21st century. In addition to the infrastructure investments including flexible AC transmission systems (FACTS), the application of technologies such as synchronized measurements is instrumental in managing grid reliability and asset management. Data analysis, model validation, instability detection, reactive power management, restoration, harmonic analysis, fast transients, and ring-down phenomenon during major equipment loss and protection equipment failures are some of the benefits offered by implementation of the technology that have made business case deployment feasible.

1.2 Grid Development History

In the 1930s, electrical power was delivered to consumers around the world by individual, not-connected electrical systems. Regional systems were created to make power systems more robust and delivery more reliable. The original function of the interconnected systems was to form the backbone for the security of supply and to reach the required high reliability level at reasonable costs. In the 1950s, power system professionals foresaw the importance of further improving delivery of reliable electricity to consumers. The grid systems have been developed to ensure mutual assistance (for example, occasional voltage support) between transmission system participants and/or national subsystems, including common use of reserve capacities to optimize the use of energy resources by allowing exchanges between the systems.

Thus, a strategy of interconnecting neighboring systems to improve reliability and security margins became a reality around the world. Coordinated rules for the mutual support of interconnected systems were defined and adopted by the power pool members between power systems, including interconnections among countries (e.g. UCTE in Europe). Since the late 1970s, the electrical transnational infrastructures have been exploited more and more for energy exchanges that take advantage of the different production costs of electricity in the various nations or interconnected grids in order to deliver lower cost energy, lower the infrastructure investment cost, and achieve maximum profits. However, the bulk power system was not originally engineered to transfer large amounts of power between neighboring systems over long ranges, but to enable neighboring utilities to support each other during stressed conditions.

The high level of power exchanges in today's deregulated energy market is technically being provided outside of the scope of the original system design. The higher demand, coupled by low-level investments in technology, infrastructure upgrades, and capacity increase have led the control area operators to run the system close to the edge (i.e. as close to the limits as permitted by the reliability criteria and, sometimes, beyond the limits). At the same time, the increased respect and awareness for the environment and the "not in my backyard" sentiments of individuals have made it difficult to site transmission lines or major local generation sources, especially in the more densely populated areas, where energy demand is high. These difficulties make system expansions expensive and difficult, and offer new challenges in the delivery of reliable power.

The complexity of the power system, coupled with many major outages worldwide, has alerted policy makers and the industry that technological deployments are required while traditional infrastructure investments continue. In recent years, major investments have been made worldwide in "smart grid" technologies (e.g. the US DOE (Department of Energy) investment grants to enhance situational awareness and automated controls using GPS-based synchronized measurement technology).

There are still isolated power systems around the world (e.g. island networks). Unlike interconnected grids, those power systems do not have flexibility to get help from the neighboring systems to optimally balance generation and load, both during normal and stressed conditions. Those systems are more vulnerable to generation and transmission system outage and require long-term, coordinated planning and investments in the complete electrical grid infrastructure to achieve reliable and cost-effective grid operation and maintenance. As the grid has evolved, there has been a corresponding need to deploy appropriate technologies to manage it. Figure 1.1 shows the time scale of physical phenomena/events and accompanying methodologies and tools for grid management.

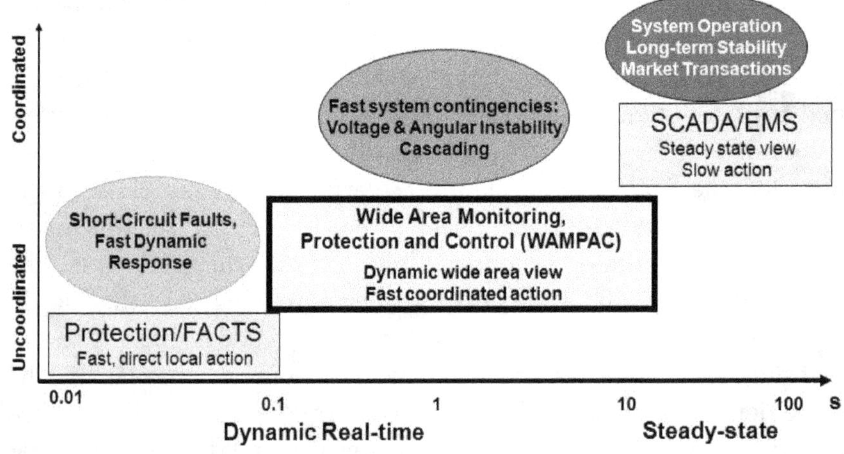

Figure 1.1. Event and solution time scale.

In the past, coordinated actions focused on steady-state events, while dynamic, fast events have been managed by automated actions that did not have information on overall system behavior. That resulted in developing new solutions that would address faster dynamic phenomena while still having a system view. Resulting WAMPAC solutions include SIPS and, recently, hardware and software products using GPS-based synchronized measurement technologies.

1.2.1 *Blackout prevention*

Within the last decade, the number of wide-area outages has rapidly increased (blackouts in India, the northeastern US and Canada, Western Electricity Coordinating Council (WECC) US, Brazil, Italy, Sweden, Denmark, England, Croatia, India, Australia, New Zealand, Greece, etc.), affecting a billion people worldwide. One can observe that the increased likelihood of low-probability events escalating into a cascading outage increases when the grid is already under stress due to pre-existing conditions.

Wide-area electrical blackouts have raised many questions about the specifics of such events and the vulnerability of interconnected power systems [1–4]. Power systems are complex interconnected machines with many components operating in harmony when the system is balanced. When a problem occurs in part of the system, the impact of the trouble may cause the system to lose its balance momentarily. In most cases, the system is immediately isolated and shortly after recovers with no further propagation observed outside of the immediate area.

Although widespread outages cannot be completely prevented, their occurrence can be reduced, and propagation (size) and consequences arrested and restoration sped up. In the last 20 years power systems around the world have been more stressed as the capacity reserves and system margins have been reduced, resulting in higher susceptibility to blackouts.

Exchange of information stemming from the recent worldwide blackouts findings and "smart grid" technology innovations shed new light on the current conditions and needs of power systems. Examination of the root causes and the resulting effects on neighboring systems, and implementation of proven solutions to help prevent propagation of such large-scale events should help us design and operate reliable "smart grid" and power delivery infrastructures for today and into the future. Power system professionals can take into consideration the costly lessons of the past, maintain a library of historical lessons about "what and why it happened" for the generations to come, and act as catalysts to achieve desired levels of power system reliability.

The high cost and the need for extensive mitigation strategies against grid congestions, combined with this type of probabilistic assessment, have led to risk management not focusing on appropriate, cost-effective mitigation actions. Understanding the complexities of the interconnected power grid and the need for proper planning, good maintenance, and sound operating practices is the key to delivering electric power to modern day consumers and to preventing the problems of tomorrow's grids.

As a consequence of major blackouts worldwide in the last two decades, utilities have hardened their electrical systems and regulatory organizations (e.g. the North American Reliability Corporation [NERC] and the Federal Energy Regulatory Commission [FERC] and state regulators in the US) have focused on defining and enforcing reliability standards. This focus has resulted in a better planned, operated, and maintained grid. However, one of the challenges facing the electric industry today is the balance of reliability, economics, environmental, and other public-purpose objectives, in order to optimize transmission and distribution of resources and thus meet the demand. Resources and transmission adequacy are necessary components of a reliable and economical supply. Though the reliability and market economics are driven by different policies and incentives, they cannot be separated when the objective is reliability and availability. Today, grid planning in the regional and inter-regional environment faces an extremely difficult task, given the challenge of achieving resource adequacy in today's restructured industry, where market economics, local concerns, and renewable energy resources often drive the decision for generation facility siting remote from major load centers. Equally difficult is planning for an adequate transmission system when the location of future generation facilities is uncertain and the lead-time for transmission construction is very long (permitting process alone may take several years).

It is more important than ever to find ways to project transmission and distribution growth, solutions to deploy, and criteria to be applied to guide prudent investment decisions. Some of the key areas to address are:

- Integration of renewable energy. As renewable resources (e.g. wind and solar) are located far from the load centers, additional stress is put on the system, causing higher vulnerability to outages.
- Price for reliability. Costs and risks transmission that owners and customers are willing to assume. The power industry is accustomed to optimizing investments and evaluating return on investments based primarily on financial aspects of trading energy and serving load within certain reliability criteria. This is often done without considering financial aspects of unavailable energy (undue service interruptions) due to low reliability and slow restoration that incurs significant costs to the society. This is an incomplete financial model that results in sub-optimal investment strategies.
- Large regional geographic areas should be included in the scope of transmission planning and decision making. However, when assets need to be built, it is not easy to identify true beneficiaries and how costs are to be shared.
- Quick restoration. As it may not be possible to completely avoid outages, it is necessary to reduce power restoration time with today's technology.

Electricity is the key resource for our society; however, strategic planning (regional and national) requires additional priorities to improve system reliability.

1.2.2 *Preconditions for outages*

Although there is a tendency to point to one or two significant events as the main reasons for triggering cascading outages, major blackouts are typically caused by a sequence of multiple low-probability contingencies with complex interactions. The three "Ts" — trees, tools, and training — have been identified as the leading focus areas to prevent widespread outages not caused by natural events. However, disturbances have occurred following extremely low-probability successive unscheduled equipment outages beyond planning criteria. There have also been cases of system disturbances caused by scheduled equipment outages when the electrical system has not been adjusted for continued safe operation, prior to the equipment being removed. Low-probability sequential outages are also not anticipated by system operators, thus rendering the power system more susceptible to wide-area blackouts. As the chain of events at various locations in the interconnected grid unfolds, operators cannot act quickly enough to mitigate the fast-developing disturbances.

Power systems are engineered to allow for reliable power delivery in the absence of one, two or more major pieces of equipment such as lines, transformers, or bulk generation, commonly referred to as contingency conditions. For example, after the 2003 blackout in northeastern US, the NERC set forth the reliability standards and performance requirements, which are enforced by audits. However, the complexity of the grid operation makes it difficult to study the permutation of contingency conditions that would lead to perfect reliability at reasonable cost. An accurate sequence of events is difficult to predict, as there is practically an infinite number of operating contingencies. Preconditions and factors influencing blackouts include:

- Congested grid with tight operating margins. Not building lines or generation as fast as required. Having wholesale merchant transactions with scheduled transactions without allowing for transmission relief when required.
- Insufficient reactive support where and when required to maintain required voltage levels.
- Uncoordinated planning between transmission and generation. Inadequate system reserve, such as generation spinning reserve.
- Inadequate planning/operation studies. No routine use of an effective contingency analysis tool and uncoordinated inter-regional transmission planning.

- Regulatory uncertainty, including renewable portfolio standards enforcement.
- Aging infrastructure, prone to failures, accompanied by insufficient level of investment in maintaining the grid. It is more and more difficult to isolate and remove equipment for maintenance.
- Lack of system and component knowledge.
- Inadequate right-of-way maintenance or environmental policies versus right-of-way vegetation management.
- Weather (high temperatures; wind, thunderstorm, fog, etc.)
- Inadequate automatic monitoring, protection, and control systems.

In general, a combination of various factors makes power systems more susceptible to disturbances.

1.2.3 *Blackout examples*

History has shown that both unscheduled and scheduled outages have affected power systems' balanced operation, hence signifying the grid complexity during managed conditions [1, 2, 10–12]. All the aforementioned blackouts have included a combination of phenomena such as line overloads, voltage and angular instability, and system separation. The recent blackouts have served as catalysts in propelling the power industry towards analyzing blackouts and finding solutions to prevent such occurrences. A comprehensive analysis of blackouts is described in an *IEEE Spectrum* article [13].

Following are some recent examples of wide-area blackouts with some key findings:

San Diego blackout, western US and Mexico, 8 September 2011

Key weaknesses and need for improvements are identified in operations planning and real-time situational awareness. Additional improvements are in the following areas:

- Need for system studies to determine impact of sub-100 kV facilities parallel to the extra high voltage system (EHV).
- Failure to recognize interconnection reliability operating limits (IROLs).

- Comprehensive study and coordination effects of protection systems and remedial action schemes (RAS) during contingency scenarios.
- Need for effective operator tools and instructions for reclosing lines with large phase angle differences.

India blackout, 30 July 2012 (Source: Report from the Enquiry Committee on Grid Disturbances in Northern Region)

Key weaknesses and need for improvements are identified in the following areas:

- Better visualization and planning of the corrective actions.
- Deployment of WAMPAC systems.
- Better regulation of interchanges.
- Better coordinated planning of outages of state and regional networks, specifically under depleted condition of the inter-regional power transfer corridors.
- Mandatory activation of primary frequency response of governors.
- Adequate reactive power compensation, specifically dynamic.
- Under-frequency and df/dt-based load shedding.
- Avoid miss-operation of protective relays.

Recommendations in both of these recent outages include deployment of wide-area monitoring technology. This is consistent with recommendations after large system disturbances in the US (August 2003) and in Europe (November 2006). Excerpts from outage reports with recommendations related to wide-area monitoring are shown below:

Northeastern US outage, 14 August 2003 (Source: US–Canada Power System Outage Task Force Report)

"A valuable lesson is the importance of having time-synchronized system data recorders. The Task Force's investigators labored over thousands of data items to determine the sequence of events, much like putting together small pieces of a very large puzzle. That process would have been significantly faster and easier if there had been wider use of synchronized data recording devices..." [30]

"*Recommendation 12a* — The reliability regions, coordinated through the NERC planning committee, shall within one year define regional criteria for application of synchronized recording devices in power plants and substations..." [30]

European blackout, 4 November 2006 (Source: UCTE Final Report)

"... On November 4, this was true more than ever — the information about the split of the system into three areas was available to some operators with significant delay. This issue might be solved via a dedicated central server collecting the real-time data and making them available to all UCTE TSOs [transmission system operators]. In this way, each TSO will obtain within a few minutes essential information about disturbances beyond their own control area."

"*Recommendation 4* — UCTE has to set up an information platform allowing TSOs to observe in real time the actual state of the whole UCTE system in order to quickly react during large disturbances."

In conclusion, real-time situational awareness using synchronized measurement technologies have been highlighted in each of the large-scale blackouts worldwide [13].

1.2.4 *Blackout prevention*

It is the cascading events that cause disturbances to propagate and turn into blackouts. The system is stressed, and as system and equipment faults occur the chain of events starts. For example, some generators and/or lines are out for maintenance and a line trips due to a fault. Other lines get overloaded and another line comes in contact with a tree and trips. There is a hidden failure in the protection system (e.g. outdated settings or hardware failures) that causes another line or generator to trip. At that stage, the power system is faced with overloaded equipment, voltage instability, transient instability, and/or small signal instability. If fast actions (e.g. load shedding or system separation) are not taken, the system cascades into a blackout.

Generally, disturbance propagation involves a combination of several phenomena:

- Equipment tripping due to faults or overloads (e.g. transmission lines and transformers). These events may cause other equipment to become overloaded, creating a cascading event contributing further to system-wide outages.
- Power system islanding (frequency instability) when a power system separates. Islands are formed, with an imbalance between generation and load, causing the frequency to deviate from the nominal value, leading to additional equipment tripping.
- Loss of synchronous operation among generators (angular or out-of-step instability) and small signal instability that may cause self-exciting inter-area oscillations if not damped.
- Voltage instability/collapse problems that usually occur when the power transfer is increased and voltage support is inadequate because local resources have been displaced by remote resources without the proper installation of needed transmission lines or voltage support devices in the "right" locations.

Deployment of a well-coordinated overall defense plan to prevent blackouts requires implementation and coordination of various schemes and actions, spanning different time periods. When events can be controlled to result in gradual shutdown of the available resources rather than permitting them to cascade, their impact could be minimized. A practical approach to identifying stressed system conditions, which are symptomatic of cascading, is feasible. This can be done by defining and modeling the power system parameters considered for reliable operation such as voltage, frequency, or phase angle at critical locations. Such findings can then be implemented through investments in hardware equipment and software tools that help manage the grid more effectively.

Weakening or splitting the grid on purpose during normal operation is not a sound alternative, as this strategy would make a full circle for the grid. For example, by operating the power grid in separate islands one could easily weaken the power system. That would effectively mean coming back to the original design of the small grid with low capacity. Separating the grid into islands would also impact deregulation (e.g. each distributed generator would be selling power to its own neighborhood). The small utility will soon need occasional support for reserve margin, voltage and reactive margins from neighboring systems. Hence, back to the interconnected grid. The solution is not to separate the grid into islands, but rather to resolve transmission problems to mitigate potential for wide-spread cascading outages.

The effective way to minimize disturbance propagation is to understand truly the common causes and design the appropriate solutions. The system needs to be addressed as a whole, implementing various planning, operations, maintenance, and regulatory measures in a coordinated way. A possibility to prevent propagation of the disturbance throughout an interconnected grid, but not weaken the grid during normal operation, is to design the interconnected power system to allow for intentional separation into stable islands or interrupt small amounts of load only when the system experiences major disturbances. As operators may not be able to act fast enough to take into account all data related to the on-line state of the system, separation actions should be done automatically. SIPS are wide-area automatic schemes that are designed to detect abnormal system conditions and initiate pre-planned automatic and corrective actions based on system studies [6–9]. They are also referred to as special protection schemes (SPS) or RAS. They detect abnormal wide-area system conditions and trigger automatic actions to restore acceptable system performance. The initiating factor in implementing a significant number of SIPS in the western part of the US (WECC) has been improved protection of the system against multiple contingencies, particularly after the 1994 and 1996 blackouts [12]. Designing the grid with appropriate measures for voltage control and advance warning systems such as wide-area protection and control would allow for both strong interconnected grids during normal operation (to make the system more reliable and secure) and creation of predetermined islands only when necessary.

In conclusion, instead of weakening the grid, the power industry needs to address deregulation as one important aspect in understanding the underlying causes of system-wide outages. The bulk power system was often not originally designed to transfer large amounts of power between neighboring systems. Individual power systems were interconnected to improve electrical network reliability by enabling neighboring utilities to support each other during stressed conditions.

Finally, the recent large-scale generation trips and remedial action responses have provided some very good benchmarks for combined small- and large-scale analysis. Re-examination of traditional planning, operating, system design, protection applications and device settings will help improve system response to slow or limit the spread of cascading outages. The frequency and varying impact levels of recent worldwide blackouts have provided the power industry with opportunities and supporting information to:

- Study the complex power system phenomenon to minimize propagation for future system-wide events using accurate and user-friendly tools.
- Validate the system studies against actual power system performance and governor modeling data.
- Ascertain the environmental and political factors limiting the addition of new generation and transmission capabilities, which highlight the needed support for regulatory measures to ease grid expansions, grid reinforcements, and well-established and measured reliability enforcement process.
- Enforce reliability requirements, for example the Planning Standards for Normal and Emergency Conditions. Operating capacity reserves and margins for transmission flows must remain available to allow system adjustments during unintended multiple contingency conditions.
- Design and set protection and control schemes that do not misoperate during major disturbance conditions, and perform protection coordination studies across regions and in coordination with equipment control and protection.
- Visit existing operating practices and real-time data exchange policies amongst control areas.

- Make use of enhanced maintenance practices and asset management tools.
- Deploy WAMPAC systems using synchronized measurements to improve grid visibility and SIPS to prevent spreading of the disturbance in a timely manner.
- Engineer computational and analysis tools to ease understanding and analyzing system performance for real-time, contingency-based analysis, as well as for post-event analysis.

Some key opportunities for improvement include coordinated adaptive protection and control systems and wide-area monitoring with advance warning systems, as elements of WAMPAC. The advanced technology today promotes the concept of the "smart grid": an integrated, electronically controlled power system that will offer unprecedented flexibility and functionality, and improve system reliability. The concept of the smart power delivery system includes automated capabilities to recognize problems, find solutions, and optimize the performance of the system.

1.3 System Integrity Protection Schemes

Examples of large blackouts in the past decade have shown that the risk of large blackouts is no longer acceptable and can lead to very large and unexpected social and financial consequences. A reduction in the risk of large system-wide disturbances and blackouts requires that system protection function be approached with the assistance of modern technologies in support of preserving system integrity under adverse conditions.

These schemes, defined as SIPS [6–9], are installed to protect the integrity of the power system or strategic portions thereof, as opposed to conventional protection systems that are dedicated to a specific power system element. The SIPS encompass SPS, RAS, as well as other system integrity schemes such as under-frequency, under-voltage, out-of-step, etc. These schemes provide reasonable countermeasures to slow and/or stop cascading outages caused by extreme contingencies.

SIPS's goal is to prevent propagation of disturbances for severe system emergencies caused by unplanned operating conditions and to ensure system security. They stabilize the power system for equipment outages, N-2 (two key elements out of service) or beyond by:

- Preventing cascading overloading of the lines and transformers.
- Arresting voltage decline.
- Initiating pre-planned separation of the power system.

Advanced detection and control strategies through the concept of SIPS offer a cohesive management of the disturbances. With the increased availability of advanced computer, communication, and measurement technologies, more "intelligent" equipment can be used at the local level to improve the overall response. Traditional dependent contingency-/event-based systems could be enhanced to include power system response-based algorithms with proper local supervisions for security.

The IEEE Power System Relaying Committee developed a worldwide survey on SIPS and summarized it in an *IEEE Transactions for Power Delivery* article [9]. Figure 1.2 shows a summary of the overall SIPS purpose classification. The numbers of SIPS performing similar types of functions have been grouped to indicate the total number of SIPS types. For each type of SIPS scheme, the number of schemes serving a similar purpose has been indicated, with the following classification:

I. Essential: Prevent cascading outages.
II. Increased Security: Minimize area affected by undesirable conditions.

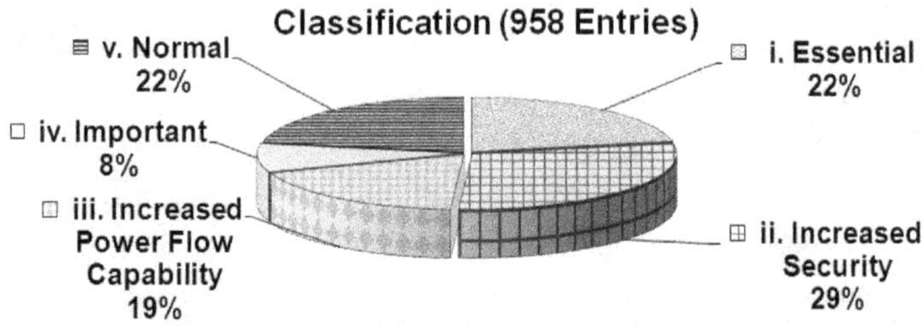

Figure 1.2. SIPS classification.

III. Increased Power Flow Capability: To extend transmission system rating without adding new transmission facilities or to delay enhancement of transmission networks.
IV. Important: Avoid difficult operating conditions.
V. Normal: A better functioning of the network.

Note that almost all classifications are evenly distributed (with the exception of "Important" which is at 8%). The approximately even distribution of classifications of SIPS highlights the important role of SIPS in grid reliability and how SIPS are an integrated part of grid development worldwide.

It is clear from Figure 1.2 that the application of SIPS has become a component of a comprehensive total grid operation and protection philosophy. The fact that 22% of the entries are applications to address "normal" system conditions demonstrates that SIPS are no longer applied solely for system security purposes. In fact, close examination of Figure 1.2 reveals SIPS applications can be viewed as two major categories:

- Operational system improvement (49% with three components: 19% Increased Power Flow, 8% Important, plus 22% Normal).
- System security (51% with two components, 22% Essential plus 29% Increased Security), which at one time was the primary intent of SIPS.

Figure 1.3 shows the intent of the various types of SIPS. The fact that voltage instability is the most often addressed phenomenon confirms

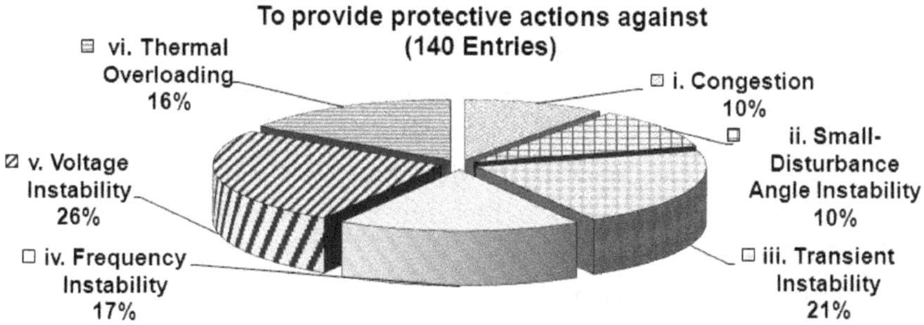

Figure 1.3. SIPS purpose.

that systems are now more complex than ever. The voltage stability phenomenon was first discovered at the beginning of the 1980s as systems were getting more complex. The information in Figure 1.3 correlates with the classifications in Figure 1.2, demonstrating that worldwide SIPS are integrated components of various aspects of grid operation.

1.3.1 *System restoration*

Another critical step in minimizing the impact of widespread blackouts is the need for effective and fast power system restoration. Returning equipment to service followed by quickly restoring power to the users is of paramount importance and can significantly minimize consequences of further outages.

Today's technology can be used to our advantage for intelligent restoration. Some of the key elements for responsive restoration are:

- Well-defined procedures that require overall coordination within the restoring area, as well as with the neighboring electric networks.
- Reliable and efficient restoration software tools, which significantly aid operators and area coordinators to execute operating procedures and to make proper decisions. This tool is a part of the SCADA/EMS (supervisory control and data acquisition/energy management system) system that provides voltage, frequency, excitation, outage status, and other data.
- Regular training sessions to ensure effectiveness of the process. These sessions should include practice drill scenarios. The drill scenarios should incorporate any regional reliability or governmental policy requirements. For example, there may be a time-delay requirements for load restoration after the bulk power system has returned to service, in order to allow the system to stabilize. There may also be critical loads, which must be given higher priority in restoration.
- Substations may need to be staffed to allow breakers or switches to be opened to clear re-energization pathways and establish an ability to control load restoration.

Today's technology allows us to design schemes to aid in quick restoration. Even if advanced tools and procedures are in place to speed up restoration, there are limits on how fast the system can be restored depending on the type and distribution of generation. After the 14 August 2003 blackout in the northeastern US, it took considerable time to restore generation. Some of the units did not have capabilities to be put in service immediately (black-start capabilities) and some units required a longer period of time to be put on-line with full power (e.g. nuclear units due to security, and steam turbines due to allowable ramp-up rates). Of equal consideration is the type of load served, the system configuration, the effects of connecting the load back to the network (cold load pickup or hot load pickup affect end-user restoration time). For example, most of the load centers were restored within five to nine hours during the Italian blackout in September 2003. In contrast, it took over a day to restore power back to Detroit and New York, and an estimated US$6 billion. While the lights stayed on in Pennsylvania, other states like Ohio, New York, Michigan, Massachusetts, and Connecticut, as well as Ontario, weren't so lucky. An *Inquirer* story headlined "Powerless" captured the disruption: "The exodus of people over bridges! The gridlock at tunnels and intersections! Jammed cell phones! Stranded subways!" [25].

In the 2003 Swedish–Danish blackout, the 400 kV power grid was restored within two hours, most customers were connected within four hours, and the last customer reconnected within six hours [13].

The low-voltage network loads in New York City and Manhattan area are a highly meshed network system that affords a very high degree of reliability against localized outages. However, under blackout conditions, when a network is to be restored, the network is isolated into 100–200 MW portions that need to be re-energized one at a time, requiring a time-consuming and careful process such that the inrush does not provide a set back to the restoration effort [13].

As discussed before, designing the power system to transfer power across large distances and not providing enough reactive power close to the load or building the accompanying transmission lines may have detrimental effects on power system operation. Similarly, designing the power system not considering the effects on restoration efforts may have detrimental effects on the speed of restoration. In conclusion, restoration time and system security could be significantly improved by planning of the generation mix and location considering not only market factors, but incorporating the value of reliable operation and faster restoration in the financial model. This approach would result in optimal, long-term investment strategies.

1.4 Synchronized Measurements

As the power grids worldwide have become more complex and are operated closer to the operating limits, applications of WAMPAC systems have become necessary to better manage the grid reliability and performance security [15, 16]. Synchronized measurement applications, using GPS-synchronized phasor measurement units (PMUs), offer large reliability and financial benefits for customers/society and the electrical grid when implemented across the interconnected grid. As measurements are reported 10–120 times per second, PMUs are well-suited to track grid dynamics in real-time. Compared to current EMS monitoring tools that use information from state estimation and SCADA over several second intervals, time-synchronized PMUs introduce the possibility of directly measuring the system state instead of estimating it based on system models and telemetry data. Due to its accuracy and wide-area coverage, synchronized measurement technology is a paradigm shift enabling unique tracking of power system dynamics. Synchronized measurement applications enable true early warning systems to detect conditions that lead to catastrophic events, help with restoration, and improve the quality of data for event analysis.

Advanced applications in WAMPAC systems offer a cost-effective solution to improve system planning, operation, maintenance, and energy trading [22]. Synchronized measurement technology and applications are an important element and enabler of WAMPAC. There are a large number of existing and potential applications of the synchronized measurement technology. As the synchronized measurement technology is deployed and as users gain experience and additional tools are developed, new applications will continue to be identified. Potential economic benefits could result in avoiding major system disturbances and in minimizing widespread blackouts. Major wide-area outages cost consumers and the power industry several billion dollars per major incident. Other benefits include reduction in congestion costs, reducing cost and time to analyze power system events, and providing means for quicker restorations following major grid outages.

A well-planned, system-wide PMU deployment, implementing optimal system architecture, is necessary to take full advantage of the technology. Once the adequate PMU system is built, incremental costs of adding applications are minimal in comparison to the added values received. Some of the major benefits result from the system-wide applications requiring PMUs to be connected across utility boundaries.

Figure 1.4 shows an example of angle measurements and alarm display. These types of displays are used both for post-disturbance analysis and as an operational tool to help during the disturbance.

The conceptual WAMPAC system has interesting parallels with the human nervous system. Figure 1.5 shows the simplest concept of a WAMPAC system, which spans a complete utility transmission system, or even an entire unified operating region. Transmission owner

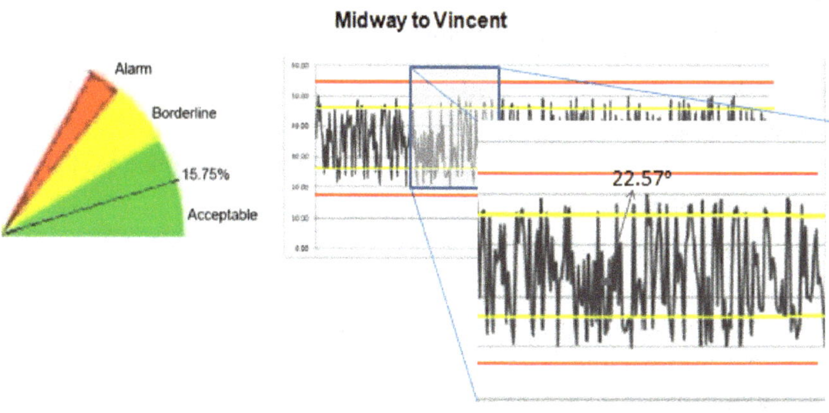

Figure 1.4. Angle measurement between buses in the WECC system and corresponding alarm display.

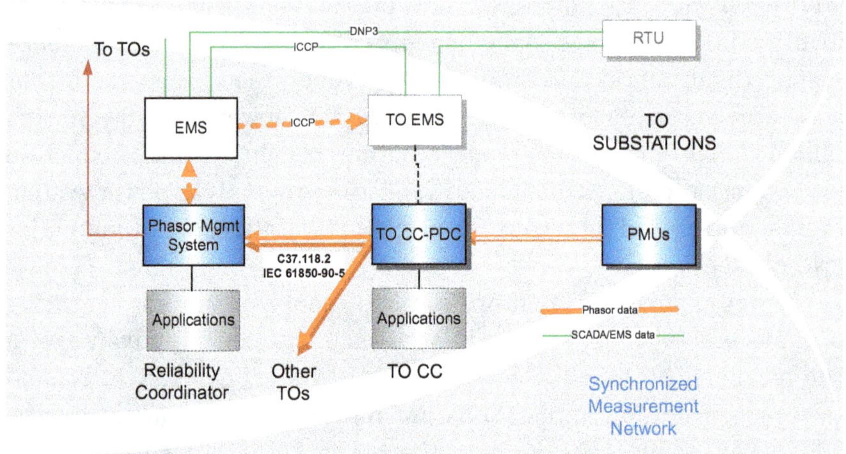

Figure 1.5. Synchronized measurement network.

(TO) PMU data is communicated to the TO phasor data concentrator (PDC). This data is also communicated to an independent system operator (ISO) phasor management system. Figure 1.5 also shows today's components like independent SCADA RTUs and connection to EMS. In the future, WAMPAC will ultimately be capable of absorbing all of the functions of today's SCADA and EMS, including not only measurement and control, but also state estimation and real-time contingency analysis.

Key success factors in implementing the technology are as follows:

- Develop a production-grade system with quality, synchronized measurements.
- Develop application and design roadmaps, based on quantifiable benefits for each user:
  - As measurements will grow over time, ensure system expandability.
  - As deployments start with small number of applications, but new applications will be added, ensure system flexibility and adaptability.
  - System integration with other enterprise systems, such as SCADA/EMS, DMS, and GIS.

- Provide norms for alarm and control thresholds.
- Major efforts in using historical data and simulations.
- Perform extensive testing and comply with standards as part of the life-cycle process.
- Develop operator guidelines and training.
- Design a system and process for interconnection data, model, and display sharing.
- Integrate asset investment and life-cycle support strategy for a successful deployment.

As present deployment status is only the tip of the iceberg for future applications, the above is necessary to ensure return of the investment and avoid unnecessary future costs.

1.5 Benefits and Roadmaps

We have established that WAMPAC is a key investment for the transmission smart grid by improving the following applications [16]:

- Data analysis and visualization — significant benefits have already been achieved with the existing PMU systems.
- System reliability improvement by preventing cascading outages due to voltage, angular, and frequency instability, thermal overloads, and low-frequency oscillations — these applications result in huge benefits to society.
- System operations and planning, modeling — enabling paradigm shift with high reporting rates.
- Market operations: Congestion management — enable large potential financial benefits.

With today's technology, it is possible to tie all the monitoring, control, and protection devices together through an information network. The key to a successful solution is fast detection, fast and powerful control devices, a communication system, smart algorithms for data mining so that actionable information are available both for real-time operation, as well as integration into contingency analysis tools.

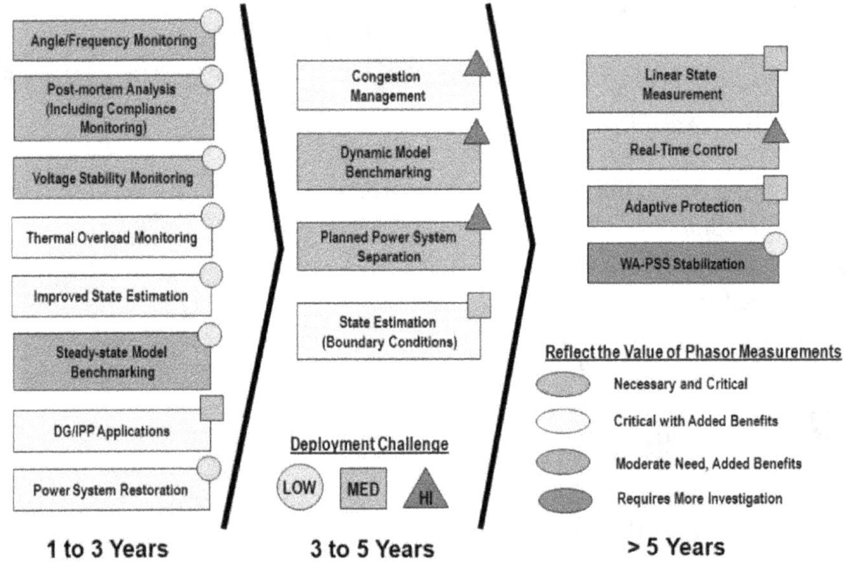

Figure 1.6. 2006 NASPI roadmap.

Given that PMU implementation requires participation of abroad base of users, the "overall industry roadmap" is an important step in designing and deploying large-scale PMU systems. The North American Synchrophasor Initiative (NASPI) developed an initial industry roadmap in 2006 (see Figure 1.6). This roadmap, based on the applications' business needs, commercial availability and cost, and complexity with deploying those applications, was based on an interview process with industry experts and users [16]. This roadmap has been updated [22] and individual users have developed their own roadmaps. However, as this roadmap served as a base for DOE three-year smart grid investment grant (SGIG) projects, the chart demonstrates the accomplishments across the US in three years. It still stands the test of time and serves as a base for creating future roadmaps.

First, industry needs are identified as critical, moderate, or unknown, regardless of the technology. Second, the value of the PMU technology for each identified application has been mapped related to importance in serving industry. This approach resulted in four categories: necessary and critical; critical with added benefits; moderate need, added benefits; requires more investigation.

Third, deployment challenges have been mapped for each application (low, medium, high). The deployment challenges are defined based on technology (communications, hardware and software requirements) and applications status (commercially available, pilot installation, research, not developed).

Deployment experiences from the three-year SGIG projects show the following are "low-hanging fruit" applications: angle/frequency monitoring and alarming, including small signal stability mode meter and oscillation detection; post mortem analysis; improved state estimation; and power system restoration. The following applications are in the process of being deployed as they are significantly improved or enabled by using PMUs: dynamic model benchmarking/validation; transient and voltage stability monitoring and control; planned power system separation; linear state measurements; real-time control, including advanced SIPS. Applications are also inter-related. For example, dynamic nomograms, angle and voltage stability monitoring are ingredients of congestion management, the implementation of which could result in major cost-savings and be the major contributor to the PMU system business case, both for asset owners and end-clients.

In addition, some of the deployment projects include applications such as integration of synchrophasor technology into state estimation and will lead to major improvements with distributed and/or linear state estimation as more and more PMUs are installed with an ultimate goal to enable full system visibility. Voltage stability monitoring falls into this category, as major benefits for the system reliability would be realized with voltage stability real-time control (based on monitoring) and contingency analysis [23].

1.6 Selecting PMU Locations

The first step in PMU deployment is a clear roadmap of the process for selecting the location of the PMU devices and establishing guidelines to assist with this decision-making process. Many of the existing optimal PMU placement approaches are mainly focused on a particular application (such as improving State Estimation).

Deployment of large-scale synchrophasor measurement system begins with the development of a comprehensive process. For large power systems involving several hundreds of transmission substations stretched across a span of a few thousands of kilometers and serving millions of customers over 180,000 square kilometers, the methodology for optimally determining the location of PMU devices should be based on a specific set of application and business requirements. The PMU siting studies can be conducted to identify observability locations for applications such as Situational Awareness, Visualization and Alarming for Operators as well as Post-Disturbance Event Analysis for Engineers. A completely different set of system studies would be needed for black start (system restoration) studies or Adaptive Protection studies where system disturbances from far away locations may appear as a local fault condition to the protective relays elsewhere in the system.

The recommended methodology considers both system studies as well as several practical implementation aspects such as infrastructure considerations, redundancy requirements, ease of maintenance, and overall constraints for a large power system. Risk management process is also key in terms of the technology deployment as well as the overall solution package. The various criteria utilized in decision-making for placement study results, including the risk management criteria, are summarized in this chapter [24].

1.6.1 *Methodology*

The overall goal is to identify optimal locations for PMU placement that maximize the benefit across multiple applications for real-time operation, as well as offer the least-cost solution by leveraging existing and planned infrastructure upgrades not only across the power company's footprint, but also across PMU placements in the neighboring systems. To achieve this objective, a methodology that is based on the analytic hierarchy process (AHP) and the weighted average criterion for prioritizing PMU placement has been pursued (Figure 1.7). This systematic approach helps in priority setting and

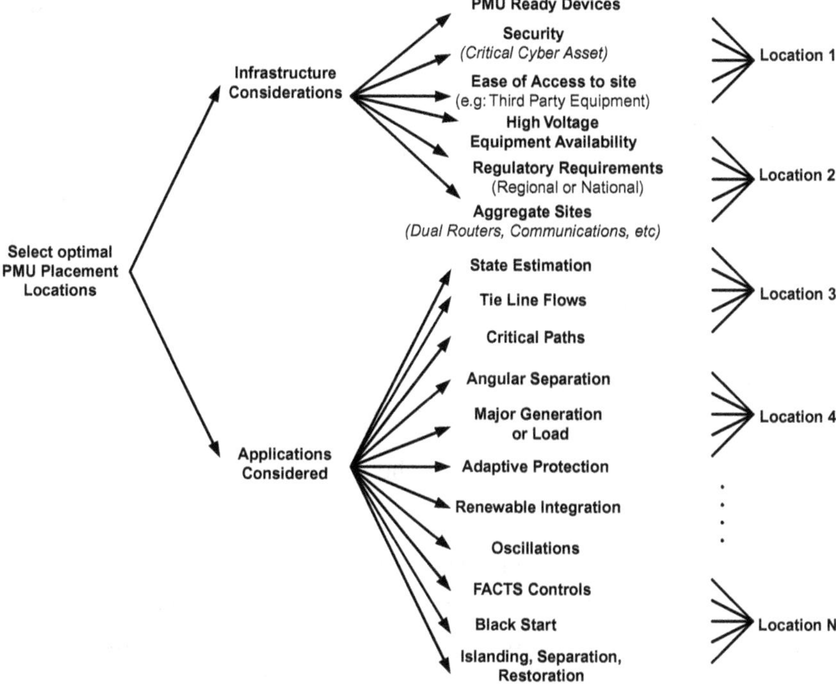

Figure 1.7. Analytic hierarchy structure for PMU placement criteria.

decision-making by decomposing any complex decision problems into more easily comprehended sub-problems. The process involves:

1. Structuring a decision problem into a hierarchy of goals, decision criteria and alternatives, as in Figure 1.7.
2. For all choices of PMU placement under consideration, a "score" is assigned to each location based on certain decision criteria such as applications needs, overall benefits (whether regional or within an identified list of beneficiaries), infrastructure considerations, etc.
3. A "weight" is assigned to each of the decision criteria. The key to weight assignment is a set of rules.

   - In the case of application requirements, the requirements are treated with a weight scale of 1 initially, and incremented upward based on the overall benefits for the given intended applications. In the case of observability, for example, a PMU on a tie line has more benefits than a PMU not on a tie line. Similar analysis can be performed for PMU locations in close proximity to planned wind integration.

- For the infrastructure categories, when serving equal purpose each has a weight scale of 1. If availability of PMU data for a given location benefits the entity deploying the PMU as well as other users (e.g. the regional reliability coordinator), then the benefits will receive an additional weight for a total score of 2. Likewise, redundancy of the PMUs and/or the availability of already existing diverse network infrastructure for a particular PMU site make the implementation more cost effective, therefore the weight assigned is 2.

4. Prioritization is then based on the weighted sum of values across all criteria.

In addition to the above steps, the PMU penetration level is impacted by factors such as types of system studies conducted (e.g. light loading, seasonal, or a maximum power flow scheduled in the future), the PMU outages for a particular day, or line contingencies impacting system equivalency.

Placement studies are then used to assign scores based on the applicability of a particular PMU allocation site to each decision criterion. Once all decision categories are filled in, the net weighted score for each PMU site under consideration is computed, and the list of candidate sites are sorted in descending order. The optimal PMU allocation sites are those with the highest weighted score and the ones towards the top of this sorted list, Figures 1.8 and 1.9 for application and infrastructure considerations, respectively.

The set of decision criteria utilized in the PMU allocation process are chosen based on the priorities described in the methodology section. These criterions can broadly be categorized into "application requirements" and "infrastructure considerations" [24].

1.6.2 *Application requirement*

The list of functions or applications served by the synchrophasor system will determine the PMU locations. The usefulness of a PMU

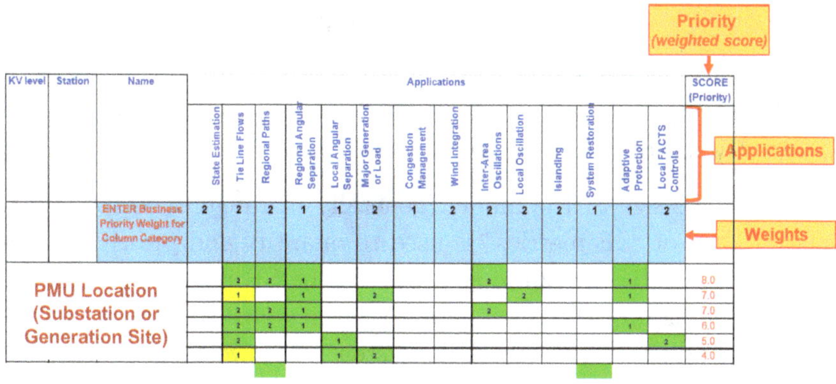

KV level	Station	Name	State Estimation	Tie Line Flows	Regional Paths	Regional Angular Separation	Local Angular Separation	Major Generation or Load	Congestion Management	Wind Integration	Inter-Area Oscillations	Local Oscillation	Islanding	System Restoration	Adaptive Protection	Local FACTS Controls	SCORE (Priority)
		ENTER Business Priority Weight for Column Category	2	2	2	1	1	2	1	2	2	2	2	1	1	2	
PMU Location (Substation or Generation Site)				2	2	1					2				1		8.0
				1		1		2				2			1		7.0
				2	2	1					2						7.0
				2	2	1									1		6.0
				2			1									2	5.0
				1			1	2									4.0

Figure 1.8. Prioritization based on weighted sum scoring — applications.

KV level	Station	Name	PMU-Ready Devices (e.g. SIPS or RAS, etc.)	COST to Build New Network to Site	On Critical Cyber Asset (CCA) list	Automation Site	Sites Ready for Upgrade (e.g. Regulatory Req.)	Ease of Life cycle Maintenance	Secure Network Exists Today	Local Network Redundancy	Wide Area Network Redundancy	Proposed Aggretate Site	SCORE (Priority)	TOTAL SCORE	PMU Location Counter
		ENTER Business Priority Weight for Column Category	1	2	1	1	1	1	1	2	2	1			
PMU Location (Substation or Generation Site)			1	2	1		1	Yes	Yes		Yes	PMU Location	10.0	18	1
			1	2	1		1	Yes	Yes		Yes		10.0	17	2
			1	2	1		1	Yes	Yes		Yes		10.0	17	3
			1	2	1		1	Yes	Yes		Yes		10.0	16	4
			1	2	1		1	Yes	Yes		Yes		10.0	15	5
			1	2	1		1	Yes	Yes		Yes		10.0	14	6

Figure 1.9. Prioritization based on weighted sum scoring — infrastructure.

at a particular location in serving an application's needs is very much application-dependent, as suggested by the various studies and analyses that have been conducted [8–13], the results of which are described below.

State estimation (SE)

The objective of this study is to identify locations where additional observability via the PMU system would improve the SE solution both in terms of accuracy and robustness. The analysis is conducted on a state estimator snapshot obtained from the most current version of the power company's model, with the following attributes:

- Comprised of buses and stations.
- SCADA injection measurements and flow measurements.
- Directly interconnected neighboring systems.

Based on the size of the model (generally in range of 3,000–15,000 buses), a set of "SE metrics" is used to quantify and prioritize locations where PMU measurements benefit the SE results. One meaningful indication of the SE function accuracy is the "variance of the SE system state errors", where the system state (voltages and angles) errors are defined as:

$$e = x_{true} - x_{estimated}, \tag{1.1}$$

where

$$\mathbf{X} = \text{Measurement (applies to voltage or angle)}$$
$$\mathbf{X}_{true} = \text{Actual Measurement (applies to voltage or angle)}$$
$$\mathbf{X}_{estimated} = \text{Calculated Measurement (applies to voltage or angle).}$$

The more actual measurements (PMU), the less need for calculated measurements, and hence the smaller the variances of system state errors for voltage and angle at a given bus and the better the SE solution. The goal would be to identify all stations above a certain transmission voltage level (e.g. 100 kV and above) where the variances are high, and consequently to help reduce the variance by PMU allocation at these locations.

Additionally, areas with observability problems (i.e. locations with high levels of pseudo-measurements) and critical measurements (i.e. non-redundant measurements) are also selected. The "residual sensitivity matrix" is utilized to identify critical measurements, and the allocation of PMUs at these locations would then increase the local redundancy and reduce the number of critical measurements. The sensitivity is determined based on the application, infrastructure, and planned architecture. When the application is deemed critical and is planned for redundancy (i.e. meets overall technical and diverse infrastructure requirements), the residual sensitivity matrix gives an additional weight to PMU location. The expected benefits from PMU placement at the suggested locations from this study should be:

- An increase in the number of valid SE solutions.
- A reduction in the number of critical measurements.
- Improvement in the SE accuracy (i.e. reduction in the "variance of state").
- Improved SE performance (i.e. reduction in the SE factorization times).

Critical paths (regional corridors, tie lines, and angular separation)

This criterion includes the allocation of PMUs to ensure adequate monitoring capabilities of angular separation as well as the power flows on each of the transmission lines that constitute the major transmission paths.

- Critical inter-tie paths.
- Critical internal paths.
- Other tie lines linking the power grid to neighboring systems.

Some of the envisioned benefits from PMU installations at these locations include the ability to monitor both static and dynamic stresses observable in the MW/MVAR flows and the angular separation across these corridors, and early detection of weakening grid conditions (such as line trips and associated impedance changes) and potential instabilities based on known historical separations when applicable.

Local and inter-area oscillations

Low-frequency electromechanical oscillations in an interconnected grid may be known to exist. While these oscillations are typically well damped and therefore harmless, there is always the danger of the oscillations gradually becoming unstable with increased loading (i.e. small-signal instability phenomena), or the possibility that severe faults can create steadily growing oscillations that may lead to partial or total power system breakdown [18]. Similarly, local oscillations at individual generators, if not properly identified and controlled, can lead to permanent damage of expensive power system equipment (such as rotor shafts). The high temporal resolution PMU measurements are capable of observing power system dynamics and characterizing the stability of such low-frequency oscillations in real-time.

The goal of this set of studies would be to utilize the model-based approach of performing an eigenvalue analysis on the dynamic model to extract the local and inter-area modal characteristics (i.e. modal oscillatory frequency, damping levels, and mode shape information). The immediate advantage of this model-based approach is that it provides both modal observability and controllability information, even at locations where measurements may not be available, and therefore can recommend new PMU locations so that grid oscillation modes can be better detected and controlled.

Both inter-area and local oscillatory modes need to be studied. Also, for each of the modes, study of the following information is recommended:

- Mode frequency (Hz) — the natural frequency of the electromechanical oscillation. (Note: Modes within the 0.1 Hz and 1 Hz range are typically "inter-area" modes, while modes within the 1 Hz and 3 Hz range are "local" modes.)
- Mode damping (%) — this characterizes the rate of decay of the oscillations—the lower the damping levels, the closer the power system is to dynamic instability.
- Mode shape — this provides the relative observability of a mode at each generation station. (Note: The locations with high observability are places where PMUs should be allocated to detect this mode.)
- Mode participation factor — this characterizes the controllability of a particular mode's behavior at each generation location. (Note: The locations with high controllability are places where PMUs should be allocated for implementing control schemes to dampen out the mode.)

Refer to [17] for more details and a table of studies conducted for a large-scale PMU deployment project.

Major generation and load

A set of general rules can be applied for selecting generation sites with significant value for PMU consideration. The combined generation is often considered as the initial site for study. In many cases, the transmission outlet is monitored for overall effectiveness, ease of implementation in existing sites, availability of network, and other infrastructure-related reasons. For example, generation facilities with a combined capacity of 1000 MW or above, or single generating units with capacity greater than 500 MW are selected as the sites for PMU placement under the criterion. Similarly, stations feeding major load centers are studied as candidates for PMU installation.

The expected benefits from the PMU allocations include the ability to monitor the performance of power system stabilizers (PSS) and other controls at the major generation stations, as well as assessing the load-response characteristics such as fault-induced delayed voltage recovery (FIDVR), which is typically associated with highly concentrated induction-motor loads (e.g. air-conditioning load without compressor under-voltage protection), which results in depressed voltages for several seconds following a fault in the system. It is important that such characteristics be represented properly in simulation programs. The ability to capture high-resolution data will be very valuable in calibrating the generator and load model parameters and keeping planning models up-to-date.

Other critical substation locations

This criterion covers all stations that are of special importance for one of the following reasons:

- Renewable integration — this includes stations that are interconnection points for a group of variable generation (e.g. feeders to large wind farms). PMU placement at these locations is expected to be useful in tracking the output of these intermittent resources and determining their response characteristics (low-voltage ride through capability, local oscillations, frequency response characteristics, etc.).

- Islanding, separation and restoration — these include interfaces at known separation points as well as locations with black-start generation capabilities. The expected benefits from PMU installations at these locations include early detection of islanding conditions, assistance with the restoration process, and resynchronization back into the main grid.
- FACTS controls — these are stations with controllable devices such as HVDC and static VAR compensator SVC controls. PMUs at these locations in the short term will provide valuable measurements to evaluate the controller performance, and in the future could be utilized in feedback control schemes that dampen inter-area oscillations or regulate voltage.
- Adaptive protection — conventional equipment protection systems (e.g. line, transformer, etc.) are designed to maintain the protected equipment and in general rely on local measurements. The PMU information from properly monitored locations on the power system can provide an additional piece of supervisory information from outside of the local protected zone of coverage for improved grid reliability during major disturbances. A series of system studies with multiple contingency analyses are required as the initial condition for identifying locations for the PMUs.

In addition to the application needs, it is equally important that several infrastructure considerations (e.g. communications availability and redundancy) are also taken into account during the PMU placement decision-making process. It's very possible that while a particular location is highly desirable from an application's perspective, the lack of required infrastructure to communicate these measurements to the control center make it cost-prohibitive. The key infrastructure factors recommended for consideration in the PMU allocation process are summarized below.

Sites ready for upgrade (e.g. regulatory requirements sites)

Local or national regulatory bodies may have requirements for continuous Disturbance monitoring and synchronized reporting requirements (real-time and sequence of events) to ensure that the TO collects adequate data needed to facilitate analysis of disturbances. For example:

- Stations that contain any combination of three or more transmission lines operated at a certain voltage level (e.g. 200 kV) or above and transformers having primary and secondary voltage ratings of 200 kV or above.
- Stations that are connected to generating plant with a specific MVA nameplate rating (e.g. 500 MVA for a single unit), or through a generator step-up unit (GSU) to a generating plant with an aggregate plant total nameplate capacity (e.g. 1500 MVA) or higher. Hence, installing PMU at those locations for system purposes would automatically provide generating plants with PMU functionality at no additional cost.

On critical cyber asset (CCA) list

PMUs cyber security compliance is a major concern. Locations that have already been identified as critical cyber assets, and thus have (or will have) the required security practices in place to meet the standards, would also be a preferred PMU allocation location from an infrastructural point-of-view.

The "weighted average criterion" is applied to the PMU placement utilizing the various application and infrastructure criteria discussed above. For all these potential PMU allocation sites, the net weighted scores are computed. Then, based on the overall project business plans (funding available and timeline for initial operation), a cutoff point is determined. Those locations with the highest scores are selected as the sites for PMU placement. The results of this exercise are described in Section 1.6.1 and shown in Figures 1.8 and 1.9.

1.7 Integrated Phasor Measurement Network Subsystem and Energy Management System

The PMUs enable synchronized measurements of voltages and currents across the power system at very high rates. This then enables a more accurate state estimation solution and also provides means for real-time displays. The fast execution cycle makes it possible to execute the state estimation algorithm in the same platforms as the communication software. The results of the state estimator can provide the basis for other functions such as voltage stability, oscillatory analysis, frequency control and islanding analysis. Voltage stability can be evaluated using the phasor measurement directly using real-time voltage instability methodology based on the equivalent Thévenin network [21] or as an add on to the EMS contingency analysis suite. Examples of deploying and implementing PMUs in the Pacific Gas and Electric (PG&E) EMS system grid are described next.

1.7.1 *Visualization — coherency within a monitored system*

Figures 1.10 and 1.11 show sample system displays. Figure 1.10 shows a high-level view of a group of generators and systems that are coherently swinging in relative unison with each other. Notice the relative flow directions (the arrows) within each of the coherent groups. Figure 1.11 shows the view of the northern and central systems swinging together, while the southern systems form their own coherent group.

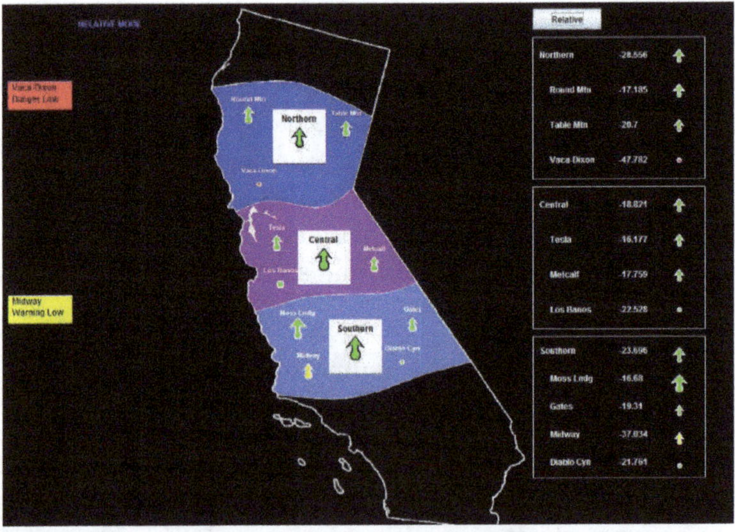

Figure 1.10. Relative flow directions in a partitioned system.

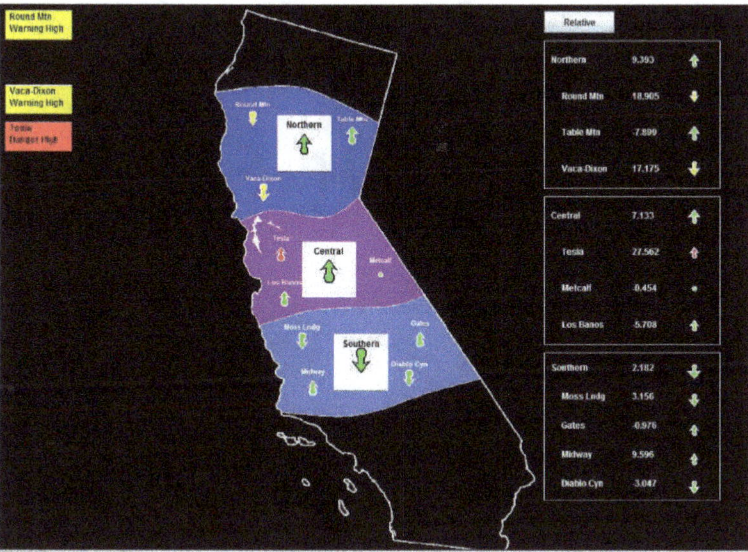

Figure 1.11. Relative flow directions with northern, central, and southern boundaries.

The angles in the center of Figure 1.11 are relative angles between the boundaries. Figure 1.11 shows that in a power system emergency requiring action, the south–central boundary is a natural cut set to consider for partitioning the grid without loss of synchronism. More detailed information about relative volt angles is provided in Section 1.7.2.

Figure 1.12 shows a wide-area view of voltage violations. Part (a) shows the pre-disturbance with some areas simulated to reflect low voltages. Part (b) shows the post-disturbance voltage violation regions in thick dark cloud formation reflecting areas whose system voltages should be first corrected to minimize potential for high voltages and ease of restoring the system.

1.7.2 *Voltage angle visualization*

In AC power systems, voltage angles govern the flow of power through the electrical system. In particular, power flows on transmission systems from locations with large voltage angles to those with smaller voltage angles. The ability to visualize these voltage angles is

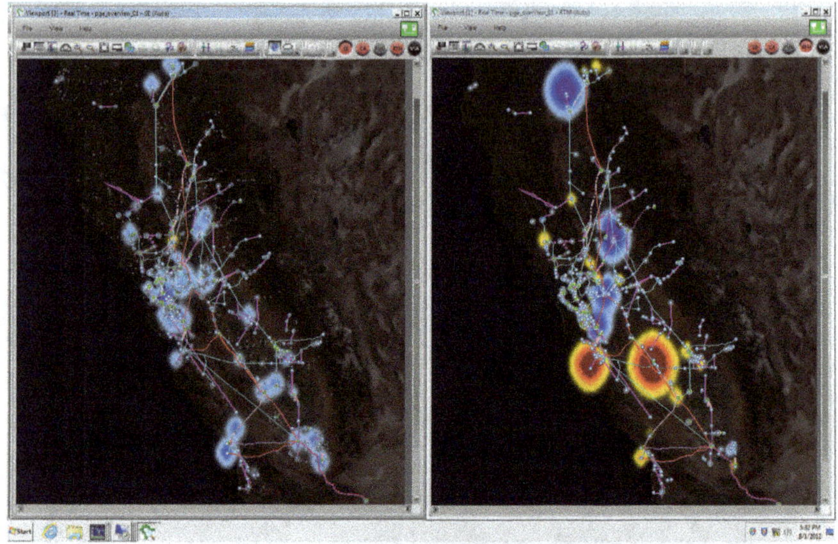

Figure 1.12. Wide area view of voltage violations in a simulated power system.

therefore valuable for real-time operations. Voltage angles are commonly viewed and understood in one of the following ways:

- As "relative voltage angles" with respect to a common "reference".
- As "voltage angle differences" between a pair of nodes in system.
- As "voltage rate-of-change" to detect sudden disturbances in the system.

Relative voltage angles

The "relative voltage angles" are computed at all locations as a difference between the measured voltage angle (from the PMU) at each of those locations, and the voltage angle at measured at a common "reference" bus:

$$\delta_A^{rel} = \delta_A - \delta_{ref}, \tag{1.2}$$

where

$\delta_A =$ measured voltage angle (from a PMU) at Location A,
$\delta_{ref} =$ measured voltage angle (from a PMU) at chosen common "reference" bus,

δ_A^{rel} = computed "relative" voltage angle at Location A with respect to the chosen "reference".

***Benefits*:** The main benefit of visualizing relative voltage angle profiles is to quickly identify the major "sources" (i.e. large voltage angles) and "Sinks" (i.e. small voltage angles) of power across the grid.

***Limitations*:** The major limitation of relative voltage angles is that they are dependent on a common reference choice, which means:

- They require prior knowledge of the "reference" choice.
- If the reference angle measurement is unavailable, the relative angles cannot be computed (i.e. unavailable) unless a different reference selection is made.
- If the reference selection changes, the relative angles are impacted by that change and their values change.

Voltage angle differences

The "Voltage Angle Difference" is computed as difference in the voltage angle between two locations: typically between the "source" and "sink" areas of the system, or across a known corridor or interface.

(Note: The two locations don't necessarily have to be at the two ends of a transmission line.)

$$\delta_{AB} = \delta_A - \delta_B, \tag{1.3}$$

where

δ_A = measured voltage angle (from a PMU) at Location A
δ_B = measured voltage angle (from a PMU) at Location B
δ_{AB} = computed "angle difference" between Location A and Location B.

***Benefits*:** The key benefits of angle differences include:

- Quick identification of the stress across known Corridors (e.g. California–Oregon inter-tie, or Georgia–Florida), or important "source" and "sink" regions (e.g. Pacific Northwest and California).

- No dependance on a “reference” selection (i.e. the “Angle Difference” does not change when the reference changes).
- Ability to specify “alert” and “alarm” limits on large “angle differences”.

***Limitations*:** Requires knowledge of the corridors or source/sink regions in the grid.

Voltage angle rate of change

The “voltage angle rate of change” is computed as change in voltage angle over a user-defined time period (e.g. one second). Since this represents relatively fast changing angles in time (e.g. pre- and post-event angle change during a disturbance), the absolute angle values themselves are less significant, and therefore the reference choice becomes unimportant.

***Benefits*:** The main benefits of voltage angle rate of change include:

- Quick detection of a disturbance in the system (e.g. line trip or generator loss).
- Ability to approximate the location of the event (PMU with largest rate of change is closest to the event).
- Ability to specify “alert” and “alarm” limits on large “angle rate of change”.

***Limitations*:** None.

1.8 Proof of Concept (POC) Test Facility

To deploy a practical synchrophasor system, several factors have to be considered. A synchrophasor system consists of a number of elements, including PMUs, PDCs, various telecommunication devices including routers and switches, telecommunication infrastructure usually spanning over several hundreds of miles, and intelligent functions and software applications running on various computers and processors throughout the synchrophasor system. A production-grade synchrophasor system's design and architecture need to satisfy a number of key requirements including cyber security, low-latency, large data throughput (bandwidth), high availability and reliability, and maintainability. Also, consistency among all measurements and interoperability among devices used are critical for the functions deployed in a wide-area system. Accordingly, ensuring accuracy of measurement devices and conformance to requirements is paramount for a well-functioning and sustainable system.

Preparation for large-scale deployment is best served by establishing a proof of concept (POC) test facility. The POC provides an environment for testing the components, validating interoperability, and various applications and is a vital step towards accelerating the deployment of a production-grade power-grid monitoring system incorporating the latest synchrophasor technology. In addition to fostering an environment for creativity and developing applications, the POC facilities also play a role in managing the risk of stranded assets in an environment where technology and standards are evolving constantly.

The POC can serve multiple purposes and accelerate the modernization of electric transmission functions. Examples include facilitation of development of implementation standards, setting of point templates, and debugging of the platform. The POC can also serve as a training facility for grid operators similar to flight simulators for pilots and astronauts. The POC facilities are often engineered to act as a small-scale replica of the power system. Figure 1.13 shows an overview example of a typical POC facility with redundant architecture that consists of PMUs provided by multiple manufacturers and fault recorders capable of generating and streaming synchrophasor measurement. The POC facilities streamline implementation of system-wide synchrophasor-based monitoring and advance warning systems that will significantly enhance existing grid monitoring capabilities and improve grid efficiency, reliability, and security.

The POC test facility helps in validating synchrophasor system interoperability and functional performance. By engineering, testing and demonstrating a production-grade system at the POC, the overall solution will be tested. For example, interoperability issues amongst various products and applications that need to comply with

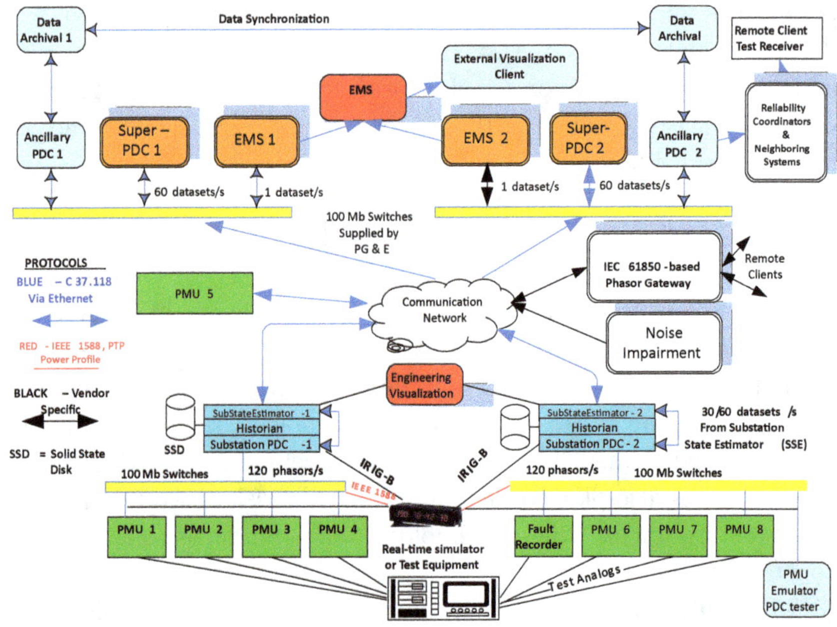

Figure 1.13. Proof of concept overview.

evolving industry standards are tested. The POC facility needs to be flexible to allow compatibility and interoperability testing against industry standards such as the IEEE C 37.118 -1 and -2, IEEE C 37.238, the IEC 61850-90-5, and the on-going efforts in the IEEE PDC guide in parallel with the production deployment efforts. The lessons learned from the POC facility can then be shared with the appropriate industry and government entities to inform the development of best practices for enhancing grid situational awareness. The POC facility is also used for demonstrating power system performance by, for example, comparing results from the load flow studies for validation of observability and the reactive power margin evaluations. A real-time digital simulator (RTDS) is used to simulate system behavior.

The POC can also be used as the training ground for operators and dispatchers learning to work with this advanced new technology.

The testing at typical POC facilities can further advance the applications of the PMU by:

- Identifying the need for more comprehensive standards for PMUs and PDCs. These findings have been coordinated with the appropriate industry liaisons for timely inclusion in industry standards. As a result, the standards are being balloted to ensure enhanced robustness and precision for interoperability and compatibility.
- Identifying field equipment and network compatibility issues that impact time synchronization.
- Performing precision time testing and performance compatibility requirements in a multi-facility (substation) environment.
- Conducting cognitive task analysis using operator use cases to ensure that synchrophasors provide operators with only the most actionable information.
- Preliminary validation and correction of field measurements using synchrophasor applications.
- Establishing a hands-on training and learning environment for diverse groups of users, technical staff and management executives.
- Developing a framework for preparation of "set points", templates, training modules, etc.
- Providing grid operators, engineering and operational staff early exposure to EMS visualization tools and an opportunity to recommend system enhancements.
- Helping vendors gain a better understanding of the anticipated system performance of a fully integrated product.

Tests conducted at the POC facility may include:

- Some of the basic tests such as individual PMU performance.
- Interoperability tests between various PMU devices as well as interoperability with PDC.
- Network testing such as TCP and UDP.
- Clock performance.
- Network impairment and impact on PDC performance.
- Network impairment and impact on overall system performance.

- Impacts of interpolation and extrapolation on analytics and visualizations.
- Analytics associated with the integrated phasor management subsystems and EMS.

Some of the tests are more application related (e.g. interoperability tests or the standards' compatibility and conformance tests). Other types of tests have a more academic contribution and lay the foundation and industry roadmaps for future work. In addition, topics such as cyber security considerations deserve a considerable amount of research and touch on broader aspects than power systems.

1.9 Data Mining and Cyber Security

This new generation of synchrophasor applications has moved beyond prototype to the POC stage. Once validated by field installation and training and accepted by end users, the tools will become part of the next-generation production systems for real-time applications. Enhanced tools to validate results and advanced simulation tools for training are other areas for development [26]. The integration tasks pose many challenges, including:

- Migrating a new application from the conceptual/development environment to production environment.
- Modeling tasks and how to make them more user-friendly and less labor-intensive.
- Learning from and adaptively tuning the new applications as they mature in the production.
- Contingency analysis and computing reactive margins.
- Information services, data mining, pattern recognition.

1.10 On-line Dimension Reduction of Synchrophasor Data

The massive data from PMUs has brought challenges to the storing, analyzing, and transmitting of results without causing a bottleneck in the available information-processing infrastructure. In addition to the amount of data, the dimensionality of synchrophasor data increases with more PMUs to support a wide-area monitoring. In order to enable real-time surveillance of the grid, high-speed synchrophasor data has to be processed before a new set of data arrives for processing. A method of dimensionality reduction of synchrophasor measurements such as voltage, current or frequency, utilizing principal component analysis (PCA) can extract correlations between measurements summarizing trends in PMU data without the loss of vital information where trends are more important than exact data [27]. Transmission, storage and computation of data become less expensive after dimensionality reduction of the synchrophasor data [26].

1.11 Cyber Security Preparedness

Deployment of a large-scale production-grade situational awareness and on-line analysis tools requires several infrastructure cyber security measures; a cyber security requirements plan that is based on the deployment architecture will be helpful in achieving a successful development plan. Some key components of a plan include:

- Security requirements conformance.
- Denial of service testing.
- Network protocol fuzzing.
- PMU and PDC security tests.
- Network port scanning and impact on PMU and PDC.
- Network fuzzing for port intrusion detection.
- Snort intrusion detection system preprocessor and rules.

Test setups, methodology, and experiences should be documented and communicated with the manufacturers of the hardware and software tools [28, 29].

1.12 Conclusions

The power system is very complex and human-made; our industry needs to keep planning, operating, and maintaining it as simply as possible. In last two decades, the number and frequency of major blackouts has increased. There is a general understanding of blackouts caused by natural disasters (earthquakes, hurricanes, etc.). However, system-wide outages created by humans and/or not arrested due to sub-optimal design (i.e. a system being operated beyond its original intended design) should be easier to prevent. Analysis of large disturbances reveals some common threads among them, leading to the following conclusions:

- There is a need to understand the symptoms and root causes of the major disturbances and learn from past blackouts.
- The power grid should not be operated under system conditions that have not been studied.
- Specific solutions should be implemented to reduce the likelihood and propagation of outages.
- Restoration time could be reduced.

In summary, although it is not possible to avoid multiple contingency-initiated blackouts when the system is not adjusted accordingly and quickly, the probability, size and impact of wide-area blackouts could be reduced and the propagation arrested.

Within the context of this approach, we can also address specific solutions to reduce the likelihood of outages, because once the overall causes of wide-area disturbances are minimized, the smaller contributing factors are easier to handle, further diminishing the incidence of failures. The advent of advancements in IT, innovations in power system monitoring, and deployment of advance warning systems enable tools to arrest the grid from wide-area blackouts and meet the expectations for reliable power delivery. For example, while investment in strengthening the electrical grid infrastructure, such as re-building T&D grid and installing new generation and controls (e.g. reactive power devices, FACTS, HVDC) is irreplaceable, "smart grid" WAMPAC deployment is a necessary and cost-effective way to improve grid reliability. Under normal conditions, and with sufficient automatic supports, operators are able to adequately control power system operation. However, the speed and complexity of disturbance phenomena make control of the grid more suited to automated WAMPAC systems that respond to fast-developing and complex disturbances. WAMPAC technology enablers, such as SIPS and synchronized measurements, provide the means to deploy transmission smart grids and prevent large blackouts.

One key step in synchrophasor technology deployment is optimal PMU placement. A methodology for optimal placement fulfils holistic criteria that consider multiple diverse factors that influence the PMU location decision-making process, and enables the incorporation of several practical implementation aspects. Key requirements for lifecycle support of investment are application needs, reliability requirements, and infrastructure challenges that drive the overall solution for optimal PMU location selection. Several new factors from technical applications to infrastructure considerations are presented for a more comprehensive and practical approach to achieve wide-area observability. Clear definitions for real-time volt-angle visualization and alarming are described. Furthermore, tying this new methodology to traditional approaches helps with the deployment transition. For example, phase angle limits, looking at multidimensional relations of different angular separations and angles change, are studied in relation to more traditional measurable parameters including voltage, apparent impedance, and power flow transfer schedules, to identify intra-area and inter-area problems. This flexible approach is required to achieve the required observability targets and support making real-time operational decisions for various applications and operating conditions.

Experiences from the deployment projects (e.g. PG&E PMU DOE project) describe practical aspects. As synchrophasor technology and standards continue to evolve (e.g. IEC 61850; IEC 37-118; cyber security), successful implementation of a production-grade system requires an innovative approach to performance and interoperability testing. Interconnected power systems and the complex nature of today's grid operation and system reliability considerations require more integrated test-beds than traditional discrete testing methods. The technology is used for a range of applications with stringent and varied requirements in order to improve grid reliability in complex and multifaceted power system conditions. The comprehensive methodology for testing equipment (PMU and PDC) and system interoperability helps to achieve high reliability and availability, system expandability and flexibility, and adaptability is designed and implemented in the unique PG&E POC test facility. This methodology helped with standard development and serves as blueprint for the whole industry.

Synchrophasor technology benefits from using the same infrastructure for a variety of applications. As the technology is still at the beginning of the wide-scale deployment and full realization of benefits, there is a pressing need for future research to improve existing applications and develop new ones.

References

[1] Novosel, D., Begovic, M. and Madani, V. (2004). Shedding light on blackouts, *IEEE Power Energy M.*, Jan./Feb. 2004, 32–43.

[2] Madani, V. and Novosel, D. (2005). Getting a grip on the grid, *IEEE Spectrum*, December 2005, 42–47.

[3] Novosel, D. and Madani, V. (2005). "Blackout Prevention" in *McGraw Hill Yearbook on Science and Technology*, McGraw Hill, New York, pp. 34–38.

[4] Madani, V., Novosel, D., Apostolov, A. *et al.* (2004). "Innovative Solutions for Preventing Wide Area Disturbance Propagation", presented at IREP Symposium, Cortina d'Ampezzo, Italy, August 2004.

[5] Horowitz, S.H. and Phadke, A.G. (2003). Boosting immunity to blackouts, *IEEE Power Energy M.*, Sep./Oct. 2003, 47–53.

[6] CIGRE WG C2.02.24 (2007). Defense plan against extreme contingencies, *ELECTRA*, April 2007, 46–61.

[7] Horowitz, S., Novosel, D., Madani V. *et al.* (2008). System-wide protection, *IEEE Power Energy M.*, Sep./Oct. 2008, 34–42.

[8] Madani, V., Novosel, D., Begovic, M. *et al.* (2008). Application considerations in system integrity protection schemes (SIPS), *GE Protection & Control Magazine*, May 2008, 25–30.

[9] Madani, V., Novosel, D., Horowitz, S. *et al.* (2010). IEEE PSRC Report on Global Industry Experiences with System Integrity Protection Schemes (SIPS), *IEEE T. Power Deliver.*, **25(4)**, 2143–2155.

[10] Western Systems Coordinating Council Disturbance Summary Reports for Power Systems Outages Occurred in December 1994, July 1996, and August 1996 respectively. Available at: www.wecc.biz. Accessed September 1996.

[11] NERC Recommendations to August 14, 2003 Blackout — Prevent and Mitigate the Impacts of Future Cascading Blackouts. Available at: www.nerc.com. Accessed September 2003.

[12] UCTE (2007). System disturbance on November 4, 2006. Available at http://www.ucte.com. Accessed February 2007.

[13] Madani V. and Novosel, D. (2005). Taming the Power Grid, *IEEE Spectrum website.* Available at: http://spectrum.ieee.org/energy/the-smarter-grid/taming-the-power-grid.
[14] Novosel, D., Bartok, G., Henneberg, G. *et al.* (2010). IEEE PSRC Report on Performance of Relaying during Wide-Area Stressed Conditions, *IEEE T. Power Deliver*, **25(1)**, 3–16.
[15] Horowitz, S., Novosel, D., Madani, V. *et al.* (2008). System-wide protection, *IEEE Power Energy M.*, Sep./Oct. 2008, 34–42.
[16] Novosel, D., Madani, V., Bhargava, B. *et al.* (2008). Dawn of the grid synchronization, *IEEE Power Energy M.*, **6**, 49–60.
[17] Phadke, A.G. and Thorp, J.S. (2008). *Synchronized Phasor Measurements and Their Applications*, Springer, New York.
[18] Amin, S.M. and Wollenberg, B.F. (2005). Toward a smart grid, *IEEE Power Energy M.*, Sep./Oct. 2005, 34–41.
[19] Taylor, C.W. (1999). Improving grid behavior, *IEEE Spectrum*, June 1999, 40–45.
[20] Kundur, P. (1994). *Power System Stability and Control*, McGraw Hill, New York.
[21] Glavic, M., Novosel, D., Heredia, E. *et al.* (2012). See it fast to keep calm, *IEEE Power Energy M.*, July/Aug. 2012, 43–55.
[22] Grigsby, L.L. (2012). "Wide Area Monitoring and Situational Awareness", Chapter 15 in Grigsby, L.L. (ed.), *Power System Stability and Control, Third Edition*, CRC Press, Boca Raton, pp. 15–45.
[23] Giri, J., Parashar, M., Madani, V. *et al.* (2012). Control center analytics for enhanced situational awareness, *IEEE Power Energy M.*, Sep./Oct. 2012.
[24] Madani, V., Parashar, M., Giri, J. *et al.* (2011). "PMU Placement Considerations — A Roadmap for Optimal PMU Placement", presented at IEEE PES Power Systems Conference & Expo, Phoenix, AZ, 20–23 March 2011.
[25] Lin, J., Currie Schaffer, M. and Ginsberg, T. (2003). POWERLESS Blackout hits 50 million in U.S., Canada NEW YORK CITY: A flashback to 9/11, then relief and tests of patience, *The Inquirer*. Available at: http://articles. philly.com/2003-08-15/news/25455362_1_cell-phones-commuters-sidewalks. Accessed August 2003.
[26] Jampala, A., Madani, V., Glavic, M. *et al.* (2012). Practical challenges of integrating synchrophasor applications into an EMS, *IEEE Proceedings Innovative Smart Grid Technology (ISGT)*, January 2012, 1–6.
[27] Dahal, N., King, R. and Madani, V. (2012). "Online Dimension Reduction of Synchrophasor Data", presented at IEEE PES Transmission and Distribution Conference and Exposition, Orlando, FL, 7–10 May 2012.
[28] Pan, S., Morris, T., Madani, V. *et al.* (2011). "Cybersecurity Risk Analysis of Substation Phasor Measurement Units and Phasor Data Concentrators", presented at IEEE SmartGridComm, Brussels, Belgium, 17–20 October 2011.
[29] Morris, T., Pan, S., Madani, V. *et al.* (2011). "Cyber Security Risk Analysis of Substation Phasor Measurement Units and Phasor Data Concentrators",

presented at 7th Annual Cyber Security and Information Intelligence Research Workshop by DOE, Oak Ridge National Lab, 12–14 October 2011.

[30] US–Canada Power System Outage Task Force (2004). Final Report on the August 14, 2003 Blackout in the United States and Canada: Causes and Recommendations. Available at: http://energy.gov/sites/prod/files/oeprod/DocumentsandMedia/BlackoutFinal-Web.pdf. Accessed April 2004.

Chapter 2

A MINLP Approach for Network Reconfiguration and Dispatch in Distribution Systems

Sergio Bruno[a] and Massimo La Scala[a]

[a]*Department of Electrical Engineering, Politecnico di Bari, Italy*

2.1 Introduction

Distribution systems, born as passive networks and operated mostly through manual procedures, are becoming active grids that integrate customers, services, and utility resources, and achieving increasing levels of automation and "smartness" through the adoption of sensors, communication systems, and computer intelligence. Smart distribution systems must be able to accommodate a fast-growing number of distributed generation (DG) units and a large variety of distributed energy resources (DERs), manage huge amounts of signals, and control multiple devices.

The improvement of distribution system automation requires the update of current distribution management system (DMS) monitoring and control schemes, which must be adapted to advanced DMS (ADMS) [1] designs and expected implementations. ADMS must achieve complete automation of DERs' dispatching and energy services, ensuring at the same time the fulfillment of reliability and economical targets. ADMS is able to provide most of the requested innovative functionalities of a smart distribution system and is responsible for managing, storing, and elaborating available data and performing several management applications that can be carried out in the medium–long term, for planning, or in extended real-time, for system operation [1]. Most of monitoring and control functions of ADMS are based on the update of common tools for power system analysis and control, such as power flow or optimal power flow, which have to be adapted in order to embed new control functions, new models, devices and technologies, and new operative requirements. An extensive description of such ADMS applications was given in [2–4], whereas this chapter is devoted to the development and integration of optimal network reconfiguration (ONR) tools in ADMS.

ONR is based on a mathematical process that is focused on finding an optimal solution, with regards to an objective function, through the combination of network switches under specific constraints [5]. ONR is a combinatorial optimization problem that requires remarkable computational efforts for its application to large electric systems. Formulation and solution of this problem have been largely discussed at transmission level, whereas nowadays, for the same abovementioned reasons, it finds growing applications at distribution level.

A number of relevant distribution network reconfiguration applications, solving multi-objective planning and off-line reconfiguration problems through heuristics and metaheuristics techniques, can be found in the literature [5–13]. These studies refer to off-line approaches, whereas, given the actual need for smarter and more efficient distribution systems, new optimization approaches to be implemented during real-time system operations must be developed. Such approaches will have to be reliable, fast, and able to achieve optimal and feasible solutions in the extended real-time framework of distribution system operation (15–30 minutes).

An example of real-time ONR for distribution systems is shown in [14], where the authors propose a robust and efficient algorithm for real-time management of smart distribution grids and loss reduction, demonstrating how, in smart distribution grids characterized by extensive networks and continuous fluctuations in demand and generation, best performances must be obtained through the implementation of advanced real-time ONR applications.

In [15], a heuristic approach for real-time ONR and loss minimization is presented. The proposed algorithm follows every change in system structure by getting a directed graph of the system to find the depth-first search discovery order and calculating precise branch currents, node voltages and system power losses. The procedure was successfully compared to other "classic" techniques, but the presented results are limited to small networks.

An innovative harmony search algorithm (HSA) is proposed in [16] to solve real-time ONR problems and get optimal switching combinations in the network. HSA bases its formulation on the behavior of musicians who search for the perfect harmony: by collectively playing their musical instruments (population members) they gradually come up with a pleasing harmony (global optimal solution). The methodology seems to be simple in concept and easy in implementation, but its efficiency has been tested so far just for small radial distribution systems (up to 119 nodes).

The approach proposed in [17] is aimed at exploring when it is appropriate to reconfigure the network, or what are, from a quantitative point of view, the benefits of the reconfiguration process. The study approaches the ONR problem from an operational point of view, giving useful indications about the opportunity to implement the reconfiguration process in real-life distribution networks. The authors, with regard to future work, introduce the idea of adopting active reconfiguration in order to increase generation hosting capacity in distribution systems.

In the aforementioned works, few papers are devoted to real-time applications or to the opportunity of adopting ONR in coordination with other ADMS management tools. In this chapter, a formulation of ONR as mixed-integer non-linear problem (MINLP) is given. The solving algorithm is based on two-staged optimization and allows the integration of a simulated annealing (SA) reconfiguration tool within ADMS extended real-time tools. It is shown how ONR gives support to any other optimization or decision tool, helping to solve several operative problems such as loss minimization, congestion management, security violations, and volt-var optimization with minimum control effort.

The feasibility of this approach for on-line applications is tested for solving operative problems such as loss minimization and congestion management. Test results are obtained by carrying out simulations on a detailed representation of a real-sized urban distribution network (about 1,000 nodes), where about 100 disconnector switches can be adopted for system reconfiguration.

2.2 Optimal Reconfiguration Functions in Advanced DMS Scheme

The idea of employing ONR functions in ADMS is based on the simple observation that most distribution network operators (DNOs) already have at their disposal supervisory control and data acquisition/distribution management systems (SCADA/DMS) with topology processor functions and a switch management architecture, usually adopted for emergency reconfigurations following faults or during maintenance operations. This means that most of the necessary communication systems and actuators are already in operation and that ONR can be implemented on both long-term planning and short-term operational time frameworks with minor adjustments.

Most distribution control centers are able to interrogate controlled switchboards via global system for mobile communication (GSM) or general packet radio service (GPRS) and obtain information on the status of each power disconnector switch. If GSM is adopted, this procedure might take several minutes and sometimes is performed just once or a few times per day. Nevertheless, since any closure/opening of controlled switches is usually promptly communicated to the control center, and since disconnectors are very seldom switched on or off (usually just after faults or during maintenance operations), at any time it is possible to have an exact description of the disconnectors' status and evaluate the topology of the network. However, GSM is often adopted because of its proved high reliability in terms of system security (for example a robust firewall to external intrusions is obtained by programming the modem in the switchboards to answer only incoming calls from known numbers), even if it does not provide top-notch technology for communication. An enhancement of the system automation level requires the implementation of faster communication channels (GPRS or optical fibers), which allows such components to be kept on-line and have a continuous flow of information from and to the control center. Despite this,

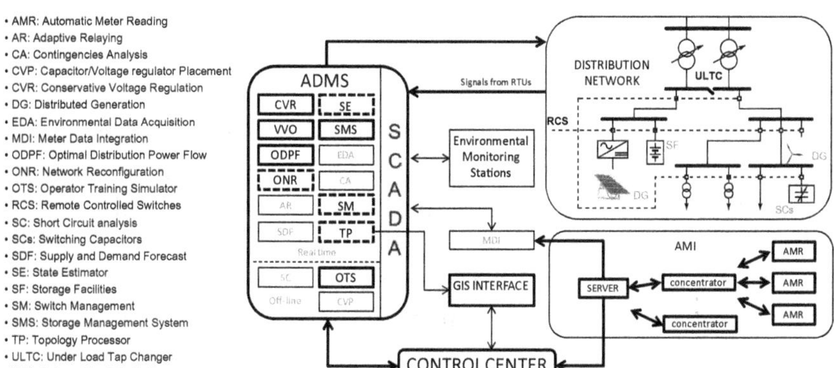

Figure 2.1. Basic ideal scheme of the proposed monitoring and control architecture.

given the expected time framework in which the system is supposed to be operated (an operative time window of about 15–30 minutes), a GSM-based monitoring and control system seems to be sufficiently capable to do the request job.

Figure 2.1, based on [1] and [4], shows a possible scheme for a monitoring and control architecture in smart distribution systems. In such a scheme the ADMS block represents a modular system combination of several intelligent functions (e.g. distribution power flow, adaptive relaying, and store management system) supported by bi-directional communications with field equipment and remote terminal units (RTUs). In this same figure, those functions framed with a bold and continuous line were fully described in [2–4], whereas bold and dotted contours identify the elements strictly necessary for developing ONR tools.

The main idea is to reconfigure the network during the day-ahead or the extended real-time (about 15–30 minutes [18]) framework of system operation. The starting configuration must be identified through a topology processor (TP) and a state estimator (SE). TP is an on-line module that collects the status of each switch and gives back an actual snapshot of the grid. Then, the state estimator module calculates voltages, currents, and angles, based on pseudo-measurements from the field. For real-time applications a snapshot of the system can be obtained by considering real-time measurements provided by automated metering infrastructure along with measurements (or generation forecasts) from all producing units and data from the topology processor.

In Figure 2.1, ONR is a tool capable of evaluating the necessary switching maneuvers for implementing the best grid configuration in terms of loss reduction or minimization of control effort during active or reactive power rescheduling. If ONR is performed in combination with other controlling techniques (for example load shedding or generation redispatch), then system optimization has to be performed through the formulation and the solution of a MINLP. In this chapter the overall MINLP is solved through a combination of soft and hard computing techniques. Soft computing techniques are usually adopted for the solution of combinatorial problems such as reconfiguration problems, whereas hard computing is the customary approach to system rescheduling problems such as optimal power flow. The chapter presents a methodology that permits the combination of both of these techniques into a two-staged optimization algorithm.

2.2.1 *Formulation of the ONR problem*

The ONR problem is a MINLP containing both integer and real variables. It can be formulated as a minimization problem subject to equality and inequality constraints:

$$\min_{\boldsymbol{x},\boldsymbol{u}} C_{obj}(\boldsymbol{V}, \boldsymbol{x}, \boldsymbol{u}) \tag{2.1}$$

$$f(\boldsymbol{V}, \boldsymbol{x}, \boldsymbol{u}) = 0 \tag{2.2}$$

$$g(\boldsymbol{V}, \boldsymbol{x}, \boldsymbol{u}) \leq 0 \tag{2.3}$$

with $\boldsymbol{x} \in \Omega_x$ and $\boldsymbol{u} \in \Omega_u$.

In equation (2.1), C_{obj} is the objective function to be minimized; $\boldsymbol{V}$, $\boldsymbol{x}$ and $\boldsymbol{u}$ represent respectively the sets of node voltages, the continuous control variables (for example generated active and reactive power) and the discrete control variables (i.e the open/closed status of each switch). Equation (2.2) takes into account the non-linear load flow equations, whereas in equation (2.3) all technical and operational requirements are taken into account (line and transformer thermal limits, minimum and maximum voltages, etc.).

MINLP can be solved by means of several techniques that might involve relaxation [19] or problem decomposition. Given the good performance of SA in solving combinatorial and reconfiguration problems [20], decomposition seems to be the most feasible approach for the solution of this specific problem. Bender decomposition [21] or two-staged optimization [22, 23] are possible approaches.

In the proposed methodology, the optimization algorithm adopts SA solely for the solution of the reconfiguration problem, whereas all operational constraints and continuous variables are taken into account by means of an optimization code based on non-linear programming techniques (basically a three-phase distribution optimal power flow or TDOPF). This means that to each configuration selected by the SA code, a single feasible solution coming from the optimization tool is associated. This methodology allows the embedding of network constraints in the OPF code and not in the SA. This might result in a higher computational burden but it avoids the definition of time varying weights or constraint relaxation rules in the first steps of SA as in [24].

2.2.2 *Objective functions*

Objective functions vary according to the specific operative problem that must be solved. In the case of minimization of system losses the objective function can be formulated as:

$$C_{obj} = \alpha_0 \left(\frac{P_{loss}}{\sum_{i=1}^{nbus} P_{Li}} \right)^2, \tag{2.4}$$

where P_{loss} represents total active power losses, P_{Li} is the load active power at the ith bus and α_0 is a weighting factor.

Other formulations can be aimed at the minimization of control effort during power system rescheduling. Hypothesizing that, at a certain moment of the day, too much power is produced causing the violation of one or more security limits and that the generated output must be rescheduled, the objective function will be formulated as in the following equation:

$$C_{obj} = \sum_{i=1}^{ngen} \alpha_{0,i} \left(\frac{P_{Gi\,sched} - P_{Gi}}{P_{Gi\,sched}} \right)^2, \tag{2.5}$$

where, for the ith generator, P_{Gi} is the generated power after rescheduling and $P_{Gi\,sched}$ is the amount of power scheduled for production, and $\alpha_{0,i}$ is a weighting factor. Clearly the solution of this problem assumes the availability of dispatchable generating power resources. Further operative constraints in redispatching can be taken into account as hard limits.

An objective function aimed at maximizing the allocation of distributed generation or hosting capacity, given local maximum generation capacity P_{Gimax} can be formulated as:

$$C_{obj} = \sum_{i=1}^{ngen} \alpha_{0,i} \left(\frac{P_{Gi} - P_{Gi\,max}}{P_{Gi\,max}} \right)^2 . \tag{2.6}$$

Other possible operative problems might be solved adopting different formulations of the objective function and assuming a different set of control variables. Other possible formulations can be found in [2–4].

2.2.3 *Penalty functions*

Inequality constraints referred to thermal limits of branches and to acceptable voltage profiles are taken into account through the introduction of penalty functions. In this chapter three penalty functions (C_{p1}, C_{p2} and C_{p3}) have been formulated. These functions are referred respectively to line, transformer and voltages constraints and are formulated as:

$$C_{p1} = \sum_{i=1}^{nlines} \alpha_{1,i} \left(\frac{I_i - I_{max,i}}{I_{max,i}} \right)^2 \tag{2.7}$$

with $\alpha_{1,i} = 0 \ \textit{if} \ I_i < I_{max,i}$, where I_i and $I_{max,i}$ are respectively current and maximum current at the ith distribution line and $\alpha_{1,i}$ is a coefficient that allows to weight penalty functions;

$$C_{p2} = \sum_{j=1}^{ntrasf} \alpha_{2,j} \left(\frac{S_j - S_{max,j}}{S_{max,j}} \right)^2 \tag{2.8}$$

with $\alpha_{2,j} = 0 \ \textit{if} \ S_j < S_{max,j}$, where S_j and $S_{max,j}$ are apparent power and maximum apparent power at the jth transformer and $\alpha_{2,j}$

is a weight factor;

$$C_{p3} = \sum_{k=1}^{nbus} \alpha_{3,k} \left(\frac{V_k - V_{lim,k}}{V_{lim,k}} \right)^2 \tag{2.9}$$

with

$$\begin{cases} V_{lim,k} = V_{max,k} & \text{if } V_k > V_{max,k} \\ V_{lim,k} = V_{min,k} & \text{if } V_k < V_{min,k} \\ \alpha_{3,k} = 0 & \text{if } V_{min,k} \leq V_k \leq V_{max,k} \end{cases}$$

where V_k, $V_{min,k}$, and $V_{max,k}$ are respectively voltage magnitude, minimum voltage, and maximum voltage at the kth bus, and $\alpha_{3,k}$ is a weight factor.

Under these assumptions the ONR problem can be formulated as

$$\min_{\boldsymbol{x},\boldsymbol{u}} C(\boldsymbol{V}, \boldsymbol{x}, \boldsymbol{u}) \tag{2.10}$$

subject to equality constraints

$$f(\boldsymbol{V}, \boldsymbol{x}, \boldsymbol{u}) = 0 \tag{2.11}$$

where

$$C = C_{obj} + C_{p1} + C_{p2} + C_{p3} \tag{2.12}$$

and $\boldsymbol{x} \in \Omega_x$ and $\boldsymbol{u} \in \Omega_u$.

2.2.4 *Solving algorithm*

The ONR algorithm proposed for the solution of the problem in equations (2.10)–(2.11) is structured in order to ensure modularity with other ADMS tools. The ONR algorithm is based on a Matlab/OpenDSS environment, built around the COM (component object model) data exchange interface available in the OpenDSS package [25], and is structured as in Figure 2.2. The solving algorithm is based on a two-staged optimization approach where the first stage is a SA-based reconfiguration algorithm that searches and selects radial network configurations and the second stage is a code that performs a distribution three-phase load flow (DTLF) or solves an optimization problem (for example a TDOPF).

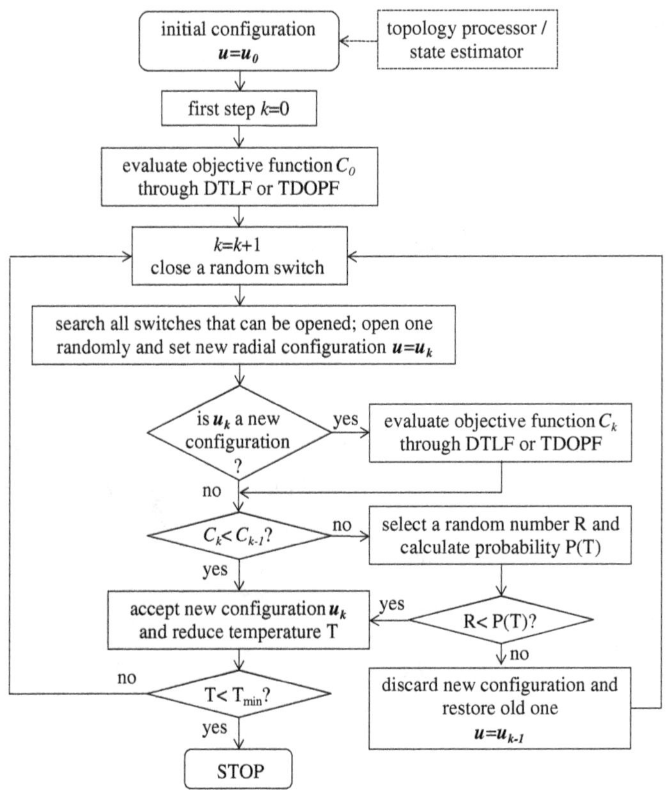

Figure 2.2. Flow chart of the proposed ONR algorithm.

In the SA stage, the algorithm looks for new radial configurations and communicates necessary topological changes to the OpenDSS grid model. Each state contains the open/closed status of all controllable disconnector switches that might interconnect laterals and backbones of distribution feeders. In realistic-sized networks, where hundreds of disconnectors can be switched, the research space is quite large and radial solutions are very few compared to its size. For this reason the search of other radial solutions follows a simple strategy, very close to the ones proposed in [21–24]. Starting from an initial radial configuration (for example the actual configuration produced by the TP), an open disconnector is randomly selected for being closed. Since a closed branch has been added to a connected radial graph, the resulting configuration is meshed. At this point, if one disconnector is opened and the system remains connected the resulting configuration is radial. The algorithm searches among all open switches for those ones that can be opened without losing the connectivity of the network, and randomly selects one of them, producing a new radial system configuration. This approach allows not only the reaching of other radial solutions, but also the obtaining of states that can be reached by the first state through a limited number of switching maneuvers, keeping a radial configuration after each maneuver.

If the status of disconnectors is the only control variable in ONR, then the second stage of the optimization algorithm is given by a simple DTLF code. In such case, the OpenDSS simulation engine performs a distribution load flow for each new state, evaluates losses, calculates voltages and power flows, and decides penalty functions.

When other control variables have to be optimized, the second stage is given by a TDOPF code that performs an optimization of all system control variables (e.g. active and reactive resources, loads, switching capacities, under-load tap changers, etc.), thereby minimizing the chosen objective function. This optimization block is developed in a Matlab/OpenDSS environment and is based on the work presented in [2–4]. An important feature of such optimization code is that it can treat concurrently both single- and three-phase system representations. Each system element, represented as a single object with its single- or three-phase model, can be controlled by the optimizing code, overcoming the limitations of the nodal approach.

Once a new configuration is selected for study, the algorithm optimizes/evaluates objective and penalty functions for that configuration by DTLF or TDOPF. Such optimization is performed only if this configuration has not been analyzed before, in order to save computation time. The objective function evaluated for this configuration is compared to the one evaluated at the previous step, and the new configuration is chosen or discarded according to SA working principles. The algorithm stops after the temperature is below a certain threshold, having reached a maximum number of iterations, or whenever a certain objective is reached (for example C is below a certain tolerance value).

2.3 Test Results

Test results have been obtained by carrying out simulations on a realistic-sized representation of the distribution system supplying electricity to the densely populated urban area of a typical middle-sized city in the south of Italy (about 60,000 inhabitants), serving also a large rural area and reaching altogether about 35,000 customers over about 100 km^2. The system under study is interconnected with the subtransmission system through a single high-voltage/ medium-voltage (HV/MV) substation and supplies energy by means of two 150 kV/20 kV transformers equipped with controllable tap changers and eleven 20 kV feeders. The two transformers have respectively a capacity of 30 MVA and 25 MVA, with a base load of 20 MW and peaks of about 35 MW. A simplified scheme of the distribution substation is given in Figure 2.3.

The system model, comprising all HV and MV elements, consists of 930 buses, 1,000 distribution lines (cabled and overhead), 100 controllable switches, and 500 load buses. Test results were obtained considering the whole representation of the system comprising an

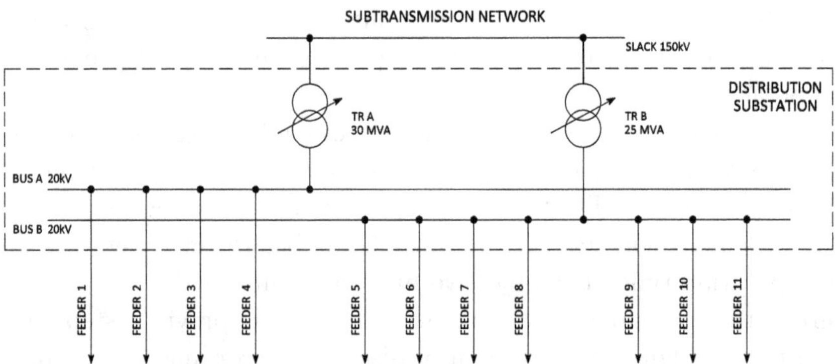

Figure 2.3. Simplified scheme of the distribution substation.

urban area, served by the 30 MVA transformer and the main four feeders, and the rural network supplied by a 25 MVA transformer.

An important feature of this network, which makes ONR applications particularly appealing, is that the network is characterized by a tangled architecture that allows reverse current feeding on several feeders. Such tangled structure is often a legacy of inhomogeneous urbanization processes that led to incremental development of the distribution network. The distributor in fact had to connect, one after the other, blocks or buildings as soon as they were completed and new connections to the grid were requested. The result is that very often laterals of a feeder can be directly connected to laterals of different feeders. Moreover each backbone has at least one back-current feeding switch at the end of the line.

2.3.1 *Case A — loss minimization*

The first case is aimed at finding the optimal network configuration for loss reduction. The adopted objective function is the one formulated in equation (2.4). The initial configuration is characterized by a loss value of about 1078 kW and several current violations ($C_{p1} > 0$). In Figures 2.4 and 2.5, the overall convergence behavior is shown. Figure 2.4 shows how the overall objective function is minimized along the iterative method. It also suggests how the method is able to move out of suboptimal areas and search for a global minimum. At the last iterations the overall amount of loss is reduced to about 758 kW. In Figures 2.6 and 2.7, line currents are compared to ampacity, showing how at first iteration several lines are congested, whereas at best and final iteration no congestion is experienced.

2.3.2 *Case B — generation rescheduling*

The second test case was carried out by introducing into the network a significant amount of distributed generation (about 13 generators, producing about 40 MW). In this case, generated power overloaded several distribution lines (see Figure 2.8). By applying the proposed

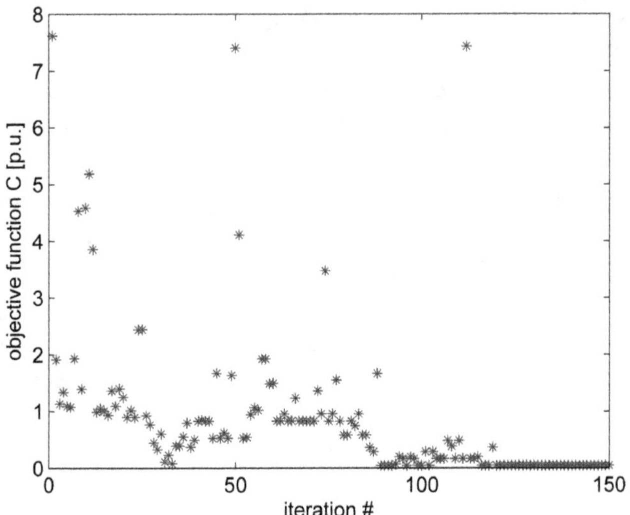

Figure 2.4. Case A, objective function C.

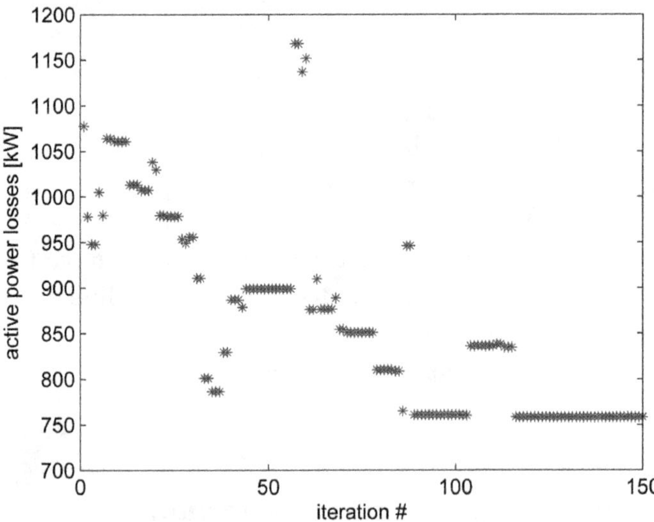

Figure 2.5. Case A, overall losses along the SA algorithm.

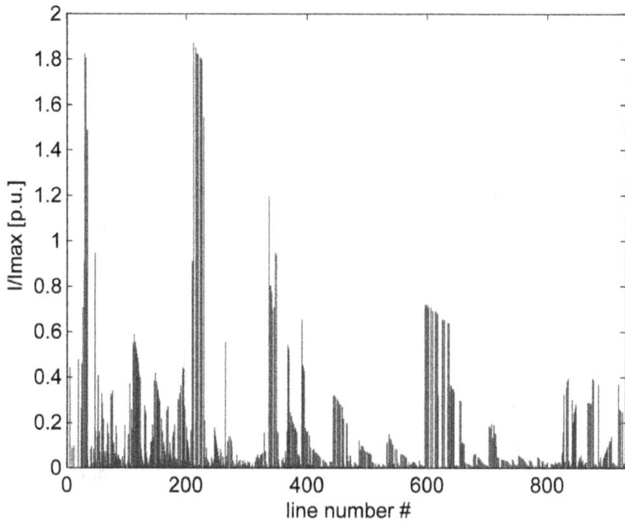

Figure 2.6. Case A, line current vs. ampacity (before ONR).

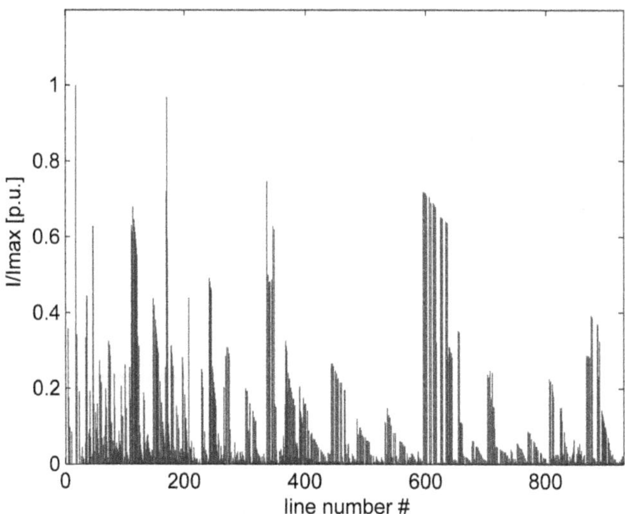

Figure 2.7. Case A, line current vs. ampacity (after ONR).

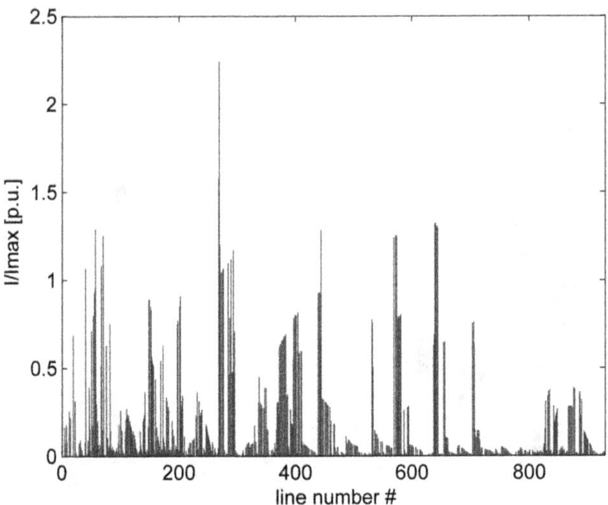

Figure 2.8. Case B, line current vs. ampacity (first configuration, no rescheduling).

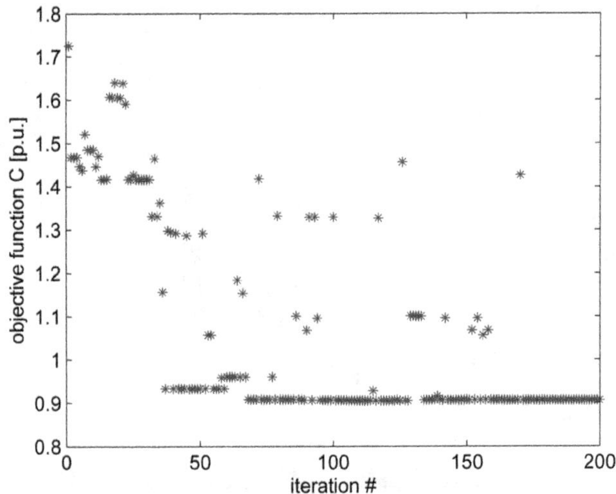

Figure 2.9. Case B, objective function C.

methodology and employing the objective function formulated in equation (2.5), an optimal configuration is found where only a minimum quantity of generated power has to be rescheduled. Figure 2.9 shows how the method converges towards an optimal solution in

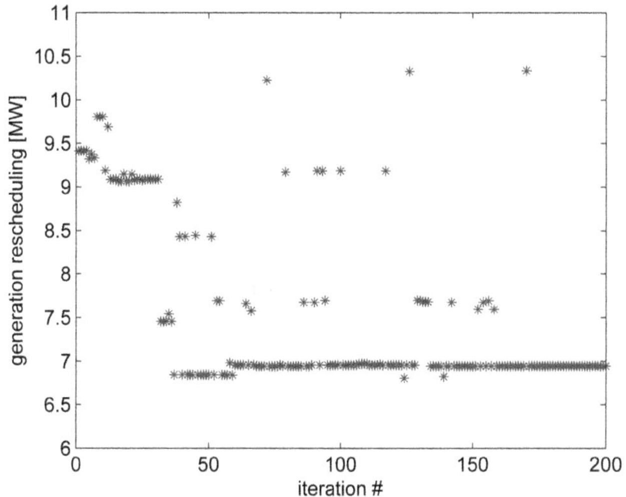

Figure 2.10. Case B, rescheduled power.

about 200 iterations. Figure 2.10 shows how the total generated power is maximized along the process. The best configuration is characterized by a generation curtailment of 7 MW only, allocating extra generation power for about 33 MW without line overloads. As shown in Figure 2.10, solutions with lower curtailment were also found (around iteration 40), but the final configuration is preferred since it is characterized by a lower overall objective function and, therefore, security constraints are better satisfied.

In Table 2.1, it is shown how the TDOPF code finds the minimum acceptable curtailment in the presence of all the above-quoted inequality constraints.

2.3.3 *Case C — maximization of generation capacity*

The amount of distributed generation for which the system performance becomes unacceptable can be defined as the hosting capacity (HC). In fact, the high penetration of dispersed generation on distribution grids can cause excessive loading of cables and wires, negative effects on the voltage regulation, power quality problems [3] etc.

Table 2.1. Case B. Optimization convergence behavior (optimal configuration).

Iter. #	C	C_{obj}	C_{p1}	C_{p2}	C_{p3}
0	35.080	0.000	35.081	0.000	0.000
1	9.180	0.389	8.789	0.000	0.000
2	1.790	1.142	0.644	0.000	0.000
3	1.410	1.290	0.120	0.000	0.000
4	1.320	1.257	0.067	0.000	0.000
5	1.260	1.206	0.052	0.000	0.000
6	1.190	1.136	0.049	0.000	0.000
7	0.960	0.936	0.022	0.000	0.000
8	1.150	0.765	0.381	0.000	0.000
9	0.920	0.904	0.016	0.000	0.000
10	0.910	0.873	0.033	0.000	0.000
11	0.910	0.877	0.027	0.000	0.000

A major problem in regulating the access of new distributed generation to grids is to define the HC of a specific network and assess this capacity at each node (nodal hosting capacity). The HC concept was also utilized by the Italian regulator Autorità per l'energia elettrica e il gas (AEEG) in Deliberation ARG/elt 39/10 as one of the key parameters for the admission to a particular number of pilot incentive schemes for judging the effectiveness of a proposed smart grid architecture. A study carried out by the AEEG and published with the ARG/elt 25/09 introduced a method to assess the HC, the results of which are very easy to apply in spite of many drastic assumptions. In this test case, the proposed approach is applied to assess the overall HC of the distribution grid in a quite natural way without introducing these particular assumptions.

In this test case, it is assumed that renewable resources are available at certain nodes up to a certain extent (it may represent the request for new access to a specific node) and that an optimal allocation of the new generation capacity has to be done in order to maximize the new installations. ONR, formulated through the objective function (2.6), allows the switching of generation areas to uncongested feeders or the consumption of "on-site" distributed generation supplying local loads.

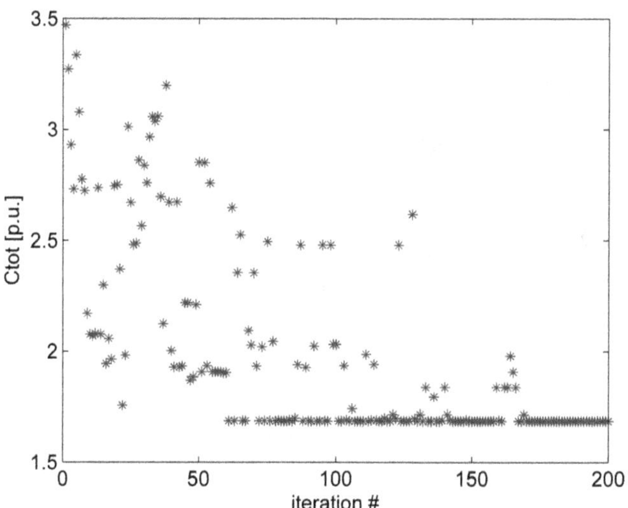

Figure 2.11. Case C, objective function C.

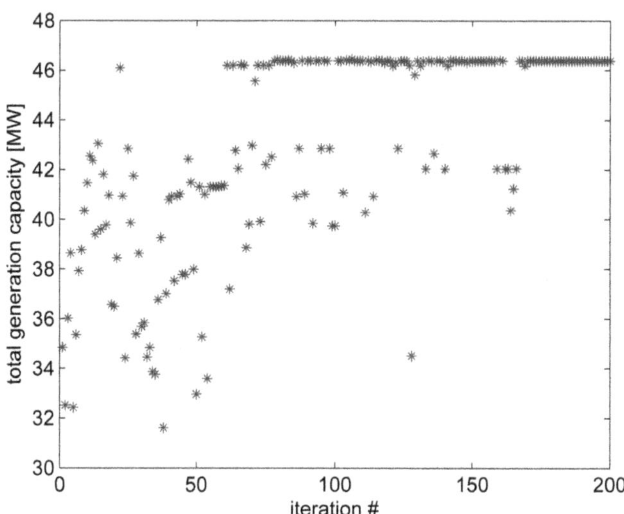

Figure 2.12. Test case C, total hosting capacity.

Figures 2.11 and 2.12 show how objective function and maximum generation capacity vary along SA iterations. The optimal configuration allows, for this specific operating case, the installation of about 47 MW of distributed generation (Figure 2.12) with

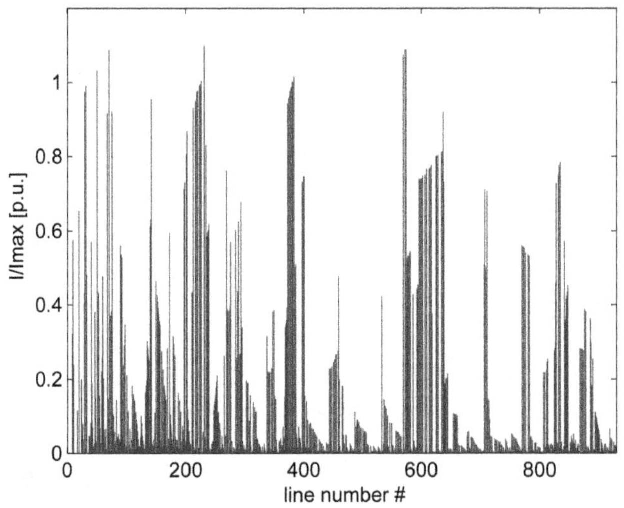

Figure 2.13. Case C, line current vs. ampacity (after ONR).

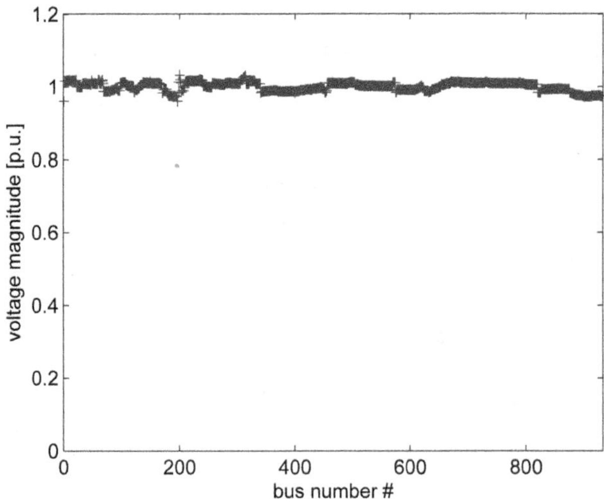

Figure 2.14. Case C, voltage magnitude (after ONR).

no significant security violations. As shown in Figures 2.13 and 2.14, only a few lines are working slightly over the ampacity, and all nodal voltages are within the interval 0.96–1.03 p.u. It is reasonable to accept slight violations of maximum current-related constraints since

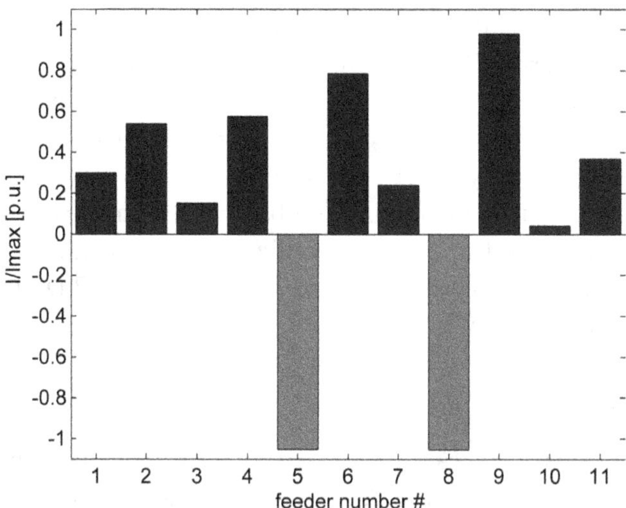

Figure 2.15. Case C, feeder current vs. ampacity (starting configuration).

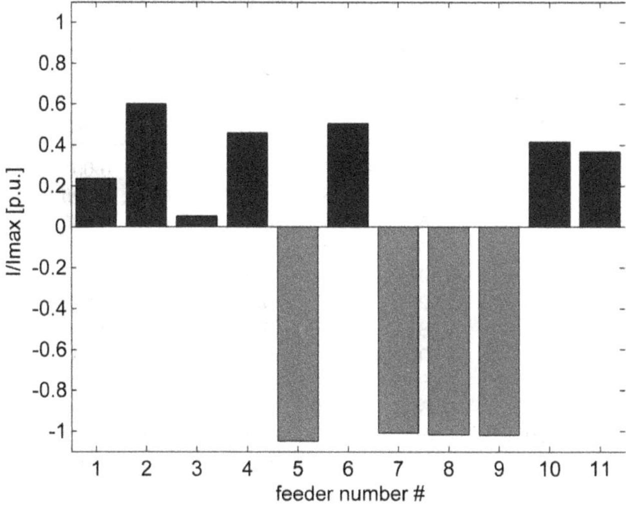

Figure 2.16. Case C, feeder current vs. ampacity (optimal configuration).

this condition, with all generators producing at full capacity, is supposed to be experienced rarely or for short periods of time.

Figures 2.15 and 2.16 show how feeder capacity is exploited. The starting configuration allows the installation of only 36 MW because generation can be increased only in nodes that are connected to congested feeders (#5 and #8). With the optimal reconfiguration, generating nodes are switched to other feeders allowing maximum capacity on feeders #5, #7, #8, and #9 to be reached, and increasingly hosting capacity by 11 MW. In order to fully exploit the potentials of the grid, it is interesting to observe that in some cases it was necessary to invert the flow on specific feeders (#7 and #9)

Table 2.2 shows the convergence behavior of the TDOPF for the optimal configuration.

2.3.4 *CPU timings*

All simulations were carried out on an ordinary desktop PC, HP Compaq 8000 Elite CMT PC, with Intel Core 2 Quad CPU Q 9650 3.00 GHz and 4.00 GB RAM. The total elapsed time is shown for each case in Table 2.3.

Table 2.2. Case C. Optimization convergence behavior (optimal configuration).

Iter. #	C	C_{obj}	C_{p1}	C_{p2}	C_{p3}
0	44.680	12.427	32.249	0.000	0.004
1	86.500	0.000	86.364	0.136	0.000
2	80.153	0.002	80.052	0.099	0.000
3	7.255	0.890	6.365	0.000	0.000
4	2.391	1.418	0.973	0.000	0.000
5	1.926	1.557	0.369	0.000	0.000
6	1.784	1.588	0.196	0.000	0.000
7	1.707	1.607	0.100	0.000	0.000
8	1.689	1.613	0.076	0.000	0.000
9	1.687	1.624	0.063	0.000	0.000
10	1.686	1.615	0.071	0.000	0.000
11	1.686	1.618	0.068	0.000	0.000

Table 2.3. CPU execution time.

Case	Time [s]
A	430
B	1678
C	2065

Timings for case A and case B appear to be compatible with extended real-time system operation and a 15–30 minutes control framework. The computation effort for case B is about 28 minutes, but it can be drastically reduced through code optimization and executing the simulation on a more powerful machine. In general, in the presence of severe time requirements, it is always possible to accept suboptimal solutions that are available to the SA algorithm after few tens of iterations. The highest computation effort was experienced for case C, but the time requirements for planning are not as strict as for system operation.

2.4 Conclusions

This chapter presented a methodology for ONR that can be easily integrated with other monitoring and control functions of an ADMS. An ONR problem was solved through a simulated annealing-based algorithm that allows easy integration with other system analysis and optimization tools such as DTLF and TDOPF.

Test results obtained by implementing such an algorithm on a detailed representation of a medium-sized urban distribution network show how the methodology can be applied in the extended real-time operative framework of such a system. The methodology is able to ensure the selection of an optimal configuration while minimizing system losses and respecting all technical and operative constraints.

When associated to other ADMS tools, such as a TDOPF, the methodology permits the evaluation of mixed-control actions that are based on both reconfiguration and system redispatch. As shown in the test results, ONR allows the minimization of the control effort requested for removing security violations during system operation, or the increase of hosting capacity during planning operation.

The main foreseeable bottleneck arises from the on-line implementation of system state estimators that will have to exploit data received from the field from smart meters and distributed generators, and build the system model to be adopted in the optimization code.

References

[1] Fan, J. and Borlase, S. (2009). The evolution of distribution, *IEEE Power Energy M.* **7**, 63–68.

[2] Bruno, S., Lamonaca, S., Rotondo, G. *et al.* (2011). Unbalanced three-phase optimal power flow for smart grids, *IEEE T. Ind. Electron.*, **58**, 4504–4513.

[3] Bronzini, M., Bruno, S., La Scala, M. *et al.* (2011). "Coordination of Active and Reactive Distributed Resources in a Smart Grid", presented at PowerTech 2011, Trondheim (Norway), 19–23 June 2011.

[4] Bruno, S., La Scala, M. and Stecchi, U. (2011). "Monitoring and Control of a Smart Distribution Network in Extended Real-Time DMS Framework", presented at Cigré International Symposium — The Electric Power System of the Future. Integrating Supergrids and Microgrids, Bologna, Italy, 13–15 September, 2011.

[5] Celli, G. and Pilo, F. (2001). Optimal distributed generation allocation in MV distribution networks, *Proc. of 22nd IEEE PES International Conf. on Power Industry Computer Applications 2001 (PICA 2001)*, 81–86.

[6] Shariatkhah, M.H., Haghifam, M.R., Salehi, J. *et al.* (2012). Duration-based reconfiguration of electric distribution networks using dynamic programming and harmony search algorithm, *Int. J. Elec. Power*, **41(1)**, 1–10.

[7] Celli, G., Ghiani, E., Mocci, S. *et al.* (2005). A multiobjective evolutionary algorithm for the sizing and siting of distributed generation, *IEEE T. Power Syst.*, **20**, 750–757.

[8] Silvestri, A., Berizzi, A. and Buonanno, S. (1999). "Distributed generation planning using genetic algorithms", presented at Conference on Electric Power Engineering, PowerTech Budapest 99 International, Budapest, Hungary, 29 August–2 September 1999.

[9] Satish Kumar, K. and Jayabarathi, T. (2012). Power system reconfiguration and loss minimization for distribution systems using bacterial foraging optimization algorithm, *Int. J. Elec. Power*, **36(1)**, 13–17.

[10] Nahamn, J.M. and Perić, D.M. (2008). Optimal planning of radial distribution networks by simulated annealing technique, *IEEE T. Power Syst.*, **23**, 790–795.

[11] Gandomkar, M., Vakilian, M. and Ehsan, M. (2005). "A combination of genetic algorithm and simulated annealing for optimal dg allocation in distribution networks", presented at Canadian Conference on Electrical and Computer Engineering, Saskatoon, SK, Canada, 1–4 May 2005.

[12] Gonzalez, A., Echavarren, F.M., Rouco, L. *et al.* (2012). Reconfiguration of large-scale distribution networks for planning studies, *Int. J. Electr. Power*, **37(1)**, 86–94.

[13] Zhigang, M. (2008). Study on distribution network reconfiguration based on genetic simulated annealing algorithm, *Proc. Electr. Distrib. CICED 2008*, 1–7.

[14] Vargas, A. and Samper, M.E. (2012). Real-time monitoring and economic dispatch of smart distribution grids: high performance algorithms for DMS applications, *IEEE Trans. Smart Grids*, **3**, 866–877.

[15] Abul' Wafa, A.R. (2011). A new heuristic approach for optimal reconfiguration in distribution systems, *Electr. Pow. Syst. Res.*, **81(2)**, 282–289.
[16] Rao, R.S., Narasimham, S.V.L., Raju, M.R. *et al.* (2011). Optimal network reconfiguration of large-scale distribution system using harmony search algorithm, *IEEE Trans. Power Syst.*, **26**, 1080–1088.
[17] Delfanti, M., Falabretti, D., Merlo, M. *et al.* (2012). "MV Networks Reconfiguration for Losses Reduction", presented at 2nd IEEE Energycon Conference & Exhibition, Florence, Italy, 9–12 April 2012.
[18] Paudyaly, S., Canizares, C.A. and Bhattacharya, K. (2011). "Three-phase distribution OPF in smart grids: Optimality versus computational burden", presented at ISGT Europe 2011, Manchester, England, 5–7 December 2011.
[19] Gomes, F.V., Carneiro, S., Pereira, J.L.R. *et al.* (2006). A new distribution system reconfiguration approach using optimum power flow and sensitivity analysis for loss reduction, *IEEE T. Power Syst.*, **21**, 1616–1623.
[20] Matos, M.A. and Melo, P. (1999). "Multiobjective Reconfiguration for Loss Reduction and Service Restoration Using Simulated Annealing", presented at Conference on Electric Power Engineering, PowerTech Budapest 99 International, Budapest, Hungary, 29 August–2 September 1999.
[21] Khodr, H.M., Martinez-Crespo, J., Matos, M.A. *et al.* (2009). Distribution systems reconfiguration based on OPF using benders decomposition, *IEEE T. Power Deliver.*, **24**, 2166–2176.
[22] Chiang, H.-D. and Jean-Jumeau, R. (1990). Optimal network reconfigurations in distribution systems. i: a new formulation and a solution methodology, *IEEE Trans. Power Deliver.*, **5**, 1902–1909.
[23] Chiang, H.-D. and Jean-Jumeau, R. (1990). Optimal network reconfigurations in distribution systems. ii: solution algorithms and numerical results, *IEEE Trans. Power Deliver.*, **5**, 1568–1574.
[24] Jeon, Y.-J., Kim, J.-C., Kim, J.-O. *et al.* (2002). An efficient simulated annealing algorithm for network reconfiguration in large-scale distribution systems, *IEEE Trans. Power Deliver.*, **17**, 1070–1078.
[25] *OpenDSS*. Available at: http://sourceforge.net/projects/electricdss/. Accessed September 2014.

Chapter 3

Multi-Objective Optimization Methods for Solving the Economic Emission Dispatch Problem

Balusu Srinivasa Rao[a] and Kanchapogu Vaisakh[b]

[a]*Department of Electrical & Electronics Engineering, V R Siddhartha Engineering College, Andhra Pradesh, India*
[b]*Department of Electrical Engineering, Andhra University College of Engineering, Andhra Pradesh, India*

3.1 Introduction

Traditionally, the economic dispatch (ED) problem [1–4] has played a vital role in the optimal operation of a power system. It is defined as the process of allocation of generation to various generating units available such that the cost of generation is optimum subject to several equality and inequality constraints. However, with the increase in public awareness over the environmental pollution caused by thermal plants, the economic emission dispatch (EED) problem [5, 6] has drawn much more attention for a good dispatch scheme because it would not only result in great economical benefit, but also reduce pollutant emissions.

Various investigations of EED have been reported in the literature to date. A direct approach using conventional methods is to convert a multi-objective EED (MOEED) problem into an equivalent single-objective problem [7, 8] by treating emission as a constraint; however, this method fails in getting a complete trade-off curve between cost and emission due to the approximation model. A linear programming-based optimization technique is proposed in [9] to solve the EED problem by considering only one objective at any point in time, but this method requires high computation time and it also fails in giving precise information about the complete trade-off curve between cost and emission. In another technique, Zahavi *et al.* converted a MOEED problem to a single-objective problem with a linear combination of different objectives as a weighted sum [10], in which a set of Pareto-optimal solutions are attained with different weights. Unfortunately, this method demands multiple runs to get Pareto-optimal solutions and is not suitable for problems having a non-convex Pareto front.

Over the last two decades, many studies on evolutionary algorithms (EAs) have revealed that they are efficiently used to solve the multi-objective optimization problem (MOOP); some of these algorithms are the multi-objective evolutionary algorithm (MOEA) [11], the strength Pareto evolutionary algorithm (SPEA) [12], the non-dominated sorting genetic algorithm (NSGA) [13], multi-objective particle swarm optimization (MOPSO) [14] and the multi-objective differential evolutionary algorithm (MODE) [15]. Since these algorithms are population-based methods, they give multiple Pareto-optimal solutions in a single run. Since the objectives are in conflict with each other in MOOP, it is natural to attain a solution set rather than single solution. Power system decision makers can select the desired solution between them by applying the fuzzy decision-making method.

Recently some other new algorithms [16–18] have been developed and successfully applied to solve combined EED problems. Chatterjee *et al.* [16] applied the concept of an opposition-based learning approach within a basic harmony search algorithm (HSA) to solve combined emission load dispatch problems. In [17] Srinivasarao *et al.* solved an EED problem by using the multi-objective adaptive clonal selection algorithm (MOACSA) method. Yasar *et al.* [18] scalarized the EED problem into a single-objective optimization problem using a conic scalarization method and then applied genetic algorithms (GAs) for the solution.

In recent years many biologically-inspired [19], swarm intelligence-[20] and artificial intelligence-based techniques [21] have been developed and applied successfully to solve EED problems. The artificial immune systems (AIS) with intrinsic characteristics [22] are capable of making these methods more appropriate for MOOP. Recently, an AIS-based algorithm has been used to solve a combined heat and power ED problem by Basu [23]. In this article a new AIS-based adaptive clonal selection algorithm (ACSA) is presented in addition to three standard algorithms, namely NSGA-II, MOPSO and MODE. All four of these methods are applied to solve multi-objective EED problems.

The rest of the chapter is organized as follows: Section 3.2 describes the mathematical formulation of the EED problem. A brief introduction of multi-objective optimization and the concept of non-dominated sorting and crowding distance techniques are described in Section 3.3. Various types of multi-objective optimization algorithms used in this chapter for solving EED problem are presented in Sections 3.4–3.7. The parameter settings of the test system to evaluate the performance of proposed methods and simulation studies are presented in Section 3.8. Finally, conclusions are drawn in Section 3.9.

3.2 Mathematical Formulation of the EED Problem

The mathematical formulation of the EED problem is treated as a MOOP. This MOOP formulation is defined well in the literature, and hence is only presented briefly in this section. The general MOOP is composed of the control variables set, objective functions, and several equality and inequality constraints that are functional relations.

3.2.1 *Problem objective functions*

In this chapter, three different objectives are considered for illustrating various multi-objective optimization methods. These objective functions are minimization of fuel cost, minimization of NO_X emissions, and minimization of real power transmission loss.

3.2.2 *Minimization of fuel cost*

The ED problem is defined as minimization of the total fuel cost by satisfying various equality and inequality constraints. The total fuel cost function of generator units can be denoted as:

$$F_1 = \sum_{i=1}^{NG} FC_i(P_{Gi}) = \sum_{i=1}^{NG} a_i + b_i P_{Gi} + c_i P_{Gi}^2 (\$/h), \tag{3.1}$$

where a_i, b_i and c_i are the quadratic fuel cost coefficients that pertain to i^{th} generator, P_{Gi} is the generating real power output of the ith generator, and NG is the total generator units.

3.2.3 *Minimization of NO_X emissions*

Thermal units may release environmental pollutant emissions due to the burning of fossil fuels for production of electrical power. The emission function includes the sum of all types of emissions like sulphur oxides (SO_X) and nitrogen oxides (NO_X). The emissions produced by each thermal unit is denoted as a quadratic function in terms of generator power output. Therefore the objective function representing minimization of NO_X or SO_X emission may be mathematically modeled as:

$$F_2 = \sum_{i=1}^{NG} (\alpha_i P_{Gi}^2 + \beta_i P_{Gi} + \gamma_i) + \xi_i e^{\lambda_i P_{Gi}}, \tag{3.2}$$

where $\alpha_i, \beta_i, \gamma_i, \xi_i$ and λ_i are emission coefficients of the ith thermal unit.

3.2.4 *Minimization of real power loss*

Active power transmission loss, P_L, is also treated as one objective function, since the loss reduction is an efficient way to decrease the generation cost and increases the social welfare. This objective function is denoted as:

$$F_3 = P_L = \sum_{k=1}^{NL} g_k [V_i^2 + V_j^2 - 2V_i V_j \cos(\delta_i - \delta_j)], \tag{3.3}$$

where g_k is the conductance of a transmission line k connected between buses i and j, V_i, V_j are the voltage magnitudes at bus i and j respectively, and δ_i and δ_j are the phase angles of voltages at bus i and j respectively.

3.2.5 *Problem constraints*

The optimal power flow (OPF) problem has to satisfy both equality and inequality constraints. The operating limits of the system are assumed as inequality constraints, while the load flow equations are equality constraints.

3.2.6 *Equality constraints*

The equality constraint represents the real power balance equilibrium condition that it must always satisfy for any power system network, i.e.:

$$\sum_{i=1}^{NG} P_{Gi} - P_D - P_L = 0, \tag{3.4}$$

where P_D is total the active power demand in the system and P_L is the total transmission losses, which can be calculated by using the NR (Newton–Raphson) load flow method.

3.2.7 *Inequality constraints*

The inequality constraints represent the system operating limits as follows:

(a) Generation constraints: generator voltages, real power outputs, and reactive power outputs are restricted by their lower and upper bounds as:

$$V_{Gi}^{\min} \leq V_{Gi} \leq V_{Gi}^{\max}, \quad i = 1, \ldots, NG, \tag{3.5}$$

$$P_{Gi}^{\min} \leq P_{Gi} \leq P_{Gi}^{\max}, \quad i = 1, \ldots, NG, \tag{3.6}$$

$$Q_{Gi}^{\min} \leq Q_{Gi} \leq Q_{Gi}^{\max}, \quad i = 1, \ldots, NG. \tag{3.7}$$

(b) Transformer constraints: transformer tap settings are restricted by their minimum and maximum limits as:

$$T_i^{\min} \leq T_i \leq T_i^{\max}, \quad i = 1, \ldots, NT, \tag{3.8}$$

where NT = number of tap changing transformers.

(c) Shunt volt-ampere reactive (VAR) constraints: reactive power injections at buses are restricted by their minimum and maximum limits as:

$$Q_{Ci}^{\min} \leq Q_{Ci} \leq Q_{Ci}^{\max}, \quad i = 1, \ldots, NC, \tag{3.9}$$

where NC = number of shunt compensators.

(d) Security constraints: these include the limits of voltage magnitudes at load buses and transmission line loadings as:

$$V_{Li}^{\min} \leq V_{Li} \leq V_{Li}^{\max}, \quad i = 1, \ldots, N_{PQ}, \tag{3.10}$$

$$S_{li} \leq S_{li}^{\max}, \quad i = 1, \ldots, NL. \tag{3.11}$$

3.2.8 *Constraints handling technique*

In the optimization process there is a possibility that the violation of inequality constraints results in an infeasible solution. When too many constraints are imposed in the problem, there is a chance of obtaining no solution satisfying all of them. In order to solve this problem a penalty factor is added to the objective functions corresponding to different security constraints, such as load bus voltage limits, line flow limits, and reactive power generation limits. If all the security constraints are satisfied then the penalty function value will be zero. All security constraint violations are handled as the sum of all the penalties which are added to one of the objective functions, given by

$$J_{pen} = J_{LF} + J_{BV} + J_{Qg}, \tag{3.12}$$

where J_{LF} is the penalty function for line flow violations,

$$J_{LF} = Kp \sum_{i=1}^{NL} (|S_{li}| - S_{li}^{\lim})^2, \tag{3.13}$$

J_{BV} is the penalty function for load bus voltage violations,

$$J_{BV} = K_v \sum_{i=1}^{N_{PQ}} (V_{\text{li}} - V_{\max})^2, \quad \text{if } V_{\text{li}} > V_{\max} \quad \text{or}$$

$$= K_v \sum_{i=1}^{N_{PQ}} (\mathrm{V_{min}} - \mathrm{V_{li}})^2, \quad \text{if } \mathrm{V_{li}} < \mathrm{V_{min}}, \tag{3.14}$$

and J_{Qg} is the penalty function for reactive power generation violation,

$$J_{Qg} = K_q \sum_{i=1}^{NG} (Q_{Gi} - Q_{\max})^2, \quad \text{if } Q_{Gi} > Q_{\max} \quad \text{or}$$
$$= K_q \sum_{i=1}^{NG} (Q_{\min} - Q_{Gi})^2, \quad \text{if } Q_{Gi} < Q_{\min}, \tag{3.15}$$

where K_p, K_v and K_q are the corresponding scaling factors for penalty functions.

3.3 Multi-Objective Optimization

In the real world, any multi-objective optimization problem consists of several objective functions that need to be optimized simultaneously, along with certain equality constraints and inequality constraints. This MOOP can be formulated mathematically as

$$Min\, F(x) = [f_1(x),\ f_2(x), \ldots, f_i(x)] \quad i = 1, 2, \ldots, N \tag{3.16}$$

subject to: $\{g_j(x) = 0, h_k(x) \leq 0\}$ $j = 1, 2, \ldots, J$; $k = 1, 2, \ldots, K$;

where f_i, h_k and g_j are i^{th} objective function, k^{th} inequality constraint, and j^{th} equality constraint respectively, x represents a decision vector, and N, K, and J are respectively the number of multiple objectives, inequality constraints, and equality constraints.

Any MOOP solution is not just one solution, as in the case of single objective OPF; it also gives a set of solutions called the trade-off. The decision maker has to select one best solution from the Pareto set, known as the compromise solution. All the solutions in the trade-off obtained for MO algorithms utilize the principle of dominance. Let x_1 and x_2 be two solutions of MOOP. Then a solution x_1 is said to dominate x_2 if it satisfies the following two conditions:

1. The solution x_1 is not worse than x_2 for all objectives, i.e.

$$\forall\, i \in \{1, 2, \ldots, N\}\colon \quad f_i(x_1) \leq f_i(x_2). \tag{3.17}$$

2. The solution x_1 is firmly better than x_2 for at least one objective, i.e.

$$\exists j \in \{1, 2, \ldots, N\}: \quad f_j(x_1) < f_j(x_2). \tag{3.18}$$

The solutions that are non-dominated within the entire search space are denoted as Pareto-optimal solutions.

All four of the multi-objective optimization algorithms utilize the concept of non-dominated sorting and crowding distance techniques [24] to find and manage the Pareto-optimal set. The detailed procedure for these two techniques is presented in the following two sections.

3.3.1 *Non-dominated sorting*

A fast sort algorithm is an improved version of the original non-dominated sorting approach proposed in [25]. In this process non-dominated solutions are identified in the population, at each generation, to form non-dominated fronts based on the concept of the non-dominance criterion. The following procedure describes a fast sort algorithm using non-dominance:

- For each individual i in main population P perform the following operations:
  - Initialize set, $S_i = \phi$, that contains all the individuals that are being dominated by i.
  - Initialize counter, $n_i = 0$, that counts the number of individuals that dominate i.
- For each individual j in P:
  - If i dominates j then add j to the set S_i, i.e. $S_i = S_i \cup \{j\}$.
  - If j dominates i then increment the domination counter for I, i.e. $n_i = n_i + 1$.
- If $n_i = 0$, i.e. no individuals dominate i, then i belongs to the first front.
  - Set rank of individual i to one, i.e $i_{rank} = 1$.
  - Update the first front set by adding i to front one, i.e $F_1 = F_1 \cup \{i\}$.

- This is carried out for all the individuals in main population P.
- Initialize the front counter to one, $k = 1$.
- The following steps are carried out if the kth front is non-empty (i.e. $F_k \neq \phi$):
  - ∘ $Q = \phi$, the set for storing the individuals for $(k+1)^{\text{th}}$ front.
  - ∘ For each individual i in front F_k.
    - — For each individual j in S_i (S_i is the set of individuals dominated by i):
    - — $n_j = n_j - 1$, decrement the domination count for individual j.
    - — If $n_j = 0$, then none of the individuals in the subsequent fronts would dominate j. Hence, set $j_{rank} = k + 1$. Update the set Q with individual j, i.e. $Q = Q \cup j$.
  - Increment the front counter by one.
  - Now the set Q is the next front and hence $F_k = Q$.

3.3.2 *Crowding distance*

Once the non-dominated sort is completed, the crowding distance value is required for the selection process. In order to select the individuals from the population, rank and crowding distance are taken into consideration. Therefore, crowding distance is assigned frontwise and is calculated as below:

- For each front F_i, n is the number of individuals.
  - ∘ Initialize the distance to be zero for all the individuals, i.e. $F_i(d_j) = 0$, where j corresponds to the jth individual in front F_i.
  - ∘ For each objective function m:
    - — Sort the individuals in front F_i based on objective m, i.e. $I = sort(F_i, m)$.
    - — Assign infinite distance to boundary values for each individual in F_i, i.e. $I(d_1) = \infty$ and $I(d_n) = \infty$.
  - ∘ For $k = 2$ to $(n-1)$:
    - — $I(d_k) = I(d_k) + \frac{I(k+1).m - I(k-1).m}{f_m^{\max} - f_m^{\min}}$.

— $I(k).m$ is the value of the mth objective of the kth individual in I.

The basic idea behind the crowding distance is to find the Euclidian distance between each individual in a front based on its m objectives in the m-dimensional hyperspace. The individuals in the boundary are always selected since they have infinite distance assignment.

3.3.3 *Best compromise solution*

After having the Pareto-optimal set, a fuzzy-based mechanism is applied to extract a the best compromise solution. Due to the imprecise nature of the decision maker's judgment, the ith objective function of a solution in the Pareto-optimal set F_i is represented by a membership function μ_i defined as [26]

$$\mu_i = \begin{cases} 1, & F_i \le F_i^{\min}, \\ \dfrac{F_i^{\max} - F_i}{F_i^{\max} - F_i^{\min}}, & F_i^{\min} < F_i < F_i^{\max}, \\ 0, & F_i \ge F_i^{\max}, \end{cases} \tag{3.19}$$

where $F_i^{\max}$ and $F_i^{\min}$ are the maximum and minimum values of the ith objective function, respectively.

For each non-dominated solution k, the normalized membership function μ_k is calculated as

$$\mu_k = \frac{\sum\limits_{i=1}^{N_{obj}} \mu_i^k}{\sum\limits_{j=1}^{M} \sum\limits_{i=1}^{N_{obj}} \mu_i^j}, \tag{3.20}$$

where M is the number of non-dominated solutions. The best compromise solution is the one having the maximum of μ_k. As a matter of fact, arranging all solutions in the Pareto-optimal set in descending order according to their membership function will provide the decision maker with a priority list of non-dominated solutions. This will guide the decision maker in view of the current operating conditions.

3.4 Particle Swarm Optimization (PSO)

Recently a new evolutionary computational intelligence technique called particle swarm optimization (PSO), has been proposed and introduced [27–31] to solve optimization problems. This technique combines social psychology principles in socio-cognition human agents and evolutionary computations. PSO has been motivated by the behavior of organisms, such as fish schooling and bird flocking. Generally, PSO is characterized as simple in concept, easy to implement, and computationally efficient. Unlike the other heuristic techniques, PSO has a flexible and well-balanced mechanism to enhance the global and local exploration abilities.

Like evolutionary algorithms, the PSO technique conducts a search using a population of particles, corresponding to individuals; each particle represents a candidate solution to the problem at hand. In a PSO system, particles change their positions by flying around in a multidimensional search space until a relatively unchanging position has been encountered, or until computational limitations are exceeded. In the social science context, a PSO system combines a social-only model and a cognition-only model [27]. The social-only component suggests that individuals ignore their own experience and adjust their behavior according to the successful beliefs of individuals in the neighborhood. On the other hand, the cognition-only component treats individuals as isolated beings. A particle changes its position using these models.

In MOPSO, a set of non-dominated solutions must replace the single global best individual in the standard single objective PSO case. In addition, there may be no single local best individual for each particle of the swarm. Choosing the global best and local best to guide the swarm particles becomes a non-trivial task in a multi-objective domain. In the MOPSO method, elitism is also considered by copying any non-dominated solution obtained to an external set in order to keep the new non-dominated solutions obtained during generations. The external set is updated regularly to hold only the non-dominated solutions.

3.4.1 *MOPSO algorithm*

The basic elements of the proposed MOPSO technique are briefly stated and defined below [32–34].

- ***Particle, $X(t)$*:** This is a candidate solution represented by an m-dimensional vector, where m is the number of optimized parameters. At time t, the jth particle, $X_j(t)$, can be described as $X_j(t) = [x_{j,1}(t), \ldots, x_{j,m}(t)]$, where the x are the optimized parameters and $x_{j,k}(t)$ is the position of the jth particle with respect to the kth dimension, i.e. the value of the kth optimized parameter in the jth candidate solution.
- ***Population, $pop(t)$*:** This is a set of n particles at time t, i.e. $pop(t) = [X_1(t), \ldots, X_n(t)]^T$.
- ***Particle velocity, $V(t)$*:** This is the velocity of the moving particles represented by an m-dimensional vector. At time t, the jth particle velocity $V_j(t)$ can be described as $V_j(t) = [v_{j,1}(t), \ldots, v_{j,m}(t)]$, where $v_{j,k}(t)$ is the velocity component of the jth particle with respect to the kth dimension. The particle velocity in the kth dimension is limited by some maximum value, $v_k^{\max}$. This limit enhances the local exploration of the problem space and it realistically simulates the incremental changes of human learning [27]. The maximum velocity in the kth dimension is characterized by the range of the kth optimized parameter and given by

$$v_k^{\max} = (x_k^{\max} - x_k^{\min})/N, \tag{3.21}$$

  where N is a chosen number of intervals in the kth dimension.
- ***Inertia weight, $w(t)$*:** This is a control parameter that is used to control the impact of the previous velocities on the current velocity. Hence, it influences the trade-off between the global and local exploration abilities of the particles. For the initial stages of the search process, a large inertia weight to enhance the global exploration is recommended while, for the last stages, the inertia weight is reduced for better local exploration. An annealing procedure is incorporated in order to make a uniform search in the initial stages and a very local search in the later stages. A decrement problem for decreasing the inertia weight, given as $w(t) = \alpha w(t-1)$, where

α is a decrement constant smaller than but close to 1, is proposed in this study.

- ***Non-dominated local set, $S_j^*(t)$:*** This is a set that stores the non-dominated solutions obtained by the jth particle up to the current time. As the jth particle moves through the search space, its new position is added to this set and the set is updated to keep only the non-dominated solutions.
- ***Non-dominated global set, $S_j^{**}(t)$:*** This is a set that stores the non-dominated solutions obtained by all particles up to the current time. First, the union of all non-dominated local sets is formed. Then, the non-dominated solutions out of this union are members in the non-dominated global set.
- ***External set:*** This is an archive that stores a historical record of the non-dominated solutions obtained during the search process. This set is updated continuously by applying the dominance conditions to the union of this set and the non-dominated global set. Then, the non-dominated solutions of this union are members in the updated external set.
- ***Local best, $X_j^*(t)$, and global best, $X_j^{**}(t)$:*** The individual distances between members in the non-dominated local set of the jth particle, $S_j^*(t)$, and members in the non-dominated global set, $S_j^{**}(t)$, are measured in the objective space. If $X_j^*(t)$ and $X_j^{**}(t)$ are the members of $S_j^*(t)$ and $S_j^{**}(t)$ respectively that give the minimum distance, then they are selected as the local best and the global best of the jth particle respectively. The size of the non-dominated local set, the non-dominated global set, and the external set could be extremely high due to accumulation of all non-dominated solutions throughout the search. To keep the sizes of these sets manageable, a clustering algorithm [35] should be implemented.

3.4.2 *MOPSO computational flow*

In the proposed MOPSO algorithm [36], the population has n particles and each particle is an m-dimensional vector, where m is the number of optimized parameters. The computational flow of the proposed MOPSO technique can be described in the following steps and is applied to solve MOEED problem.

***Step 1 (initialization)*:** Initialize the counter $t = 0$ and randomly generate n particles, i.e.

$$\{X_j(0),\ j = 1, \ldots, n\}, \tag{3.22}$$

where $X_j(0) = [x_{j,1}(0), \ldots, x_{j,m}(0)]$. The value $x_{j,k}(0)$ is generated by randomly selecting a value with uniform probability over the kth optimized parameter search space $[x_k^{\min}, x_k^{\max}]$. Similarly, randomly generate initial velocities for all particles, $\{V_j(0), j = 1, \ldots, n\}$, where $V_j(0) = [v_{j,1}(0), \ldots, v_{j,m}(0)]$. The value $v_{j,k}(0)$ is generated by randomly selecting a value with uniform probability over the kth dimension $[-v_k^{\max}, v_k^{\max}]$. Each particle in the initial population is evaluated using the objective functions of problem. For each particle, set $S_j^*(0) = \{X_j(0)\}$ and the local best $X_j^*(0) = X_j(0), j = 1, \ldots, n$. Search for the non-dominated solutions and form the non-dominated global set $S^{**}(0)$. The nearest member in $S^{**}(0)$ to $X_j^*(0)$ is selected as the global best $X_j^{**}(0)$ of the jth particle. Set the external set equal to $S^{**}(0)$. Set the initial value of the inertia weight, $w(0)$.

***Step 2 (time updating)*:** Update the time counter $t = t + 1$.

***Step 3 (weight updating)*:** Update the inertia weight $w(t) = \alpha w(t-1)$.

***Step 4 (velocity updating)*:** Using the local best $X_j^*(t)$ and the global best $X_j^{**}(t)$ of each particle, $j = 1, \ldots, n$, the jth particle velocity in the kth dimension is updated according to the following equation:

$$\begin{aligned} v_{j,k}(t) = {} & w(t)v_{j,k}(t-1) + c_1 r_1(x_{j,k}^*(t-1) - x_{j,k}(t-1)) \\ & + c_2 r_2(x_{j,k}^{**}(t-1) - x_{j,k}(t-1)), \end{aligned} \tag{3.23}$$

where c_1 and c_2 are positive constants and r_1 and r_2 are uniformly distributed random numbers in [0,1]. If a particle violates the velocity limits, set its velocity equal to the appropriate limit.

***Step 5 (position updating)*:** Based on the updated velocities, each particle changes its position according to the following equation:

$$x_{j,k}(t) = v_{j,k}(t) + x_{j,k}(t-1). \tag{3.24}$$

If a particle violates its position limits in any dimension, set its position at the corresponding limit.

***Step 6 (non-dominated local set updating)*:** The updated position of the jth particle is added to $S_j^*(t)$. The dominated solutions in $S_j^*(t)$ will be truncated and the set will be updated accordingly. If the size of $S_j^*(t)$ exceeds a pre-specified value, the hierarchical clustering algorithm [35] will be invoked to reduce the size to its maximum limit.

***Step 7 (non-dominated global set updating)*:** The union of all non-dominated local sets is formed and the non-dominated solutions out of this union are members in the non-dominated global set $S_j^{**}(t)$. The size of this set will be reduced by hierarchical clustering algorithm [35] if it exceeds a prespecified value.

***Step 8 (external set updating)*:** The external Pareto-optimal set is updated as follows:

(a) Copy the members of $S^{**}(t)$ to the external Pareto set.
(b) Search the external Pareto set for the non-dominated individuals and remove all dominated solutions from the set.
(c) If the number of the individuals externally stored in the Pareto set exceeds the maximum size, reduce the set by means of clustering.

***Step 9 (local best and global best updating)*:** The individual distances between members in $S_j^*(t)$ and members in $S^{**}(t)$ are measured in the objective space. If $X_j^*(t)$ and $X_j^{**}(t)$ are the members of $S_j^*(t)$ and $S^{**}(t)$ respectively that give the minimum distance, they are selected as the local best and the global best of the jth particle respectively.

***Step 10 (stopping criteria)*:** If the number of iterations exceeds the maximum then stop; otherwise go back to Step 2.

3.5 Differential Evolution (DE)

In the recent past, powerful EA such as differential evolution (DE) techniques have been employed for power system optimization problems. DE, developed by Storn *et al.* [37], is a numerical optimization approach that is simple to implement, fast, and robust. These methods, when used with real-valued parameters, optimize non-differentiable and non-linear continuous space problems. One of the significant features of DE is that it utilizes the variation of sampled object vector pairs obtained at random to conduct mutation operations, rather than using probability function like other EAs.

DE merges classical with simple arithmetic operators of crossover, mutation, and selection operations to emerge from a randomly generated starting population to a final solution. The best fit offspring competes one-to-one with its corresponding parent. This one-to-one competition makes it different from other EAs and thus results in a high convergence rate.

DE uses population P of size N_p, composed of floating-point-encoded individuals that develop over G generations to attain the optimal solution. Each vector individual X_i consists of parameters that are equal in number to the problem decision variables D. The population size N_P is an algorithm control parameter selected by the user that remains constant over the entire optimization process.

$$P^{(G)} = [X_1^{(G)}, \ldots, X_{N_P}^{(G)}] \tag{3.25}$$

$$X_i^{(G)} = [X_{1,i}^{(G)}, \ldots, X_{D,i}^{(G)}], \quad i = 1, \ldots, N_P \tag{3.26}$$

Three basic operators are used in DE optimization: mutation, crossover, and selection. This process starts by creating an initial population with N_P vectors, and random values assigned to each decision parameter in every vector as defined by equation (3.27).

$$X_{j,i}^{(0)} = X_j^{\min} + \eta_j (X_j^{\max} - X_j^{\min}), \tag{3.27}$$

where $i = 1, \ldots, N_P$ and $j = 1, \ldots, D$, $X_j^{\min}$ and $X_j^{\max}$ are respectively the lower and upper limits of jth decision parameter, η_j is a uniform random variable within [0, 1], and $X_{j,i}^{(0)}$ is the jth parameter of the ith individual of the initial population.

The mutant vectors X_i' are created by perturbing a random vector X_a with a difference function of two more randomly selected vectors, (X_b, X_c).

$$X_i'^{(G)} = X_a^{(G)} + F|(X_b^{(G)} - X_c^{(G)})|, \quad i = 1, \ldots, N_P, \tag{3.28}$$

where X_a, X_b, and X_c are randomly selected vectors from every parent vector, where X_a, X_b, $X_c \in \{1, \ldots, N_P\}$ and $a \neq b \neq c \neq i$. To control the size of perturbation and improve convergence rate, an algorithmic scaling parameter/control constant F is used.

The crossover operator produces test vectors X_i'' by combining the parameters of mutant and target vectors X_i, as per a particular probability distribution.

$$X_{j,i}''^{(G)} = \begin{cases} X_{j,i}'^{(G)}, & \text{if } \eta_j' \leq C_R \quad \text{or} \quad j = q, \\ X_{j,i}^{(G)}, & \text{otherwise,} \end{cases} \tag{3.29}$$

where $i = 1, \ldots, N_P$ and $j = 1, \ldots, D$, q is a randomly selected index $\in \{1, \ldots, N_P\}$ that ensures that a minimum of one parameter is selected from mutant vector for a trial vector, η_j' is a uniform random variable distributed over (0, 1) for every j, the crossover constant, C_R, is an algorithmic scaling parameter that helps the algorithm to move away from local minima and controls population diversity, and $X_{j,i}^{(G)}$, $X_{j,i}'^{(G)}$, and $X_{j,i}''^{(G)}$ are the jth parameter of ith target, mutant, and trial vectors at generation G, respectively.

Finally, the selection operation that generates population from either the trial (test) vector or its predecessor (target vector) is based on better optimal or higher fitness according to equation (3.30).

$$X_i^{(G+1)} = \begin{cases} X_{j,i}'^{(G)}, & \text{if } f(X_{j,i}'^{(G)}) \leq f(X_{j,i}^{(G)}) \quad \text{or} \\ & \quad j = q, \;\; i = 1, \ldots, N_p \\ X_i^{(G)}, & \text{otherwise} \end{cases} . \tag{3.30}$$

The above optimization is repeated to achieve better fitness while the solution space is explored for best optima over several generations.

3.5.1 *Multi-objective differential evolution (MODE)*

In multi-objective differential evolution (MODE) [38, 39], Pareto-based, non-dominated sorting, and crowded techniques are used to implement the selection of the best individuals. The first step of this algorithm is random generation of a population whose size is N_P and evaluation of each objective function value corresponding to its initial state. At a given generation of the evolutionary search, the initial population is sorted based on non-dominated sorting and assigned ranks using crowding distance. Secondly, DE operations like crossover and mutation are carried out over the individuals of the population. The trial vectors of size N_P are generated and objective functions are evaluated. Now both the parent vectors and trial vectors are combined to form a population of size $2N_P$. Then, the ranking of the combined population is carried out followed by the crowding distance calculation. The best N_P individuals are selected based on ranking and crowding distance. These individuals act as the parent vectors for the next generation. The algorithm of MODE can be described in the following steps and is applied to solve MOEED problems.

***Step 1*:** Randomly generate initial vectors P of size N_P and store them in an archive X.

***Step 2*:** Classify all these vectors into fronts using the non-dominated sorting described in Section 3.3.1 and store them in an archive X'.

***Step 3*:** After non-dominated sorting, the crowding distance (I_{dist}) is calculated for all the vectors in X'. The following procedure is adopted to identify the better of the two vectors. Vector i is better than vector j if $I_i, rank < I_j, rank$ or if $I_i, rank = I_j, rank$ and $I_i, dist > I_j, dist$.

***Step 4*:** Create a new empty box X'' of size N_P. Perform DE operations over N_P vectors in X' to generate N_P trial vectors and store these vectors in X''.

(a) Select a target vector, i in X'.
(b) Start with $i = 1$.

(c) Choose two vectors, r_1 and r_2 randomly from the N_P vectors in X'. Find the vector difference between these two vectors and multiply this difference with the scaling factor F_s to get the weighted difference.
(d) Choose a third random vector r_3 from the N_P vectors in X' and add this vector to the weighted difference to obtain the noisy random vector.
(e) Perform crossover between the target vector and noisy random vector to find the trial vector. This is carried out by generating a random number and if random number $> C_R$ (crossover factor), copy the target vector into the trial vector else copy the noisy random vector into the trial vector and put it in box X''.
(f) Increment i by one. If $i \leq N_P$, go to (c); otherwise go to Step 5.

***Step 5*:** Copy all N_P parent vectors from X' and all N_P trial vectors from X'' into box X'''. Now the box X''' has $2N_P$ vectors.

(a) Classify these $2N_P$ vectors into fronts based on non-domination and calculate the crowding distance of each vector.
(b) Take the best N_P vectors from box X''' and put into box X''''.

This completes one generation. Stop if generation number is equal to maximum number of generations. Otherwise, copy N_P vectors from box X'''' to the starting box X and go to Step 2.

3.6 Genetic Algorithm

Genetic algorithm (GA) is a directed random search method used to find a global minimum solution in a huge multidimensional search area. Holland proposed GA for the first time [40] and it has been effectively applied to many optimization problems [41]. GA makes use of genetic operators to progressively develop the fitness of a population and control individuals in a solution population over numerous generations. Generally, all the optimization parameters are considered as binary numbers. The GA optimization uses a random number generator to generate a random initial population. This method is useful when prior knowledge is unavailable.

There are three basic genetic operators, namely crossover, mutation, and selection, that are used to create, search the neighborhood of a population, and decide on a new population. The randomly generated initial population of size N undergoes genetic operations to produce N different solutions for each iteration. The selection operator evaluates each current solution population by its fitness value, which is represented by an objective function. Individuals from the population with higher fitness are selected based on either stochastic or ranking-based selection.

Crossover operation is performed on a pair of selected population solutions with a crossover rate. The rate of crossover for a selected solution pair is described as the probability of applying crossover. One of the common definitions of the operator is one-point crossover that would randomly choose a bit position to swap corresponding bits in the given strings.

Mutation operation is a probabilistic random alteration of the string position of a binary value. This operator will avoid GA from getting stuck at a local minimum. The fitness estimation takes place at the interface of the optimization unit and GA. The fitness value gives information about solution quality which is used for the selection operation. More details about GA can be found in [41–43].

3.6.1 *Multi-objective optimization using NSGA-II*

NSGA [24] is a popular non-domination-based genetic algorithm for multi-objective optimization. It is a very effective algorithm but has been generally criticized for its computational complexity, lack of elitism, and for choosing the optimal parameter value for the sharing parameter. A modified version of NSGA, NSGA-II [25] was developed, which has a better sorting algorithm, incorporates elitism, and does not need a sharing parameter to be chosen *a priori*. NSGA-II is discussed in detail in this section and applied to solve MOEED problems.

3.6.2 *Step-by-step procedure of NSGA-II*

***Step 1 (population initialization)*:** The initial population is generated randomly based on the problem range and constraints, if any.

***Step 2* (*non-dominated sorting*):** The initial population is sorted based on non-dominated sorting described in Section 3.3.1.

***Step 3* (*crowding distance*):** Once the non-dominated sort is complete, the crowding distance is assigned as discussed in Section 3.3.2. Since the individuals are selected based on rank and crowding distance, all the individuals in the population are assigned a crowding distance value.

***Step 4* (*selection*):** After non-dominated sorting and crowding distance is assigned, the selection process is carried out using a crowded-comparison-operator (p_n) as described below.

(1) Non-domination rank p_{rank}, i.e. individuals in front F_i will have their rank as $p_{rank} = i$.
(2) Crowding distance $F_i(d_j)$

- $p \prec_n q$ if
    - $p_{rank} < q_{rank}$
    - or if p and q belong to the same front F_i then $F_i(d_p) > F_i(d_q)$, i.e. the crowding distance should be more.

The individuals are selected by using a binary tournament selection with a crowded-comparison operator.

***Step 5* (*genetic operators*):** Real-coded GAs use a simulated binary crossover (SBX) [44, 45] operator for crossover and polynomial mutation [45, 46].

(a) ***Simulated binary crossover*:** Simulated binary crossover simulates the binary crossover observed in nature and is given as below.

$$c_{1,k} = \frac{1}{2}[(1 - \beta_k)p_{1,k} + (1 + \beta_k)p_{2,k}], \tag{3.31}$$

$$c_{2,k} = \frac{1}{2}[(1 + \beta_k)p_{1,k} + (1 - \beta_k)p_{2,k}], \tag{3.32}$$

where $c_{i,k}$ is the ith child with k^{th} component, $p_{i,k}$ is the selected parent and $\beta_k(\geq 0)$ is a sample from a random number generated having the density

$$p(\beta) = \frac{1}{2}(\eta_c + 1)\beta^{\eta_c}, \quad \text{if } 0 \leq \beta \leq 1, \tag{3.33}$$

$$p(\beta) = \frac{1}{2}(\eta_c + 1)\frac{1}{\beta^{\eta_c+2}}, \quad \text{if } \beta > 1. \tag{3.34}$$

This distribution can be obtained from a uniformly sampled random number u between (0, 1). η_c is the distribution index for crossover. That is

$$\beta(u) = (2u)^{\frac{1}{(\eta+1)}}, \quad \text{if } u > 0.5, \tag{3.35}$$

$$\beta(u) = \frac{1}{[2(1-u)]^{\frac{1}{(\eta+1)}}}, \quad \text{if } u \leq 0.5. \tag{3.36}$$

(b) ***Polynomial mutation:*** The polynomial mutation is one of the genetic operation and is given by

$$c_k = p_k + (p_k^u - p_k^l)\delta_k, \tag{3.37}$$

where c_k is the child and p_k is the parent with p_k^u being the upper bound on the parent component, p_k^l being the lower bound and δ_k being a small variation which is calculated from a polynomial distribution by using

$$\delta_k = (2r_k)^{\frac{1}{\eta_m+1}} - 1, \quad \text{if } r_k < 0.5, \tag{3.38}$$

$$\delta_k = 1 - [2(1-r_k)]^{\frac{1}{\eta_m+1}}, \quad \text{if } r_k \geq 0.5, \tag{3.39}$$

where r_k is a uniformly sampled random number between (0, 1) and η_m is mutation distribution index.

Step 6 (recombination and selection): The offspring population is combined with the current generation population and selection is performed to set the individuals of the next generation. Since all the previous and current best individuals are added to the population, elitism is ensured. Population is now sorted based on non-domination. The new generation is filled by each front subsequently until the population size exceeds the current population size. If by adding all the individuals in front F_j the population exceeds N, then individuals in front F_j are selected based on their crowding distance in the descending order until the population size is N. Hence the process repeats to generate the subsequent generations.

3.7 Clonal Selection Algorithm

With the growth of computational intelligence in recent years, the branch of AIS has greatly influenced engineering applications. The AIS-based algorithms are developed using biological principles such as clone generation, proliferation, and maturation. These principles are mimicked then included into an AIS-based algorithm termed the clonal selection algorithm (CSA) [47, 48]. The CSA named CLONALG, proposed by Leandro and Fernando [49], is a population-based stochastic technique. This CSA more extensively uses artificial immune-based optimization methods in pattern recognition and multimodal optimization problems with binary representation of variables. The implementation of CSA for AIS involves the following steps [50]:

- Initialization of antibodies.
- Cloning and selection.
- Maturation and diversification.
- Removal of differentiated immune cells.

In the process of optimization with an AIS-based CSA, affinity is nothing but the fitness or objective function evaluation and constraint satisfaction. Here the constraints are represented by antigens while the constraint satisfaction is attained by antibody–antigen affinity. In other words, the more the affinity, the higher is the constraint satisfaction. Apart from the above, if two solutions equally satisfy their constraints, the one with a better value of the corresponding objective attains larger affinity or fitness value.

The first step in a CSA is populating a set of randomly generated initial solutions. This set of population, called antibodies, undergoes proliferation and maturation. The process of proliferation of antibodies is nothing more than cloning each member of the initial pool, i.e. copying each initial solution based on its affinity value. The rates of proliferation and maturation (or hypermutation) [51, 52] are two key factors associated with affinity value. The proliferation rate is proportional to its affinity value, and therefore an immunity cell with higher affinity generates more offspring. Obviously, higher affinity antibodies experience a smaller maturation rate.

In CSA the total number of clones generated per antibody directly depends on the affinity or fitness value. Thus, a higher number of clones is produced for the antibodies with a larger fitness value and a lower number of clones is generated for the antibodies with a smaller fitness value. The cloning population size is evaluated using equation (3.40):

$$TC = \sum_{i=1}^{Nsel} Nc_i. \tag{3.40}$$

Each term in the summation of the above equation represents the clone size of selected antibody i and is denoted as:

$$Nc_i = round\left(\frac{\beta N_{sel}\, cc}{i}\right), \tag{3.41}$$

where β is the multiplication factor of clone size, N_{sel} is the population size, and cc is the accelerating factor.

The accelerating factor cc is considered as a fixed value of 1 for all generations in conventional CSA, while in ACSA the value of cc is updated dynamically so that its value varies for every generation. At the end of every generation the acceleration factor is updated as $cc = cc \times \gamma$. The starting value of cc is less than 1 and the γ value lies between 0.5 and 1.1. The idea here is to use a dynamic accelerating factor instead of a fixed value to obtain best clonal population size, Nc_i. With the increase in generation count the cloning population size decreases so that fast convergence can be obtained.

3.7.1 *Implementation of MOACSA for an EED problem*

This section deals with the step-by-step procedure of the MOACSA method for solving an EED problem with consideration of transmission loss, generation limits, and all security constraints.

***Step 1*:** Generate randomly distributed antibodies of initial population with size ($N_{pop} \times N$) and store them in archive X

$$X = [X_1 X_2 \ldots X_i \ldots X_{N_{pop}}]^T, \tag{3.42}$$

where $X_i = [P_G\ V_G\ Tap\ Q_c]_{1xN}$.

Each element of vector X_i is a set of decision variables called molecules of a particular antibody. The vector consists of these antibody populations, evaluated and denoted by:

$$\left.\begin{aligned} P_G &= [P_{G1}\ P_{G2} \ldots P_{Gi} \ldots P_{G_{NG}}] \\ V_G &= [V_{G1}\ V_{G2} \ldots V_{Gi} \ldots V_{G_{NG}}] \\ Tap &= [T_1\ T_2 \ldots T_i \ldots T_{NT}] \\ Q_C &= [Q_{C1}\ Q_{C2} \ldots Q_{Ci} \ldots Q_{C_{NC}}] \end{aligned}\right\}. \tag{3.43}$$

***Step 2*:** For each antibody, satisfy the equality and inequality constraints. That means adjusting the sum of P_{Gi} values in an antibody equal to total load demand P_D, i.e. $\sum_{i=1}^{NG} P_{Gi} = P_D$.

***Step 3*:** Run an NR load flow program for each antibody and calculate the transmission losses, slack bus power, and line flows.

***Step 4*:** Evaluate the affinity for each antibody which is nothing but objective function values.

a. Cost function, F_1, evaluated from equation (3.1).
b. NO_x emission function, F_2, estimated from equation (3.2).
c. Loss, P_L, estimated from equation (3.3).

***Step 5*:** Sort the initial population using the non-dominated sorting technique described in Section 3.3.1 and then assign crowding distance [53].

***Step 6*:** Set iteration counter $k = 0$.

***Step 7*:** $k = k + 1$.

***Step 8*:** Select the best population N_{sel} of antibodies which gives a non-dominated solution from the archive X_{nds} and store them at an archive X_{best} for cloning and maturate operation.

a. Cloning of population set $C = [C_1\ C_2 \cdots C_i \ldots C_{N_{sel}}]$, where C_i represents number of copies of the ith antibody from X_{best}.

b. The population of clones undergoing somatic hyper-maturation resulting in a new antibody is given by:

$$C_{new}(i) = C(i) + \alpha_i * (R_{d1} - R_{d2}) * \max(f_i), \tag{3.44}$$

where R_{d1} and R_{d2} are two randomly generated numbers in the range of 1 to N, and α_i is mutation rate and given as:

$$\alpha_i = \exp(-f_i \rho), \tag{3.45}$$

where ρ controls decay of the exponential function, f_i is normalized antigenic affinity over the interval (0,1),

$$f_i = \frac{F_i}{\sum_{i=1}^{N_{sel}} F_i}, \tag{3.46}$$

where F_i is the fitness or affinity of ith best population.

Step 9**:** Again test each molecule of the new mutated antibody for any constraint violation.

Step 10**:** Recalculate the affinity of all mutated clones as in Step 4 and sort again based on non-dominated sorting.

Step 11**:** Modify the acceleration factor $cc = cc \times \gamma$, where the γ value lies in between 0.5 and 1.1.

Step 12**:** Check for the stopping criterion. If the iterations have reached the maximum go to the next step, otherwise go to Step 7.

Step 13**:** Obtain a Pareto-optimal set of solutions from the final iteration.

Step 14**:** Obtain the best compromised solution from a Pareto-optimal front using a fuzzy membership function approach.

3.8 Simulation Results

The proposed multi-objective optimization algorithms presented in this chapter are tested on a six-unit IEEE 30-bus test system. This system has six generators, 41 transmission lines, four transformers, and nine reactive power injections at various buses. The detailed data of the test system is available in [54]. The generator voltage limits, transformer taps, and Qshunts are assumed to have their upper and lower limits as shown in Table 3.1.

For this test system three objectives have been considered for optimization, namely fuel cost, emission, and loss. For comparison purposes the simulations carried out on test system are categorized into two cases:

***Case (i)*:** Bi-objective optimization (fuel cost and NO_x emission).

***Case (ii)*:** Tri-objective optimization (fuel cost, NO_x emission, and loss).

This MOEED problem has also been solved by implementing and comparing the results of four different algorithms, namely MOACSA, NSGA-II, MOPSO, and MODE. The control parameters of the four algorithms are given in Table 3.2.

3.8.1 *Bi-objective optimization*

This case study is an example of a two-dimensional EED problem. The Pareto-optimal fronts for all four methods are depicted in Figure 3.1. It is understood that the MOACSA method preserves the

Table 3.1. Limits of control variables.

Variables	Vgs	Taps	Qshunts
Min	0.95	0.9	0
Max	1.1	1.1	0.05

Table 3.2. Control parameters of various algorithms used for computation.

MOACSA	NSGA-II	MOPSO	MODE
Population = 50	Population = 50	Population = 50	Population = 50
Best pop = 40	No. of gen = 200	No. of gen = 200	No. of gen = 200
No. of iterations = 200	Crossover = 5	$C1 = 2$	Crossover = 0.98
Clonal size factor = 1	Mutation = 50	$C2 = 2$	FF = 0.5
$cc = 0.8971$	Tournament = 2		Tournament = 1

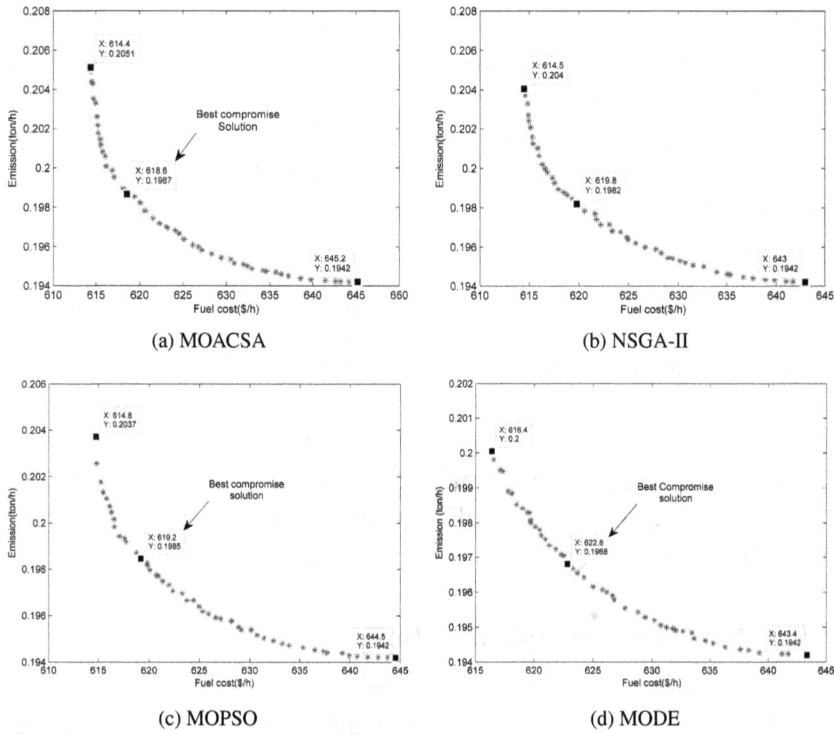

(a) MOACSA

(b) NSGA-II

(c) MOPSO

(d) MODE

Figure 3.1. Pareto-optimal front of test system with cost and emission objectives — case (i).

diversity of the non-dominated solutions over the entire trade-off surface. From the Pareto front, the two non-dominated solutions representing best cost and best emission are indicated in Table 3.3 for case (i). The optimal settings of the control variables along with the best compromise solution are also tabulated.

3.8.2 *Tri-objective optimization*

This case study is an example of three-dimensional multi-objective optimization of an EED problem with all security constraints. Here, three objectives are optimized simultaneously by all four methods. The Pareto fronts of various methods are indicated in Figure 3.2 for case (ii). The optimal settings of control variables along with function are tabulated in Table 3.4 for case (ii). The best compromised

Table 3.3. Optimal solution of test system with all the four methods — case (i).

Multi objectives	MOACSA			NSGA-II			MOPSO			MODE		
	Best cost	Best emission	Best compr.	Best cost	Best emission	Best compr.	Best cost	Best emission	Best compr.	Best cost	Best emission	Best compr.
Pg1(MW)	15.4653	40.9322	28.3580	16.7663	40.6827	28.3066	15.8526	41.5089	29.0575	27.6492	40.4104	33.4318
Pg2(MW)	33.8221	47.4213	37.6017	33.2185	45.4834	40.4514	34.9596	46.0687	40.4133	35.9876	45.2813	39.2416
Pg3(MW)	62.1445	53.8723	53.7232	61.7705	54.1864	54.0268	64.7771	53.7845	55.2162	52.9199	55.0446	52.6250
Pg4(MW)	64.7625	38.6180	62.8406	64.9319	40.0552	62.8006	64.8055	38.5714	59.2423	64.3155	39.5335	58.5257
Pg5(MW)	70.5150	54.2995	58.5444	67.6318	54.6008	54.0649	63.1951	55.1360	57.1243	63.6160	54.3423	55.8479
Pg6(MW)	38.4887	51.0988	44.5149	40.9471	51.1235	46.1214	41.7896	50.9674	45.1455	40.6990	51.2706	45.7523
V1 (p.u.)	1.0367	1.0240	1.0215	1.0282	1.0540	1.0563	1.0672	1.0519	1.0528	1.0990	1.0965	1.0980
V2 (p.u.)	1.0319	1.0205	1.0173	1.0305	1.0543	1.0445	1.0583	1.0443	1.0569	1.0959	1.0909	1.0940
V3 (p.u.)	1.0325	0.9986	1.0174	1.0301	1.0356	1.0410	1.0593	1.0419	1.0467	1.0916	1.0981	1.0919
V4 (p.u.)	1.0132	0.9984	1.0112	1.0121	1.0039	1.0010	1.0164	1.0311	1.0317	1.0881	1.0953	1.0971
V5 (p.u.)	1.0117	1.0051	1.0068	1.0207	1.0380	1.0300	1.0393	1.0490	1.0421	1.0796	1.0953	1.0817
V6 (p.u.)	1.0226	1.0015	1.0261	1.0325	0.9999	1.0165	1.0253	1.0315	1.0129	1.0799	1.0768	1.1000
T1	0.9817	1.0002	0.9597	0.9859	0.9676	0.9625	0.9966	0.9996	0.9731	1.0283	1.0655	1.0325
T2	0.9850	0.9792	0.9900	1.0089	1.0054	0.9863	0.9965	1.0005	0.9760	0.9027	0.9707	1.0245
T3	1.0071	1.0037	1.0135	1.0028	0.9772	1.0222	1.0004	0.9992	1.0003	0.9333	1.0746	1.0819
T4	0.9997	0.9632	0.9940	1.0052	0.9941	1.0251	1.0157	1.0083	1.0042	0.9846	1.0601	1.0320
Qc10(p.u)	0.0247	0.0188	0.0213	0.0345	0.0330	0.0343	0.0243	0.0319	0.0353	0.0164	0.0092	0.0030
Qc12(p.u)	0.0211	0.0275	0.0267	0.0315	0.0269	0.0306	0.0151	0.0107	0.0093	0	0.0229	0.0033
Qc15(p.u)	0.0302	0.0267	0.0306	0.0192	0.0190	0.0213	0.0321	0.0251	0.0326	0.0500	0.0201	0.0446
Qc17(p.u)	0.0275	0.0176	0.0235	0.0271	0.0311	0.0217	0.0097	0.0155	0.0164	0.0500	0.0295	0.0457
Qc21(p.u)	0.0342	0.0414	0.0290	0.0267	0.0298	0.0301	0.0302	0.0308	0.0295	0	0.0163	0.0267
Qc22(p.u)	0.0227	0.0219	0.0164	0.0299	0.0313	0.0329	0.0299	0.0290	0.0281	0.0498	0.0474	0.0500
Qc23(p.u)	0.0216	0.0199	0.0161	0.0253	0.0303	0.0229	0.0309	0.0265	0.0296	0.0240	0.0166	0.0098
Qc24(p.u)	0.0300	0.0233	0.0278	0.0319	0.0315	0.0321	0.0265	0.0256	0.0217	0.0500	0.0317	0.0421
Qc29(p.u)	0.0270	0.0266	0.0264	0.0255	0.0215	0.0204	0.0238	0.0272	0.0258	0.0069	0.0002	0.0483
Cost($/h)	614.3815	645.1734	618.5855	614.4651	642.9556	619.7896	614.7530	644.5323	619.1630	616.3886	643.3583	622.8253
Emission	0.2051	0.1942	0.1987	0.2040	0.1942	0.1982	0.2037	0.1942	0.1985	0.2000	0.1942	0.1968
Loss(MW)	1.7981	2.8422	2.1828	1.8661	2.7319	2.3718	1.9795	2.6369	2.2821	1.7871	2.4828	2.0245
ΣP_{gi}(MW)	285.20	286.24	285.5828	285.27	286.13	285.7718	285.38	286.04	285.6821	285.19	285.88	285.4245

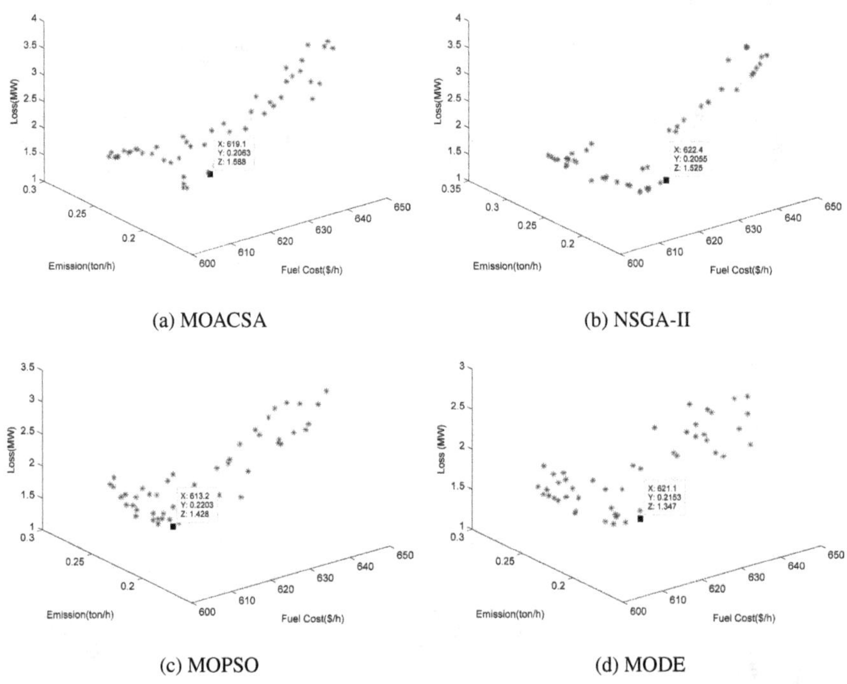

Figure 3.2. Pareto-optimal front of test system with cost, emission, and loss as objectives — case (ii).

solution with each method for tri-objective optimization is given in Table 3.5.

3.9 Conclusions

In this chapter four types of multi-objective optimization methods for solving MOEED problems are presented, namely MOPSO, MODE, NSGA-II, and MOACSA. The main target of the proposed methods is to find the Pareto-optimal set of solutions for power system control that satisfy both security and operational constraints simultaneously. The most important purpose of all four methods is the obtaining of a Pareto-optimal front, allowing the system operator to use their order of preference in selecting the best solution for implementation. The feasibility of all four methods for solving MOEED problem is tested on standard IEEE 30-bus test system for two- and tri-objective case

Table 3.4. Optimal solution of test system with various methods for cost, emission, and loss objectives — case (ii).

Method	MOACSA			NSGA-II			MOPSO			MODE		
Variables	Min. cost	Min. emission	Min. loss	Min. cost	Min. emission	Min. loss	Min. cost	Min. emission	Min. loss	Min. cost	Min. emission	Min loss
P_{G1} (MW)	11.1752	41.2880	6.2139	11.1706	40.6724	6.2721	11.4414	39.3378	6.3699	12.1408	42.4797	6.2734
P_{G2} (MW)	29.7040	46.2594	31.7717	30.4959	46.3320	32.6688	30.5673	47.4179	24.2273	29.4058	44.4386	24.1763
P_{G3} (MW)	49.8639	54.5698	40.6684	48.6156	54.3400	45.4479	49.2656	55.6444	36.0631	50.2645	54.6859	50.3077
P_{G4} (MW)	98.4056	39.2474	73.9788	99.6893	39.0773	68.7522	99.7133	38.2066	82.1996	99.3312	41.2023	73.6692
P_{G5} (MW)	60.8407	54.1692	98.4977	60.0850	54.7380	99.8029	58.8156	54.3895	99.8895	58.6216	51.9644	98.6881
P_{G6} (MW)	35.2904	51.4756	33.4835	35.3764	51.6968	31.7282	35.7228	51.5777	36.0205	35.6772	51.3260	31.5587
V_1 (p.u.)	1.0165	1.0383	1.0500	1.0458	1.0439	1.0479	1.0155	1.0295	1.0194	1.0600	1.0595	1.0600
V_2 (p.u.)	1.0138	1.0145	1.0500	1.0451	1.0226	1.0470	1.0215	1.0201	1.0157	1.0599	1.0535	1.0541
V_3 (p.u.)	1.0240	0.9792	1.0474	1.0482	1.0027	1.0495	1.0209	1.0021	1.0229	1.0571	1.0588	1.0595
V_4 (p.u.)	1.0500	0.9866	1.0500	1.0622	1.0913	1.0484	1.0489	1.0052	1.0409	1.0600	1.0444	1.0600
V_5 (p.u.)	1.0040	0.9523	1.0466	1.0354	0.9895	1.0467	1.0098	0.9708	1.0139	1.0600	1.0546	1.0555
V_6 (p.u.)	1.0486	1.0187	1.0500	1.0417	1.0928	1.0651	1.0214	1.0385	1.0398	1.0405	1.0360	1.0600
T_1	0.9584	1.0447	0.9873	0.9600	1.0578	0.9647	0.9944	1.0302	0.9796	1.0628	1.1000	1.0239
T_2	1.0400	0.9773	1.0353	1.0008	1.0756	1.0130	0.9890	0.9699	0.9686	0.9326	0.9049	0.9190
T_3	0.9475	0.9616	0.9478	1.0587	0.9012	1.0099	0.9856	0.9575	0.9812	1.0587	1.1000	1.0327
T_4	0.9595	0.9624	0.9606	0.9847	0.9530	0.9846	0.9779	1.0375	0.9784	0.9821	0.9784	0.9830
Q_{c10} (p.u)	0.0500	0.0013	0.0500	0.0456	0.0202	0.0393	0.0368	0.0269	0.0308	0.0146	0.0009	0
Q_{c12} (p.u)	0.0134	0.0070	0.0500	0.0159	0.0344	0.0385	0.0260	0.0311	0.0196	0.0421	0.0500	0.0500
Q_{c15} (p.u)	0.0427	0.0203	0.0500	0.0500	0.0097	0.0142	0.0215	0.0282	0.0211	0.0447	0.0345	0.0500
Q_{c17} (p.u)	0.0500	0.0500	0.0460	0.0254	0.0392	0.0352	0.0282	0.0342	0.0320	0.0500	0	0.0500
Q_{c21} (p.u)	0.0500	0.0109	0.0500	0.0186	0.0065	0.0324	0.0291	0.0220	0.0396	0.0143	0.0286	0.0383
Q_{c22} (p.u)	0.0371	0.0351	0.0368	0.0167	0.0344	0.0476	0.0238	0.0344	0.0134	0.0361	0.0365	0.0140
Q_{c23} (p.u)	0.0500	0.0460	0.0500	0.0024	0.0331	0.0498	0.0172	0.0317	0.0307	0.0347	0.0049	0.0195
Q_{c24} (p.u)	0.0039	0.0098	0.0390	0.0153	0.0412	0.0275	0.0368	0.0200	0.0407	0.0430	0.0500	0.0500
Q_{c29} (p.u)	0.0341	0.0254	0.0386	0.0349	0.0400	0.0384	0.0223	0.0187	0.0298	0.0273	0.0044	0.0178
Cost($/h)	**604.6608**	646.2704	616.7591	**604.9608**	645.7921	619.0763	**605.0620**	645.4718	616.1043	**604.8634**	642.8147	617.0217
Emission	0.2434	**0.1942**	0.2249	0.2211	**0.1942**	0.2224	0.2477	**0.1942**	0.2354	0.2475	**0.1943**	0.2264
Loss (MW)	1.8798	3.6094	**1.2139**	2.0400	3.4565	**1.2721**	2.1260	3.1739	**1.3699**	2.0411	2.6970	**1.2734**
$\sum$PGi(MW)	285.28	287.0094	284.6139	285.440	286.86	284.67	285.5260	286.5739	284.7699	285.44	286.10	284.67

Table 3.5. Best compromise solution of test system with various methods for tri-objectives.

Variables	MOACSA	NSGA-II	MOPSO	MODE
P_{G1} (MW)	22.2703	25.8574	11.1516	15.7933
P_{G2} (MW)	31.6977	33.9013	29.8121	30.1736
P_{G3} (MW)	46.0220	49.3873	44.2015	51.0804
P_{G4} (MW)	61.4704	56.5892	76.0960	61.7237
P_{G5} (MW)	84.8146	85.1319	90.0778	96.4820
P_{G6} (MW)	38.7134	34.0577	33.4891	29.4941
V_1 (p.u.)	1.0360	1.0507	1.0177	1.0600
V_2 (p.u.)	1.0366	1.0482	1.0151	1.0585
V_3 (p.u.)	1.0447	1.0534	1.0248	1.0599
V_4 (p.u.)	1.0435	1.0389	1.0482	1.0568
V_5 (p.u.)	1.0500	1.0379	1.0205	1.0533
V_6 (p.u.)	1.0479	1.0447	1.0358	1.0600
T_1	0.9508	0.9570	0.9841	1.0386
T_2	1.0932	1.0171	0.9742	0.9072
T_3	0.9720	1.0085	0.9757	0.9984
T_4	0.9527	0.9836	0.9753	0.9999
Q_{c10} (p.u)	0.0208	0.0381	0.0273	0.0179
Q_{c12} (p.u)	0.0333	0.0403	0.0210	0.0500
Q_{c15} (p.u)	0.0190	0.0176	0.0203	0
Q_{c17} (p.u)	0	0.0341	0.0325	0.0256
Q_{c21} (p.u)	0.0264	0.0303	0.0360	0.0064
Q_{c22} (p.u)	0.0500	0.0500	0.0146	0.0378
Q_{c23} (p.u)	0.0007	0.0500	0.0293	0.0196
Q_{c24} (p.u)	0.0417	0.0241	0.0391	0.0285
Q_{c29} (p.u)	0.0500	0.0365	0.0261	0.0229
Cost($/h)	619.0551	622.4143	613.1925	621.0733
Emission	0.2063	0.2055	0.2203	0.2153
Loss (MW)	1.5883	1.5248	1.4281	1.3469
$\sum$PGi(MW)	284.9883	284.9248	284.8281	284.7469

studies. In two-objective case studies only cost and emission objectives are considered with different operational constraints, while in tri-objective cases fuel cost, emission, and loss objectives are considered with all security constraints.

References

[1] Jeyadevi, S., Baskar, S. and Babulal, C.K. (2011). Solving ultiobjective optimal reactive power dispatch using modified NSGA-II, *Int. J. Elec. Power*, **33(2)**, 219–228.

[2] Cai, J., Ma, X., Li, L. *et al.* (2007). Chaotic particle swarm optimization for economic dispatch considering the generator constraints, *Energ. Convers. Manage.*, **48(2)**, 645–653.
[3] Coelho, L.S., and Lee, C.-S. (2008). Solving economic load dispatch problems in power systems using chaotic and Gaussian particle swarm optimization approaches, *Int. J. Elec. Power*, **30(5)**, 297–307.
[4] Srinivasa Reddy, A. and Vaisakh, K. (2013). Shuffled differential evolution for economic dispatch with valve point loading effects, *Int. J. Elec. Power*, **46**, 342–352.
[5] Zahavi, J. and Eisenberg, L. (1977). An application of the economic-environmental power dispatch, *IEEE T. Syst. Man Cyb.*, **7(7)**, 523–530.
[6] King, T.D., El-Hawary, M.E. and El-Hawary, F. (1995). Optimal environmental dispatching of electric power systems via an improved Hopfield neural network model, *IEEE T. Power Syst.*, **10(3)**, 1559–1565.
[7] Palanichamy, C. and Sundar Babu, N. (2008). Analytical solution for combined economic and emissions dispatch, *Electr. Pow. Syst. Res.*, **78(7)**, 1129–1137.
[8] Tuan, T.Q., Fandino, J., Hadjsaid, N. *et al.* (1994). Emergency load shedding to avoid risks of voltage instability using indicators, *IEEE T. Power Syst.*, **9(1)**, 341–351.
[9] Farag, A., Al-Baiyat, S. and Cheng, T.C. (1995). Economic load dispatch multiobjective optimization procedures using linear programming techniques, *IEEE T. Power Syst.*, **10(2)**, 731–738.
[10] Zahavi, J. and Eisenberg, L. (1975). Economic-enviromental power dispatch, *IEEE T. Syst. Man Cyb.*, **(5)**, 485–489.
[11] Jeyakumar, D.N., Venkatesh, P. Lee, K.Y. (2007). Application of multi-objective evolutionary programming to combined economic emission dispatch problem, *Int. Joint Conf. Neur.*, **2007**, 1162–1167.
[12] Abido, M.A. (2003). Environmental/economic power dispatch using multi-objective evolutionary algorithms, *IEEE T. Power Syst.*, **18(4)**, 1529–1537.
[13] Abido, M.A. (2003). A novel multiobjective evolutionary algorithm for environmental/economic power dispatch, *Electr. Pow. Syst. Res.*, **65(1)**, 71–81.
[14] Bo, Z. and Cao, Y.-j. (2005). Multiple objective particle swarm optimization technique for economic load dispatch, *Journal of Zhejiang University SCIENCE A*, **6(5)**, 420–427.
[15] Varadarajan, M. and Swarup, K.S. (2008). Solving multi-objective optimal power flow using differential evolution, *Generation, Transmission & Distribution*, IET, **2(5)**, 720–730.
[16] Chatterjee, A., Ghoshal, S.P. and Mukherjee, V. (2012). Solution of combined economic and emission dispatch problems of power systems by an opposition-based harmony search algorithm, *Int. J. Elec. Power*, **39(1)**, 9–20.
[17] Srinivasa Rao, B. and Vaisakh, K. (2013). Multi-objective adaptive Clonal selection algorithm for solving environmental/economic dispatch and OPF problems with load uncertainty, *Int. J. Elec. Power*, **53**, 390–408.

[18] Yaşar, C. and Özyön, S. (2012). Solution to scalarized environmental economic power dispatch problem by using genetic algorithm, *Int. J. Elec. Power*, **38(1)**, 54–62.

[19] Hota, P.K., Barisal, A.K. and Chakrabarti, R. (2010). Economic emission load dispatch through fuzzy based bacterial foraging algorithm, *Int. J. Elec. Power*, **32(7)**, 794–803.

[20] Cai, J., Ma, X., Li, Q. *et al.* (2010). A multi-objective chaotic ant swarm optimization for environmental/economic dispatch, *Int. J. Elec. Power*, **32(5)**, 337–344.

[21] Raglend, I.J., Veeravalli, S., Sailaja, K. *et al.* (2010). Comparison of AI techniques to solve combined economic emission dispatch problem with line flow constraints, *Int. J. Elec. Power*, **32(6)**, 592–598.

[22] Coello, C.A.C. and Cortés, N.C. (2005). Solving multiobjective optimization problems using an artificial immune system. *Genet. Program. Evol. M.*, **6(2)**, 163–190.

[23] Basu, M. (2012). Artificial immune system for combined heat and power economic dispatch, *Int. J. Elec. Power*, **43(1)**, 1–5.

[24] Srinivas, N. and Deb, K. (1994). Multiobjective optimization using nondominated sorting in genetic algorithms, *Evol. Comput.*, **3**, 221–248.

[25] Deb, K., Pratap, A., Agarwal, S. *et al.* (2002). A fast elitist multiobjective genetic algorithm: NSGA-II, *IEEE T. Evolut. Comput.*, **6(2)**, 182–197.

[26] Abido, M.A. (2006). Multiobjective evolutionary algorithms for electric power dispatch problem, *IEEE T. Evolut. Comput.*, **10(3)**, 315–329.

[27] Kennedy, J. (1997). "The Particle Swarm: Social Adaptation of Knowledge", presented at IEEE International Conference on Evolutionary Computation, Indianapolis, IN, USA, 13–16 April 1997.

[28] Angeline, P. (1998). Evolutionary optimization versus particle swarm optimization: philosophy and performance differences, *Proc. 7th Conf. Evolut. Prog.*, 601–610.

[29] Shi, Y. and Eberhart, R. (1998). Parameter selection in particle swarm optimization, *Proc. 7th Conf. Evolut. Prog.*, 591–600.

[30] Ozcan, E. and Mohan, C. (1998). Analysis of a simple particle swarm optimization system, *Intelligent Engineering Systems Through Artificial Neural Networks*, **8**, 253–258.

[31] Abido, M.A. (2002). Optimal design of power system stabilizers using particle swarm optimization, *IEEE T. Energy Conver.*, **17(3)**, 406–413.

[32] Abido, M.A. (2007). Two-level of non-dominated solutions approach to multiobjective particle swarm optimization, *Proc. GECCO 2007*, 726–733.

[33] Abido, M.A. (2007). Multiobjective particle swarm for environmental/economic dispatch problem, *Proc. IPEC 2007*, 1894–1899.

[34] Abido, M.A. (2009). Multiobjective particle swarm optimization for environmental/ economic dispatch problem, **79**, 1105–1113.

[35] Morse, J.N. (1980). Reducing the size of the non-dominated set: pruning by clustering, *Comp. Oper. Res.*, **7(1–2)**, 55–66.

[36] Abido, M.A. (2008). Multiobjective particle swarm optimization for optimal power flow problem, *Proc. MEPCON 2008*, 392–396.

[37] Price, K.V., Storn, R.M. and Lampinen. J.A. (2005). *Differential Evolution: A Practical Approach to Global Optimization*, Springer, New York.

[38] Babu, B.V. and Anbarasu, B. (2005). "Multi-objective differential evolution (MODE): an evolutionary algorithm for multi-objective optimization problems (MOOPs)", presented at The Third International Conference on Computational Intelligence, Robotics, and Autonomous Systems (CIRAS-2005), Singapore, 13–16 December 2005.

[39] Babu, B.V. (2006). *Process Plant Simulation*, Oxford University Press, New Delhi.

[40] Holland, J.H. (1975). *Adaptation in Natural and Artificial Systems: An Introductory Analysis with Applications to Biology, Control, and Artificial Intelligence*, University of Michigan Press, Ann Arbor, MI.

[41] Caponetto, R., Fortuna, L., Graziani, S. *et al.* (1993). Genetic algorithms and applications in system engineering: a survey, *T. I. Meas. Control*, **15(3)**, 143–156.

[42] Glodberg, D.E. (1989). *Genetic Algorithms in Search, Optimization, and Machine Learning*, Addison-Wesley, Boston.

[43] Davis, L. (1991). *Handbook of Genetic Algorithms*, Van Nostrand Reinhold, New York.

[44] Beyer, H.-G. and Deb, K. (2001). On self-adaptive features in real-parameter evolutionary algorithm, *IEEE T. Evolut. Comput.*, **5(3)**, 250–270.

[45] Deb, K. and Agarwal, R.B. (1995). Simulated binary crossover for continuous search space, *Complex Systems*, **9**, 115–148.

[46] Raghuwanshi, M.M. and Kakde, O.G. (2004). Survey on multiobjective evolutionary and real coded genetic algorithms, *Proceedings of the 8th Asia Pacific Symposium on Intelligent and Evolutionary Systems*, 150–161.

[47] De Castro, L.N. and Von Zuben, F.J. (2002). Learning and optimization using the clonal selection principle, *IEEE T. Evolut. Comput.*, **6(3)**, 239–251.

[48] De Castro, L.N. and Von Zuben, F.J. (2000). *Artificial Immune Systems: Part II — A Survey of Applications*, FEEC/Univ. Campinas, Campinas, Brazil.

[49] Burnet, F.M. (1978). Clonal selection and after, *Theoretical Immunology*, **63**, 85.

[50] Burnet, F.M. (1959). *The Clonal Selection Theory of Acquired Immunity, Vol. 3*, Vanderbilt University Press, Nashville, TN.

[51] Berek, C. and Ziegner, M. (1993). The maturation of the immune response, *Immunology Today*, **14(8)**, 400–404.

[52] George, A.J.T. and Gray, D. (1999). Receptor editing during affinity maturation, *Immunology Today*, **20(4)**, 196.

[53] Rahman, T.K.A., Suliman, S.I. and Musirin, I. (2006). Artificial immune-based optimization technique for solving economic dispatch in power system, *Proc. 16th Italian Conference on Neural Nets*, 338–345.

[54] Lee, K.Y., Park, Y.M. and Ortiz, J.L. (1985). A united approach to optimal real and reactive power dispatch, *IEEE T. Power Ap. Syst.*, **5**, 1147–1153.

Chapter 4

Voltage Security Assessment and Optimal Load Shedding Using the CBR Approach

Narayan Prasad Patidar[a]

[a]*Maulana Azad National Institute of Technology, Bhopal, India*

4.1 Introduction

In this chapter the case-based reasoning (CBR) system for voltage security assessment and optimal load-shedding plan is described. Decision trees are used for case indexing and optimal load shedding in the developed CBR system.

Heavy loadings on transmission facilities with limited reactive power control of a large-size power system may lead to voltage collapse. Since voltage collapse can occur suddenly, there may not be sufficient time for analysis of system operating conditions and operator actions to stabilize the system. In such emergencies load shedding is the most effective and practical way to mitigate the voltage collapse. Therefore, after voltage security assessment, providing a real-time optimal load-shedding plan for insecure operating states can help the operators to avoid the voltage collapse.

A power system enters into a state of voltage instability when a disturbance, an increase in load demand, a change in system conditions, or a combination of the three causes progressive and uncontrolled decline of bus voltages. If the system is found to be insecure, analysis proceeds to determine the appropriate corrective strategy. If the system is secure, then contingency analysis is performed. It is performed in three distinct stages: contingency definition, selection and evaluation. The ranking of insecure contingencies according to their severity is known as contingency ranking. The purpose of security assessment is to provide information to the operating personnel about the secure or insecure nature of the near-future power system operating states under hundreds of contingencies analyzed every 10 to 20 minutes, so that proper control action can be initiated within a safe time limit. The timeframe requirement of voltage security assessment function varies across utilities and operators. The total time taken for voltage security assessment function is less than one minute by the 700-bus system of the Tokyo Electric Power Company (TEPCO) in Japan [1] and the more-than-3000-bus system of the Independent Electricity System Operator (IESO) in Ontario [2]. In large-size power systems, a long list of contingencies has to be assessed; therefore, exhaustive power flow or continuation power flow (CPF) evaluations are very time-consuming and not suitable for real-time applications.

In a large-size power system the possible number of contingencies including multiple ones will be astronomical. However, the probability of occurrence of a large number of these contingencies is quite low. Hence, keeping in mind the real-time requirement of the security function, the aim of contingency definition is to reduce this list to a shorter one containing only credible contingencies. The probability of occurrence of credible contingencies is very high. Even the number of credible contingencies is so large that they cannot be evaluated in a timeframe of interest. Hence, the credible contingencies are first ranked in order of their severity and then the most severe contingencies are shortlisted for evaluation of their effects in a timeframe of interest so that necessary preventive control action can be undertaken. Figure 4.1 shows the overview of voltage security function [3, 4].

Voltage security function forms an integral part of the modern energy management system, but its real-time implementation is still a challenging task. For real-time application there is a need for fast detection of the potentially dangerous situations of voltage instability so that necessary corrective actions can be taken to avoid voltage collapse. The traditional methods of contingency selection based

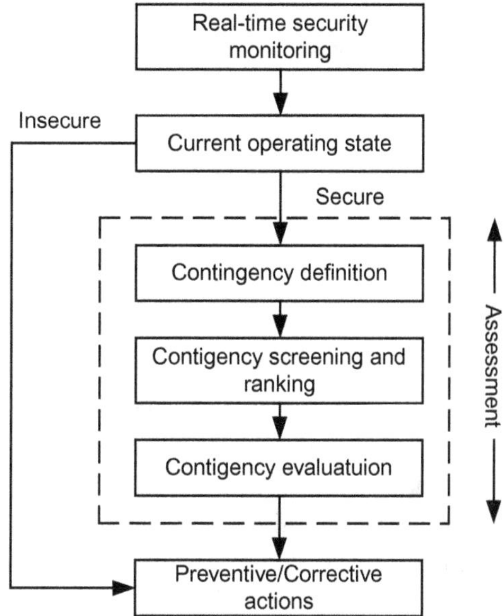

Figure 4.1. Overview of voltage security function.

on approximate or full AC load flow are either inaccurate or time-consuming. To overcome these difficulties, there is a pressing need to develop fast, accurate, and transparent security assessment tools.

The application of artificial intelligence techniques for real-time diagnosis and decision making in power system operation and control is nowadays recognized as an area of growing interest. Machine learning is a broad area of artificial intelligence, concerned with design and development of algorithms and techniques that allow computers to learn. In a very broad sense machine learning is based on two types of learners, namely eager learners like some of the artificial neural networks (ANN), decision trees (DT), etc., and lazy learners like CBR.

Voltage security assessment function must be evaluated as quickly as possible so that operators can have sufficient time for setting controls to alleviate voltage instability problems. In the past decade artificial intelligence approaches have been employed for the assessment of voltage security [5–15], but it is also essential that effective and practical solutions should be proposed in real-time to mitigate voltage collapse conditions in addition to voltage security assessment. Load shedding is one of the most effective and practical solutions to restore the system solvability during emergencies. Many researchers have proposed analytical methods [16–18] to compute minimum load shedding to mitigate the voltage collapse. These methods are not computationally efficient and therefore not suitable for on-line applications, especially during emergencies.

In the past CBR has been applied to various problems of electrical engineering [19–27]. In this chapter, a novel approach based on CBR is presented for on-line voltage security assessment of the power system and to determine the optimal load-shedding plan for insecure operating states. A case-base for the CBR is generated by computer simulation and maximum loadability margins of the power system are used as a security index. Decision trees are used for indexing of the case-base so that the case retrieval process becomes faster. The same DTs as used for case indexing have also been used for the determination of a load-shedding plan. The Manhattan distance function [28] is used for determination of similarity between the new case and old cases in the case-base. In this chapter one of the categories of single-case adaptation [29], known as null adaptation, is used for voltage security assessment. In null adaptation, the solution of the most similar case from the case-base is directly assigned to the empty solution set of the new case. The accuracy of CBR depends on the number of old cases in the case-base. As the number of solved cases is added to the case-base, accuracy greatly increases because the probability of finding a similar case to the new case is increased. The effectiveness of the case-based reasoning methodology is tested on IEEE-30 bus and IEEE-118 bus test systems [30].

4.2 Case-Based Reasoning

In real-world problem solving, people usually use experience that was successful in solving previous similar problems. Knowledge-based techniques in artificial intelligence mimic the reasoning process people use by modeling the experiences, storing them in a knowledge base, and reusing those experiences when solving new problems. In expert systems, the experiences are usually modeled as rules, which will be used to construct the solutions for new problems. In CBR [31], experiences are modeled into a different form as concrete problems with their solutions (*cases*). New problems are solved based on the solutions of retrieved cases in previous similar situations from the knowledge base (*case-base*). CBR is a problem-solving artificial intelligence methodology that uses past experiences to solve the newly encountered problems. Whenever a new problem is encountered, the CBR system retrieves a similar solved problem (*old case*) from the case-base and the solution of the old case is assigned to the new one. The new case along with its solution is also stored into the case-base for future use. Short descriptions of the main components of the CBR are given below. For details about CBR, readers may also refer to [32].

4.2.1 *Case representation*

A case represents a piece of knowledge of the system for which it is made. It consists of the determiner (input) attribute and outcome (output) attribute. A good representation method supports effective and efficient retrieval of cases from the case-base. Most of the CBR systems represent the cases as a plain structure composed of set of attribute value pairs as

$$X = [x_1, x_2, \ldots, x_a, x_c],$$

where $\mathrm{x}_1, \mathrm{x}_2, \ldots, \mathrm{x}_\mathrm{a}$ are the determiner attributes (numeric or symbolic) and x_c is a set of solutions, i.e. outcome attribute (class).

4.2.2 *Case-base*

Cases are the foundation of case-based reasoning. The case-base (or case database) is thus the most important element in a case-based system. The case-base is the database of solutions to previous problems and it is the foundation of every part of the process of augmentation.

4.2.3 *Case indexing*

A good indexing of the cases in the case-base allows only relevant cases to be retrieved. Without indexing, the retrieval time will become large because it has to test each case of the case-base (which may have thousands of cases) for similarity measure. A decision tree is good option for indexing in CBR systems [33]. The case-base is structured into several groups, each group according to a leaf in the decision tree, if this method is used. In the decision tree each node represents an attribute, and each edge represents the according value of the attribute of the parent node. The small groups are often organized in a linear manner. Thus it is only necessary to traverse the decision tree, following for each node the according branch with the correct value of the attribute, until a leaf is reached. Then, every case in this small group of cases may be a possible solution for the problem.

4.2.4 *Case retrieval and adaptation*

CBR begins with the cases and these are obtained by retrieval. Case retrieval is the process of selecting the past solved case that best matches the present case. Case retrieval is a two-step process. The index scheme is used to find the set of similar cases in the case-base. Then, a suitable similarity-matching function is used to determine the most similar case to the new case from the group of cases. Case adaptation is the problem-specific area of the CBR system. In this chapter, one of the categories of single-case adaptation [29], known as null adaptation, is used for voltage security assessment. In null adaptation, the solution of the most similar case from the case-base is directly assigned to the empty solution set of the new case.

4.2.5 *Learning*

The learning mechanism is achieved by inserting newly solved cases into the case-base. Before inserting a new case into the case-base, the CBR system will check its redundancy. If a case that has already been included in the case-base is presented to the CBR system, it will not be inserted in the case-base again. It is one of the important aspects of the CBR system in which it learns more cases for future use. As the number of cases increases in the case-base, the accuracy of the system is enhanced.

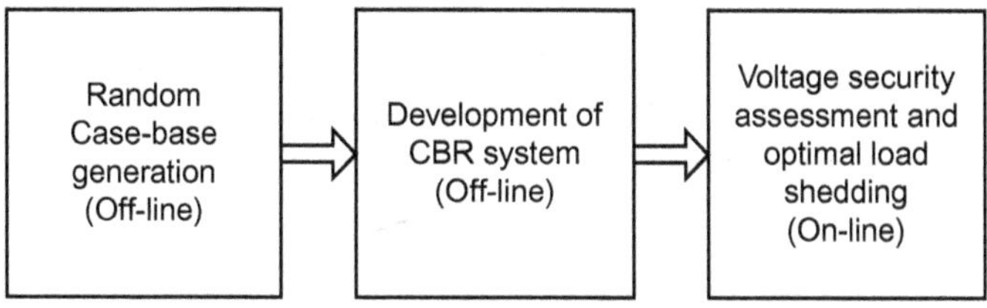

Figure 4.2. Overall voltage security and optimal load-shedding framework.

4.3 Methodology

Figure 4.2 highlights the overall voltage security framework. For a power system under study, the case-base is generated by varying the real and reactive loads at all the buses randomly, in a sufficiently wide range to screen all the situations deemed relevant. First, a load pattern, line-outage number, and corresponding security class characterize each case. Second, decision trees are generated for each line-outage to index the group of cases for the CBR model, which belongs to a particular class. Third, the CBR model is used for on-line voltage security assessment and optimal load shedding against voltage collapse.

4.3.1 *Performance index for voltage security assessment*

Several performance indices have been proposed in the past for evaluating voltage stability. The objective of these indices is to define a scalar magnitude that can be monitored as the system parameters change. The most basic and widely accepted index is loading margin [34]. Figure 4.3 shows voltage vs. real power variation for a power system. In the case of contingency, the loadability margin is reduced to a lower value. The voltage stability margin is defined as distance with respect to the bifurcation parameter, from the current operating point to the voltage collapse point. The system is said to be voltage secure if this margin is reasonably high or greater than a predefined critical value (λ_{cr}) of the loadability margin; otherwise it is said to be insecure. In this chapter, this voltage stability margin

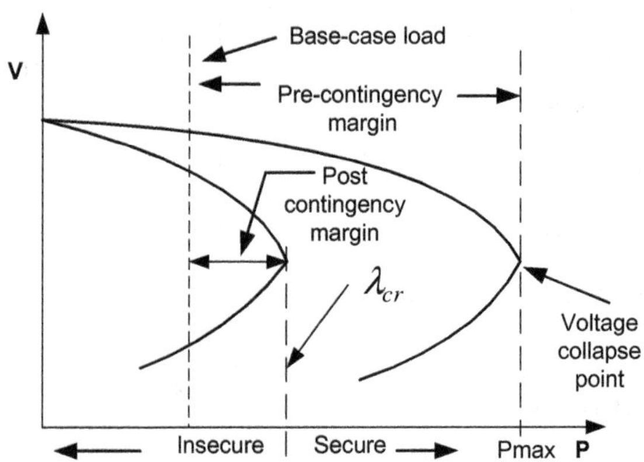

Figure 4.3. PV diagram of power system.

is referred as the maximum loadability margin and calculated by the continuation power flow method using the software UWPFLOW.

4.3.2 *Case-base generation*

To realize the effectiveness of the CBR for voltage security assessment the cases are generated by computer simulation. A case-base consists of the operating states of the power system, generated by generating a large number of load patterns randomly to screen all the possible operating states deemed necessary to solve a particular task. Then maximum loadability margins (MLM) are calculated corresponding to each pattern and under each single line outage. The CPF method is used to calculate the MLM of the power system using the program UWPFLOW [37]. MLMs mainly depend upon the real and reactive loads of the PQ[1] buses, hence the real and reactive loads of the PQ buses and the real load of the PV[2] buses are selected as input features and MLM (λ_m) is considered to be a dependent variable (output). To identify the pattern and its relation to the particular line outage case of the system, an additional feature, a contingency number L_n,

[1]In power flow analysis, PQ denotes the list of buses in which the active and reactive power are fixed.

[2]In power flow analysis, PV indicates the list of buses in which the active power and the voltage magnitude are fixed.

is introduced into the input pattern. MLM corresponding to each pattern is divided as secure and insecure with respect to a critical value of λ_m as λ_{cr} so that if $\lambda_m \leq \lambda_{cr}$, then the operating state under a particular line outage will be insecure; otherwise it will be a secure one. Thus X describes the case along with security status (class λ_k) as given below.

$$\begin{aligned} X = [&P_1, P_2, \ldots, P_{pq}, P_{pq+1}, P_{pq+2}, \ldots, P_{pq+pv}, \\ &Q_1, Q_2, \ldots, Q_{pq}, L_n, \lambda_k, \lambda_m], \end{aligned} \tag{4.1}$$

where P_i and Q_i $(i = 1, 2, \ldots, pq)$ are the real and reactive loads respectively on the ith PQ bus, P_i $(i = pq+1,\ pq+2, \ldots, pq+pv)$ is the real load on the ith PV bus, and λ_k $(k = 1, 2)$ is the output class.

4.3.3 *Decision tree for case indexing*

Case indexing makes the retrieval process faster because fewer cases have to undergo similarity matching. Also, the retrieval accuracy is enhanced because partitioning the cases by the index prevents irrelevant cases from being considered in the similarity matching. Here DT [35, 36] is used for indexing of the case-base. The training data examples (cases) are kept in the leaves. During retrieval, this index guides the search to the group of cases stored in a leaf node. The decision tree has a self-contained ability of feature selection, hence most relevant features are selected for decision making or indexing. General steps to build the decision tree are described below.

Proceeding from the root node, an attribute is chosen, say a_i, and a threshold value of the a_i, say V_{is}. The dichotomy test T is defined as

$$a_i \leq V_{is}. \tag{4.2}$$

This test is applied to all the values of the attribute a_i; it decomposes the training cases into two subsets corresponding to the two successors of the root node. Attribute and threshold value are chosen so as to obtain the maximum information gain about the classification.

Let N_{c1} and N_{c2} be the number of training cases which belong to the two output classes y and n respectively and $H_c(S)$ be the prior classification entropy of set of training cases S, measuring the impurity of S:

$$H_c(S) = -\left[\left(\frac{N_{c1}}{S}\right) Log_2\left(\frac{N_{c1}}{S}\right) + \left(\frac{N_{c2}}{S}\right) Log_2\left(\frac{N_{c2}}{S}\right)\right]. \quad (4.3)$$

Let $H_{c/T}(S)$ be the mean posterior classification entropy of S, given the outcome of test T. Set S splits into subsets S_y and S_n. Those states, which satisfy the condition $a_i \leq V_{is}$, are members of set S_y and the remaining states are members of set S_n.

$$H_{c/T}(S) = -\left[\left(\frac{S_y}{S}\right) H_c\left(S_y\right) + \left(\frac{S_n}{S}\right) H_c\left(S_n\right)\right]. \quad (4.4)$$

Using equations (4.3) and (4.4), information gain is calculated as

$$I(s) = H_c(s) - H_{c/T}(s). \quad (4.5)$$

Maximum information gain is used for decomposing the learning cases at the current node. The above procedure is repeated recursively until the stopping criterion is met.

The decision tree's growing is to be stopped if the number of cases corresponding to the particular node becomes less than a minimum number. This type of node is defined as a leaf of the tree.

4.3.4 *Similarity measure for case retrieval*

When a new case is presented to the CBR system, it is directed towards the group of relevant cases by the decision tree index and then the most similar case from the group of cases in the leaf of the tree is selected. A number of methods have been proposed in the literature for similarity measure. In this chapter, a simple Manhattan distance function [28] is used for similarity matching. The Manhattan distance function measures the attribute-to-attribute distance between the new case and a previous case. The Manhattan distance function is defined as

$$D = \sum_{i=1}^{a} \frac{|x_i^n - x_i^p|}{r_a}, \quad (4.6)$$

where

$D =$ Manhattan distance
$x_i^n =$ i^{th} attribute in a new case
$x_i^p =$ i^{th} attribute in an old case (previous case)
$r_i =$ range of variation of ith attribute in a case
$a =$ number of attribute in a case.

If one of the attributes has a relatively large range, then it can overpower the other attributes. Therefore attribute distances are often normalized by dividing the distance for each attribute by the range r_i, i.e. the difference of the maximum and minimum value of that attribute, so that the distance for each attribute is in the range of 0 to 1. Using this distance, the similarity function is defined as

$$SM = \sum_{i=1}^{a} \left(1 - \frac{|x_i^n - x_i^p|}{r_i}\right). \tag{4.7}$$

4.3.5 *Load shedding*

To drive the system from an insecure to a secure region under a particular line outage, the load at specified buses is to be curtailed. A method proposed for load shedding is described below.

In the proposed method, a DT under a particular line outage is used for optimal load shedding as well as case indexing of a case-base. The procedure for building the DT is explained in Section 4.3.3. Mathematically, each leaf of a DT represents a set of constraints on the attribute values that intervene in the tree. The constraints of the leaf of the DT define the hypercube (box) in the attribute space. The problem of computing the distance from the new case to a nearest voltage secured leaf is viewed as a minimization problem. The nearest secure leaf to a new case is determined by computing the smallest incremental vector δ in the attribute space such that summation of the new case vector and δ satisfy the box constraints, which represent the nearest secure leaf.

The incremental vector δ is defined as attribute-to-attribute difference between the two cases c_1 and c_2, each of which having 'a' number of attributes

$$\delta(c_1, c_2) = [\Delta x_1, \Delta x_2, \ldots, \Delta x_a], \tag{4.8}$$

where $\Delta x_i = \lfloor x_i(c_2) - x_i(c_1) \rfloor$ for $i = 1, 2, \ldots, a$.

The general form of the scalar distance between two cases is

$$d(c_1, c_2) = \sqrt[k]{\left(\frac{|\Delta x_1|^k}{r_1} + \frac{|\Delta x_2|^k}{r_2} + \cdots + \frac{|\Delta x_a|^k}{r_a}\right)}, \tag{4.9}$$

where $r_1 \ldots r_a$ are weights, which are equal to the range of the respective attributes.

A class is defined as the union of the leaves of a DT and characterized by as many multidimensional and scalar distances as the number of leaves. If E represents a set of constraints over the DT variables for one of the secure leaves, then the incremental vector between the new case and set E is given as

$$\delta_E = \left| \begin{array}{ll} E_{x_i} - x_i = 0 & \text{if } E_{x_i}^{\min} \leq x_i \leq E_{x_i}^{\max} \\ E_{x_i}^{\max} - x_i = -\Delta x_i & \text{if } x_i > E_{x_i}^{\max} \\ E_{x_i}^{\min} - x_i = \Delta x_i & \text{if } x_i < E_{x_i}^{\min} \end{array} \right\rangle, \tag{4.10}$$

and the minimum distances between the new case (if insecure) and all the secure leaves is given by

$$(d(c, E))_{\min} = D_{\min} = \min\{d(c, E_1), d(c, E_2), \ldots d(c, E_{sl})\}, \tag{4.11}$$

where $d(c, E_{sl})$ is the scalar distance between the new case and one of the secure leaves and sl is the total number of secure leaves.

For the nearest secure leaf, the third condition in equation (4.10) (i.e. Δx_i for $x_i < E_{x_i}^{\min}$) is very rare but even if it occurs, the positive element of the vector δ_E can be set to zero ($\Delta x_i = 0$), and then the δ_E for load shedding can be modified as

$$(\delta_E)_{sh} = \left| \begin{array}{ll} E_{x_i} - x_i = 0 & \text{if } E_{x_i}^{\min} \leq x_i \leq E_{x_i}^{\max} \\ E_{x_i}^{\max} - x_i = -\Delta x_i & \text{if } x_i > E_{x_i}^{\max} \\ E_{x_i}^{\min} - x_i = 0 & \text{if } x_i < E_{x_i}^{\min} \end{array} \right\rangle, \tag{4.12}$$

where $(\delta_E)_{sh}$ is the minimum incremental load vector which is to be added to the insecure new case to bring it into the secure region. Hence, modified loads on the specified buses are given by

$$[S_s] = [S_{ins}] + [(\delta_E)_{sh}], \tag{4.13}$$

where S_s and S_{ins} are PQ load vectors for secure and insecure cases respectively, on the specified buses only.

The DT of respective line outage determines the potential buses for load shedding. Loads on other buses remain the same.

4.3.6 *Algorithm*

The algorithm to develop the CBR model for voltage security assessment and optimal load shedding is given below.

***Step 1*:** A large number of load patterns are generated randomly by perturbing the real and reactive loads at all buses.

***Step 2*:** MLM is calculated for all the load patterns under each line outage using the CPF method.

***Step 3*:** Cases are represented by load patterns in p.u. (per unit), labeled with classes as secure or insecure with respect to the threshold value of MLM. A separate set of cases is generated for each line outage and an additional feature, the line outage number L_n, is introduced into a case vector.

***Step 4*:** Initial cases of the case-base are used to build the DT using equations (4.2)–(4.5) for each line outage separately. All cases under a particular line outage are stored in their respective leaves of the DT.

***Step 5*:** A new case is presented to the CBR system, and directed to the respective DT by traveling over the tree branches. Finally it reaches the leaf of the tree where the group of similar cases are stored.

***Step 6*:** The most similar case to the new case from the case-base is determined using equation (4.11).

***Step 7*:** The output class corresponding to the most similar case from step 6 is assigned to the new case.

***Step 8*:** Repetition is checked by comparing the features of the new case and the most similar case found in step 6. If all the features match exactly, then this case is not included in the case-base; otherwise it is retained for future use.

Step 9: The new case included in the case-base in step 8 is also kept separate into a temporary case-base, and tested off-line at regular intervals using the CPF method. Off-line testing of new cases keeps track of the accuracy of the newly added cases. This off-line testing does not affect the on-line performance. Off-line testing intervals may be once a day, week, or month, and depend on operators.

Step 10: If the current new case is found insecure then the nearest secure leaf is determined using equations (4.9)–(4.11).

Step 11: For optimal load shedding, the incremental load-shedding vector $(\delta_E)_{sh}$ is calculated between an insecure new case and a set E of the constraints for the nearest secure leaf using equation (4.12).

Step 12: To bring the system into a secure region, the final load on the specified buses is obtained using equation (4.13).

Figure 4.4 shows the flowchart of the CBR system for voltage security assessment and optimal load shedding.

4.4 Results and Discussion

The effectiveness of the CBR approach has been tested on IEEE-30 bus and IEEE-118 bus systems. The test results of the two systems are presented below. A total of 300 load patterns for each line outage with load variation in the range of 50% to 150% of the base-case load are generated randomly. Post-contingent MLM (p.u.) are calculated for each load pattern and under each line outage. Post-contingent MLM (p.u.) are classified into two classes, namely secure and insecure, with respect to a threshold or critical value ($\lambda_{cr} = 0.15$ p.u.). Out of 300 patterns for each line outage, 250 are used for the initial case-base and remaining 50 patterns are used for testing purposes. DTs are built, using the 250 cases of each line outage, which were reserved for the initial case-base.

4.4.1 *IEEE-30 bus system*

To determine the severity of each line outage contingency, 50 unseen test cases are presented to the CBR system for testing. The CBR system determines the severity of each line outage based on the

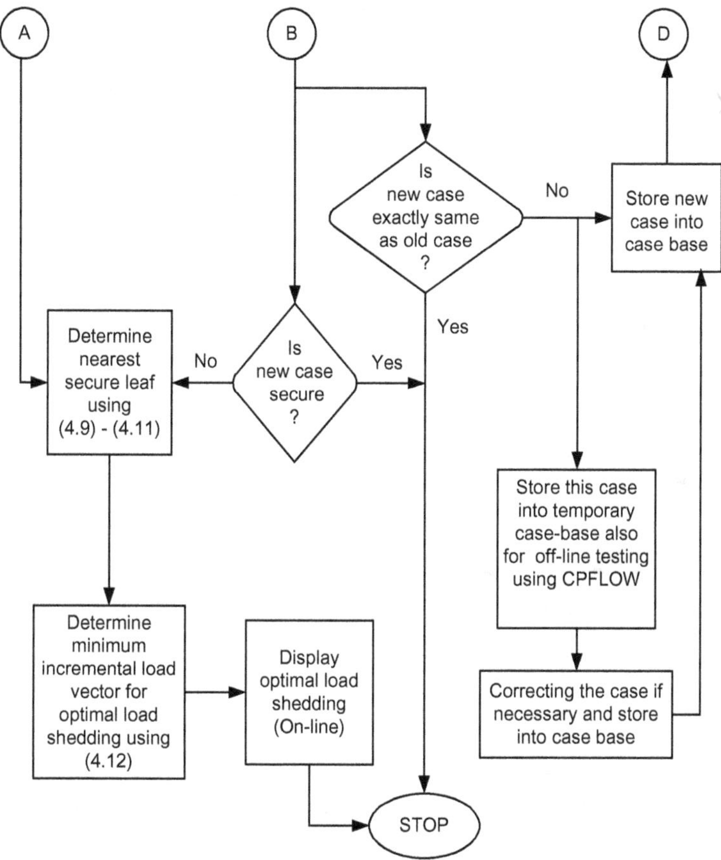

Figure 4.4. Flow chart of proposed CBR system for voltage security assessment and optimal load shedding.

percentage of insecure cases pertaining to that line outage, and ranks them in the order of their severity. Table 4.1 presents the ranking of the five most critical line outage cases. Results show that the ranking of line outage severity determined by the CBR system is same as that determined by the CPF method.

When unseen test cases are presented to the CBR system, almost all are classified correctly. Some of the new cases, which are misclassified by the DT, are classified correctly by the CBR system. This positive feature is mainly due to the effectiveness of the CBR system in reliably classifying the test cases, even in the presence of

Table 4.1. Contingency ranking of the five most severe line outages of an IEEE-30 bus system.

Rank	CPF method *Line outage number	CPF method From bus- to bus	CBR approach Line outage No.	CBR approach From bus- to bus
1	1	(1–2)	1	(1–2)
2	5	(2–5)	5	(2–5)
3	36	(28–27)	36	(28–27)
4	2	(1–3)	2	(1–3)
5	4	(3–4)	4	(3–4)

*Line numbers are given in the sequence as they appear in IEEE format [30].

Table 4.2. Results for an IEEE-30 bus system.

No. of test cases	Classifier	Performance of CBR and DT: No. of false alarms	% false alarms	No. of misses	% Misses
250	CBR	5	2.0	3	1.2
250	DT	11	4.4	6	2.4

Mean retrieval time per case is 6.98 ms.

ambiguities that are not correctly managed by the DT. Table 4.2 shows the test results for 250 new cases, which belong to the most severe line outages as shown in Table 4.1. Table 4.2 shows the number of false alarms and misses. A false alarm occurs when a secure case has been classified as an insecure case and a missed case is when an insecure case has been classified as a secure case. False alarms do not bring any danger to power system operation, because these are further evaluated through a conventional contingency algorithm. The average time to solve per case of the CBR system is found to be 6.98 ms, which can be considered fast enough from the viewpoint of real-time applications.

Table 4.3 shows the features that influence the MLM most, under a particular line outage and selected by the DTs of the five most severe line outages. Figure 4.5 shows the DT for a line-1 (bus1-bus2) outage, in which leaves L1, L2, L4, L5 represent a secure class (class 2) and leaves L3, L6, L7, L8, and L9 represents an insecure

Table 4.3. Features selected for the most severe line outages of an IEEE-30 bus system.

Real loads	Reactive loads
P2, P3, P5, P7, P8, P15, P29	Q5, Q7, Q10, Q26, Q29, Q30

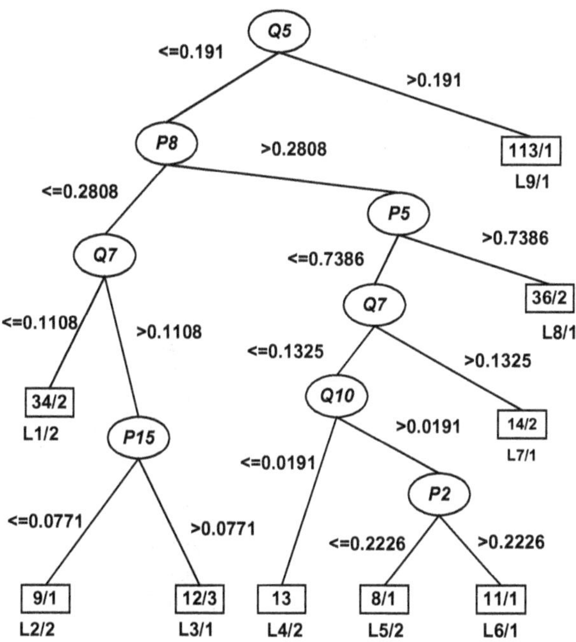

Figure 4.5. Decision tree for line-1 (bus1-bus2) outage of an IEEE-30 bus system.

class (class 1). The variables inside the ovals are real and reactive loads on the respective buses, which influence the MLM most for a line-1 (bus1-bus2) outage. The numbers inside the rectangles are the number of cases in that leaf and the lower number represents the number of cases belonging to a minority class in that leaf.

The proposed CBR system determines an on-line optimal load-shedding plan to enhance the MLM above the threshold value, for each insecure case under any line outage. Observing the DT under a line-1 (bus1-bus2) outage from Figure 4.5, can easily extract the union of leaves and set of constraints over the real and reactive power. Table 4.4 shows the union of leaves, which define the particular class as "secure" and "insecure". Each leaf is defined by a set of constraints over the real and reactive loads. Using equations (4.5)–(4.9) and

Table 4.4. Leaves of DT for line-1 (bus1-bus2) outage for an IEEE-30 bus system.

Leaf	Secure class Leaf1 v Leaf1 v Leaf2 v Leaf4 v Leaf5	Leaf	Insecure class Leaf3 v Leaf6 v Leaf7 v Leaf8 v Leaf9
L1	$[0.1087 < P2 \le 0.3248] \wedge$ $[0.4738 < P5 \le 1.4122] \wedge$ $[0.0956 < Q5 \le 0.191] \wedge$ $[0.0546 < Q7 \le 0.1108] \wedge$ $[0.1514 < P8 \le 0.2808] \wedge$ $[0.0101 < Q10 \le 0.03] \wedge$ $[0.0411 < P15 \le 0.1230]$	L3	$[0.1087 < P2 \le 0.3248] \wedge$ $[0.4738 < P5 \le 1.4122] \wedge$ $[0.0956 < Q5 \le 0.191] \wedge$ $[0.0546 < Q7 \le 0.1108] \wedge$ $[0.1514 < P8 \le 0.2808] \wedge$ $[0.0101 < Q10 \le 0.03] \wedge$ $[0.0771 < P15 \le 0.1230]$
L2	$[0.1087 < P2 \le 0.3248] \wedge$ $[0.4738 < P5 \le 1.4122] \wedge$ $[0.0956 < Q5 \le 0.191] \wedge$ $[0.1108 < Q7 \le 0.1628] \wedge$ $[0.1514 < P8 \le 0.2808] \wedge$ $[0.0101 < Q10 \le 0.03] \wedge$ $[0.0411 < P15 \le 0.0771]$	L6	$[0.2226 < P2 \le 0.3248] \wedge$ $[0.4738 < P5 \le 0.7386] \wedge$ $[0.0956 < Q5 \le 0.191] \wedge$ $[0.0546 < Q7 \le 0.1325] \wedge$ $[0.2808 < P8 \le 0.4498] \wedge$ $[0.0191 < Q10 \le 0.03] \wedge$ $[0.0411 < P15 \le 0.1230]$
L4	$[0.1087 < P2 \le 0.3248] \wedge$ $[0.4738 < P5 \le 0.7386] \wedge$ $[0.0956 < Q5 \le 0.191] \wedge$ $[0.0546 < Q7 \le 0.1325] \wedge$ $[0.2808 < P8 \le 0.4498] \wedge$ $[0.0101 < Q10 \le 0.0191] \wedge$ $[0.0411 < P15 \le 0.1230]$	L7	$[0.1087 < P2 \le 0.3248] \wedge$ $[0.4738 < P5 \le 0.7386] \wedge$ $[0.0956 < Q5 \le 0.191] \wedge$ $[0.1325] < Q7 \le 0.1628] \wedge$ $[0.2808 < P8 \le 0.4498] \wedge$ $[0.0101 < Q10 \le 0.03] \wedge$ $[0.0411 < P15 \le 0.1230]$
L5	$[0.1087 < P2 \le 0.2226] \wedge$ $[0.4738 < P5 \le 0.7386] \wedge$ $[0.0956 < Q5 \le 0.191] \wedge$ $[0.0546 < Q7 \le 0.1325] \wedge$ $[0.2808 < P8 \le 0.4498] \wedge$ $[0.0191 < Q10 \le 0.03] \wedge$ $[0.0411 < P15 \le 0.1230]$	L8	$[0.1087 < P2 \le 0.3248] \wedge$ $[0.7386 < P5 \le 1.4122] \wedge$ $[0.0956 < Q5 \le 0.191] \wedge$ $[0.0546 < Q7 \le 0.1628] \wedge$ $[0.2808 < P8 \le 0.4498] \wedge$ $[0.0101 < Q10 \le 0.03] \wedge$ $[0.0411 < P15 \le 0.1230]$
		L9	$[0.1087 < P2 \le 0.3248] \wedge$ $[0.4738 < P5 \le 1.4122] \wedge$ $[0.191 < Q5 \le 0.2848] \wedge$ $[0.0546 < Q7 \le 0.1628] \wedge$ $[0.1514 < P8 \le 0.4498] \wedge$ $[0.0101 < Q10 \le 0.03] \wedge$ $[0.0411 < P15 \le 0.1230]$

Table 4.4, the optimal load shedding is determined for insecure cases under a line-1 (bus1-bus2) outage. Table 4.5 shows 10 numbers of insecure cases (INC) and respective optimal load-shedding (LS) plans to drive the system from an insecure to a secure region. The minimum distance (D_{min}) between an insecure leaf belonging to an insecure case (INC) and leaves belong to secure classes is given in Table 4.5. The nearest secure leaf (NSL) for each leaf that belongs to insecure cases is also given in Table 4.5. It is important to note that optimal load shedding is needed only on one or two buses out of the seven buses indicated by the DT in Figure 4.5. Hence the proposed method determines the load-shedding plan on a minimum number of buses with minimum amount of load shedding. Let us say that in case 1 in Table 4.5, the load shedding is required only on two buses, i.e. bus5 (to shed reactive power Q5) and bus8 (to shed real power P8). Since a purely reactive load is rarely found, a minimum required real power must also be curtailed at that bus in order to shed a reactive power.

4.4.2 *IEEE-118 bus system*

To test the proposed method on this system, the system is modified in terms of its base load. The base load is increased by 40% and then a total of 300 load patterns for each line outage, with load variation in the range of 50% to 150% of their base-case load, are generated randomly.

DTs are built for 20 line outages, for which the post-contingent MLM are found below the acceptable value (λ_{cr}) for most of the load patterns. All other line outages have no significant reduction in MLM. Under each of the 20 line outages, a set of 50 unseen test cases is presented to the CBR system for testing. Based on the percentage of insecure cases found under a particular line outage, each line outage is ranked in order of its severity. The line outage having the highest percentage of insecure cases is kept on top of the list. Table 4.6 presents the ranking of the six most critical line outage cases. Results show that the ranking of line outage severity determined by the CBR system is the same as that determined by the CPF method. Table 4.7

Table 4.5. Load-shedding plan for insecure cases of an IEEE-30 bus system.

Case		Case features								
No.		P2	P5	Q5	Q7	P8	Q10	P15	NSL	$D_{\min}$
1.	INC	0.1240	1.2464	0.2514	0.0952	0.4404	0.0166	0.1128	L1	0.8540
	LS	0	0	−0.0604	0	−0.1596	0	0		
2.	INC	0.2507	0.8609	0.1736	0.1431	0.3636	0.0134	0.1060	L4	0.1809
	LS	0	−0.1223	0	−0.0106	0	0	0		
3.	INC	0.2714	0.6629	0.1337	0.1331	0.2881	0.0249	0.0945	L1	0.2304
	LS	0	0	0	−0.0223	−0.0073	0	0		
4.	INC	0.2274	1.3447	0.2712	0.1193	0.1739	0.0271	0.1158	L1	0.5023
	LS	0	0	−0.0802	−0.0085	0	0	0		
5.	INC	0.3227	1.1207	0.2260	0.0554	0.3257	0.0188	0.1006	L1	0.3353
	LS	0	0	−0.035	0	−0.0449	0	0		
6.	INC	0.3131	0.9421	0.1900	0.1608	0.3911	0.0233	0.1155	L1	0.6338
	LS	0	0	0	−0.05	−0.1103	0	0		
7.	INC	0.2922	0.8218	0.1658	0.1437	0.2227	0.0266	0.0792	L2	0.0256
	LS	0	0	0	0	0	0	−0.0021		
8.	INC	0.2369	0.9691	0.1955	0.1300	0.1904	0.0288	0.0905	L2	0.1873
	LS	0	0	−0.0045	0	0	0	−0.0134		
9.	INC	0.1232	1.2928	0.2607	0.1051	0.2745	0.0120	0.0610	L1	0.3683
	LS	0	0	−0.0697	0	0	0	0		
10.	INC	0.1129	0.8282	0.1670	0.1307	0.4463	0.0254	0.1118	L5	0.0954
	LS	0	−0.0954	0	0	0	0	0		

Table 4.6. Contingency ranking for an IEEE-118 bus system.

	CPF Method		CBR Method	
Rank	*Line outage No.	From bus to bus	Line outage No.	From bus to bus
1	179	(75–118)	179	(75–118)
2	93	(38–65)	93	(38–65)
3	157	(100–103)	157	(100–103)
4	51	(38–37)	51	(38–37)
5	113	(74–75)	113	(74–75)
6	161	(100–106)	161	(100–106)

*Line numbers are given in the sequence as they appear in IEEE format in [30].

Table 4.7. Test results for an IEEE-118 bus system.

		Performance of CBR and DT			
No. of test cases	Classifier	No. of false alarms	% false alarms	No. of misses	% Misses
300	CBR	7	2.34	5	1.67
300	DT	16	5.34	8	2.67

Mean retrieval time per case is 7.1 ms

shows the test results for 300 new cases, which belong to the most severe line outages that are given in Table 4.6. The average retrieval time or time to solve per case of the CBR system is 7.1 ms. In Table 4.7 the marginal increase in misclassifications (% false alarm and misses) in comparison to the IEEE-30 bus system is due to the reduction in size of the DT and it does not depend on the system size. If the size of the DT is allowed to increase up to the maximum possible, its classification accuracy improves drastically. The size of the DT increases as the system size increases without losing accuracy. In this work, the size of the DT for an IEEE-118 bus system is intentionally reduced for simplicity. Since the DTs are used for indexing in the CBR system, the accuracy of CBR is also reduced slightly but not in direct proportion. In practical implementation we can go up to the full size of the DT for indexing.

Figure 4.6 shows the DT for a line-179 (bus75-bus118) outage, in which leaves L1, L3, L4, L6, and L9 represent a secure class (class 2) and leaves L2, L5, L7, L8, and L10 represent an insecure class

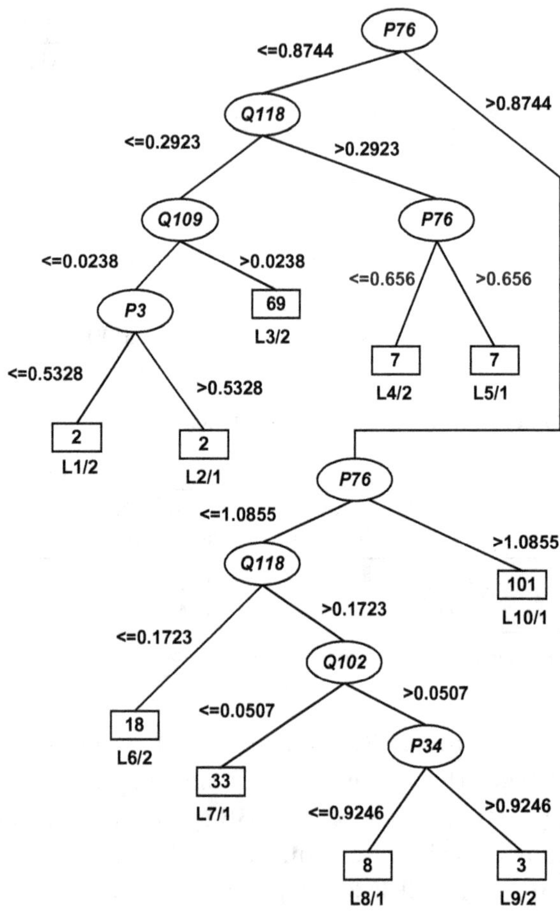

Figure 4.6. Decision tree for a line-179 (bus75-bus118) outage of an IEEE-118 bus system.

(class 1). Also the features selected by a DT of a line-179 (bus75-bus118) outage are shown in Figure 4.6. Table 4.8 presents the features selected for all the critical line outages as given in Table 4.6. By observing the DT of a line-179 (bus75-bus118) outage from Figure 4.6, the union of the leaves and a set of constraints over the real and reactive power can easily be extracted. Table 4.9 shows the union of leaves, which define the particular class as "secure" and "insecure". Each leaf is defined by a set of constraints over the real and reactive

Table 4.8. Features selected for most severe line outages of an IEEE-118 bus system.

Real loads	Reactive loads
P3, P7, P15, P16, P19, P28, P31, P34, P39, P41, P42, P48, P49, P67, P74, P75, P76, P83, P94, P101, P104, P105, P106, P107, P110, P115	Q15, Q16, Q22, Q27, Q33, Q34, Q35, Q52, Q57, Q60, Q67, Q74, Q82, Q102, Q103, Q104, Q106, Q107, Q109, Q118

Table 4.9. Leaves of a DT for a line-179 (bus75-bus118) outage for an IEEE-118 bus system.

Leaf	Secure class Leaf1 v Leaf2 v Leaf4 v Leaf5	Leaf	Insecure class Leaf3 v Leaf6 v Leaf7 v Leaf8 v Leaf9
L1	$[0.2748 < P3 \leq 0.5328] \wedge$ $[0.4148 < P34 \leq 1.2374] \wedge$ $[0.4786 < P76 \leq 0.8744] \wedge$ $[0.0211 < Q102 \leq 0.0629] \wedge$ $[0.0211 < Q109 \leq 0.0238] \wedge$ $[0.1051 < Q118 \leq 0.2923]$	L2	$[0.5328 < P3 \leq 0.8182] \wedge$ $[0.4148 < P34 \leq 1.2374] \wedge$ $[0.4786 < P76 \leq 0.8744] \wedge$ $[0.0211 < Q102 \leq 0.0629] \wedge$ $[0.0211 < Q109 \leq 0.0238] \wedge$ $[0.1051 < Q118 \leq 0.2923]$
L3	$[0.2748 < P3 \leq 0.8182] \wedge$ $[0.4148 < P34 \leq 1.2374] \wedge$ $[0.4786 < P76 \leq 0.8744] \wedge$ $[0.0211 < Q102 \leq 0.0629] \wedge$ $[0.0238 < Q109 \leq 0.0629] \wedge$ $[0.1051 < Q118 \leq 0.2923]$	L5	$[0.2748 < P3 \leq 0.8182] \wedge$ $[0.4148 < P34 \leq 1.2374] \wedge$ $[0.6560 < P76 \leq 0.8744] \wedge$ $[0.0211 < Q102 \leq 0.0629] \wedge$ $[0.0211 < Q109 \leq 0.0629] \wedge$ $[0.2923 < Q118 \leq 0.3150]$
L4	$[0.2748 < P3 \leq 0.8182] \wedge$ $[0.4148 < P34 \leq 1.2374] \wedge$ $[0.4786 < P76 \leq 0.6560] \wedge$ $[0.0211 < Q102 \leq 0.0629] \wedge$ $[0.0211 < Q109 \leq 0.0629] \wedge$ $[0.2923 < Q118 \leq 0.3150]$	L7	$[0.2748 < P3 \leq 0.8182] \wedge$ $[0.4148 < P34 \leq 1.2374] \wedge$ $[0.8744 < P76 \leq 0.1.0855] \wedge$ $[0.0211 < Q102 \leq 0.0507] \wedge$ $[0.0211 < Q109 \leq 0.0629] \wedge$ $[0.1723 < Q118 \leq 0.3150]$
L6	$[0.2748 < P3 \leq 0.8182] \wedge$ $[0.4148 < P34 \leq 1.2374] \wedge$ $[0.4786 < P76 \leq 1.4215] \wedge$ $[0.0211 < Q102 \leq 0.0629] \wedge$ $[0.0211 < Q109 \leq 0.0629] \wedge$ $[0.1051 < Q118 \leq 0.1723]$	L8	$[0.2748 < P3 \leq 0.8182] \wedge$ $[0.9246 < P34 \leq 1.2374] \wedge$ $[0.8744 < P76 \leq 0.1.0855] \wedge$ $[0.0507 < Q102 \leq 0.0629] \wedge$ $[0.0211 < Q109 \leq 0.0629] \wedge$ $[0.1723 < Q118 \leq 0.3150]$
L9	$[0.2748 < P3 \leq 0.8182] \wedge$ $[0.9246 < P34 \leq 1.2374] \wedge$ $[0.8744 < P76 \leq 1.0855] \wedge$ $[0.0507 < Q102 \leq 0.0629] \wedge$ $[0.0211 < Q109 \leq 0.0629] \wedge$ $[0.1723 < Q118 \leq 0.3150]$	L10	$[0.2748 < P3 \leq 0.8182] \wedge$ $[0.4148 < P34 \leq 1.2374] \wedge$ $[0.8744 < P76 \leq 1.4215] \wedge$ $[0.0211 < Q102 \leq 0.0629] \wedge$ $[0.0211 < Q109 \leq 0.0629] \wedge$ $[0.1051 < Q118 \leq 0.3150]$

Table 4.10. Load-shedding plan for insecure cases for an IEEE-118 bus system.

Case No.		Case features						NSL	$D_{\min}$
		P3	P34	P76	Q102	Q109	Q118		
1.	INC	0.7739	1.1368	1.3247	0.0365	0.0302	0.3059	L9	0.2536
	LS	0	0	−0.2392	0	0	0		
2.	INC	0.2946	0.4436	1.2713	0.0254	0.0604	0.2231	L9	0.2420
	LS	0	0	0	0	0	−0.0508		
3.	INC	0.6509	0.8088	0.8849	0.0472	0.0532	0.2974	L3	0.0353
	LS	0	0	−0.0105	0	0	−0.0051		
4.	INC	0.8066	0.5061	1.3457	0.0371	0.0412	0.2698	L6	0.4645
	LS	0	0	0	0	0	−0.0975		
5.	INC	0.2811	0.4188	0.9888	0.0342	0.0235	0.2001	L1	0.1213
	LS	0	0	−0.1144	0	0	0		
6.	INC	0.6309	0.9666	0.9848	0.0323	0.0262	0.3055	L3	0.1798
	LS	0	0	−0.1104	0	0	−0.0132		
7.	INC	0.3742	0.6832	0.8991	0.0530	0.0322	0.3062	L3	0.0923
	LS	0	0	−0.0247	0	0	−0.0139		
8.	INC	0.6984	1.0358	1.1521	0.0540	0.0397	0.2169	L9	0.0706
	LS	0	0	−0.0666	0	0	0		
9.	INC	0.5572	0.6867	1.1244	0.0247	0.0464	0.2580	L3	0.2651
	LS	0	0	−0.25	0	0	0		
10.	INC	0.6979	0.5618	0.9457	0.0401	0.0549	0.2317	L3	0.0756
	LS	0	0	−0.0713	0	0	0		

loads. Using equations (4.5)–(4.9) and Table 4.9, the optimal load shedding is determined for insecure cases under a line-179 (bus75-bus118) outage. Table 4.10 shows 10 numbers of insecure cases and respective optimal load-shedding plans to drive the system from an insecure to a secure region. Table 4.10 also shows the real and reactive power with respective bus numbers on which load shedding is to be done. By analyzing these data it is worth noting that, thanks to the application of the proposed technique, only a limited number of buses should reduce their load demand.

4.5 Conclusions

In this chapter, a CBR system is presented for on-line voltage security assessment and optimal load shedding to mitigate the voltage collapse under different line outages. MLM is used as a voltage security index. Tables 4.2 and 4.7 show the classification accuracies of the CBR system for the IEEE-30 and 118-bus systems respectively, which are quite high. The following conclusions are drawn from this chapter:

- After voltage security assessment, the proposed CBR system also gives a real-time optimal load-shedding plan for insecure operating states of the power system to mitigate the voltage collapse during emergencies.
- DTs are used for case indexing in the case-base and consequently the retrieval process becomes faster; otherwise it has to test each and every case in the case-base, for each new case.
- CBR is based on a case-base in which the real values of operating variables are stored as cases. Since DTs, used for indexing in the proposed CBR system, are directly formulated in terms of the operating variables, it can easily be understood by the operators and can therefore guide decision making in real-time operation and control. In the case of ANN, the knowledge is embedded into connection weights (black box in nature), and hence not easily comprehensible to the operators.
- In the case of any new installation of equipment or addition of transmission lines, the Y-bus matrix will be modified, and hence

the non-deterministic models previously trained for security assessment would not respond accurately and have to be reformulated. In such situations, as compared to the ANN approach, the case-base of CBR can easily be modified. Using the modified Y-bus and past load profiles from the case-base, the MLM for each load profile and under each selected contingency will be calculated off-line. The old cases would be replaced by these modified cases in the case-base. Because of non-iterative training, the DTs for indexing can be created very quickly. The algorithm of CBR will remain the same for real-time operation.

- After solving the new case, CBR also stores the new case into the case-base along with its solution for future use; hence the accuracy of CBR enhances in the future.
- To make the CBR system more accurate and transparent, it can be made to go through regular off-line testing (using CPF) for newly added cases and remove irrelevant cases if found. This off-line testing will not affect the on-line working of CBR. After reviewing the cases off-line, they are included in a case-base if necessary.
- In the CBR approach, execution time mainly depends on the number of system variables selected (DT variables under a particular line outage) for similarity matching, and least depends on the system size.
- The execution time per case by CPF is 75 ms and 600 ms, and by proposed method is 6.98 ms and 7.1 ms, on IEEE-30 and -118 bus test systems respectively. Hence the proposed method is much faster than the CPF method and found to be suitable from the viewpoint of real-time applications.

References

[1] Suzuki, M.,Wada, S., Sato, M. *et al.* (1992). Newly developed voltage security monitoring system, *IEEE T. Power Syst.*, **7(3)**, 965–973.

[2] IESO (2006). *Reliability Coordinator/Balancing Authority/Transmission Operator Readiness Audit Report*, IESO, Mississauga, ON, Canada, 16–19 October 2006.

[3] Ejebe, G.C., Irisarri G.D., Mokhatari S. *et al.* (1996). Methods for contingency screening and ranking for voltage stability analysis of power systems, *IEEE T. Power Syst.*, **11(1)**, 350–356.

[4] Canizares, C.A. (2002). Voltage stability assessment, procedures and guides, Technical Report, *IEEE/PES Power system stability subcommittee*, Final Document. Available at: www.power.uwaterloo.ca. Accessed August 2002.

[5] Cote, J.W. and Liu, C.-C. (1993). Voltage security assessment using generalized operational planning knowledge, *IEEE T. Power Syst.*, **8**, 28–34.

[6] Van Cutsem, T., Wehenkel, L., Pavella M. *et al.* (1993). Decision tree approaches to voltage security assessment, *IEE P-Gener. Transm. D.*, **140(3)**, 189–198.

[7] Mansour, Y., Vaahedi, E. and El-Sharkawi M.A. (1997). Dynamic security contingency screening and ranking using neural networks, *IEEE T. Neural Networ.*, **8(4)**, 942–950.

[8] Matos, M.A., Hatziargyriou N.D. and Pecaslopes J.A. (2000). Multicontingency steady state security evaluation using fuzzy clustering techniques, *IEEE T. Power Syst.*, **15**, 177–183.

[9] Nara, K., Kodam, H., Tanak, K. *et al.* (1985). On-line contingency selection algorithm for voltage security analysis, *IEEE T. Power Ap. Syst.*, **104(4)**, 847–856.

[10] Pandit, M., Srivastav, L. and Sharma J. (2001). Contingency ranking for voltage collapse using parallel self-organizing hierarchical neural network, *Int. J. Elec. Power*, **23(5)**, 369–379.

[11] Pandit, M., Srivastava, L. and Sharma J. (2003). Fast voltage contingency selection using fuzzy parallel self-organizing hierarchical neural network, *IEEE T. Power Syst.*, **18(2)**, 657–664.

[12] Suzuki, M., Wada, S., Sato, M. *et al.* (1992). Newly developed voltage security monitoring system, *IEEE T. Power Syst.*, **7(3)**, 965–973.

[13] Wehenkel, L. and Pavella, M. (1993). Decision tree approach to power system security assessment, *Int. J. Elec. Power*, **15(1)**, 13–36.

[14] Wehenkel, L., Van Cutsem, T., Gilliard M. *et al.* (1991). Decision trees for preventive voltage stability assessment, *Proceedings of the 2nd International NSF Workshop on Bulk Power System Voltage Phenomenon — Voltage Stability and Security*, Deep Creek Lake, MA, 217–228.

[15] Zhang, Z.Z., Hope, G.S. and Malik, O.P. (1989). Expert systems in electric power systems-a bibliographical survey, *IEEE T. Power Syst.*, **4(4)**, 1355–1362.

[16] Berg, G.J. and Sharaf, T.A. (1994). System loadability and load shedding, *Electr. Pow. Syst. Res.*, **28(3)**, 165–170.

[17] Arnborg, S., Andersson G., Hill D.J. *et al.* (1997). On under voltage load shedding in power systems, *Int. J. Elec. Power*, **19(2)**, 141–149.

[18] Feng, Z., Ajjarapu, V. and Maratukulam, D.J. (1998). A practical minimum load shedding strategy to mitigate voltage collapse, *IEEE T. Power Syst.*, **3(4)**, 1285–1291.

[19] Islam, S. and Chowdhury, N. (1999). A case-based expert system for power system restoration, *Proceedings of the 1999 IEEE Canadian Conference on Electrical and Computer Engineering*, 1159–1163.

[20] Islam, S. and Chowdhury, N. (2001). A case-based windows graphic package for the education and training of power system restoration, *IEEE T. Power Syst.*, **16(2)**, 181–187.

[21] Chowdhury, N. and Zhou, B. (1998). An intelligent training agent for power system restoration, *Proceedings of the 1998 IEEE Canadian Conference of Electrical and Computer Engineering*, 786–789.

[22] Long, D., King, R.L. and Luck, R. (1995). Control of power system using case-based reasoning, *Proceedings of the 1995 SSST*, 73–77.

[23] Leib, P. and Weib, P. (1999). Operating data estimation of overhead transmission lines by combining field measurements with the principle of case-based reasoning, *High Voltage Engineering Symposium, IEE conference Publication No. 467*, 2.155–2.118.

[24] Lifeng, L., Zengqiang, M., Zhe, Z. *et al.* Research on case organization and retrieval of case and rule based reasoning approaches for electric power engineering design, *Proceedings of the 1998 International Conference on Power System Technology*, 1082–1085.

[25] Mora, J., Carrillo, G., James, J. *et al.* (2003). "Strategies for the electric supply restoration in Colombian transmission substations", presented at IEEE Bologna Power Tech. Conference, Bologna, Italy, 23–26 June 2003.

[26] Lambert-Torres, G., Gonzaga Martins, H., Rossi, R. *et al.* (2003). "Using similarity assessment in case-based reasoning to solve power system substation problems", presented at IEEE CCECE 2003, Montreal, Canada, 4–7 May 2003.

[27] Lambert-Torres, G., Martins, H.G., Rossi, R. *et al.* (2003). "Using similarity assessment in case-based reasoning to solve power system substation problems", presented at IEEE conference, Montreal, Canada, May 2003.

[28] Randall, W.D. and Martinez, T.R. (1997). Improved heterogeneous distance functions, *Journal of Artificial Intelligence Research*, **6**, 1–34.

[29] Chang, C.-G., Cui J.-J., Wang D.-W. *et al.* (2000). Research on case adaptation techniques in case-based reasoning, *Proc. of the Third Int. Conf. on Machine Learning and Cybernetics*, 26–29.

[30] Power system test cases. Available at http://www.ee.washington.edu/research/pstca. Accessed October 2014.

[31] Kolodner J.L. (1993). *Case-Based Reasoning*, Morgan Kaufmann, San Mateo, CA.

[32] Pal, S.K. and Shiu, S.C.K. (2004). *Foundations of Soft Case-Based Reasoning*, Wiley, Hoboken, NJ.

[33] Craw S. (2003). Introspective learning to build case-based reasoning knowledge containers, *Proc. of the IAPR Int. Workshop on Machine Learning and Data Mining in Pattern Recognition*, 1–6.

[34] Lof, P.A., Smed, T., Andersson G., *et al.* (1992). Fast calculation of a voltage stability index, *IEEE T. Power Syst.*, **7(1)**, 54–64.

[35] Wehenkel, L., and Pavella, M. (1993). Decision tree approach to power system security assessment, *Int. J. Elec. Power*, **15(1)**, 13–36.

[36] Quinlan, J.R. (1986). Induction of decision trees, *Machine learning*, **1(1)**, 81–106.

[37] Canizares, C.A. (1999). UWPFLOW: Continuation and direct methods to locate fold bifurcations in AC/DC/FACTS power systems, University of Waterloo, Canada.

Chapter 5

A Novel State Estimation Paradigm Based on Artificial Dynamic Models

Francesco Torelli[a] and Alfredo Vaccaro[b]

[a]*Department of Electrical Engineering, Politecnico di Bari, Italy*
[b]*Department of Engineering, University of Sannio, Benevento, Italy*

5.1 Introduction

State estimation (SE) is recognized as one of the most promising enabling methodologies for power systems control and monitoring. It aims at computing the voltage phasor at each network bus by processing the available set of grid measurements. The latter include both data acquired by remote terminal units (i.e. real/reactive power flows, active and reactive power injections, and bus voltage magnitudes) and synchronized measurements acquired by phase measurement units.

The literature on SE is vast, and [1–3] outline the major contributions in this domain. In particular, many classes of programming algorithms based on weighted least squares (WLS) [4], iteratively reweighted least squares (IRLS) [5], and least absolute value (LAV) [6] methods have been traditionally adopted for solving power system SE. These algorithms formalize the SE problem by an unconstrained non-linear optimization programming problem. In detail, WLS-based methods aim at identifying the state vector that minimizes the squared weighted sum of the measurement residuals (namely the difference between the available grid measurements and the corresponding values calculated by the power flow equations). To solve this problem Newton–Raphson-based iterative algorithms are typically deployed. A similar solution paradigm is adopted in

IRLS-based methods. The only difference is that in this case the sum weights are updated at each iteration in function of the current value of the measurement residuals. As far as the LAV-based methods are concerned, they aim at minimizing the sum of the absolute value of the measurement residuals. To solve this problem, simplex-based linear programming algorithms are typically adopted.

These programming algorithms represent a useful tool for SE but, as evidenced by the many discussions reported in the literature [7–9], although they usually work quite well for solving SE problems characterized by a well-defined normal matrix, they could become unstable when the attraction region of the initial solution guess is far away from the actual problem solution or when the system is operating close to voltage collapse points. In the latter case the Jacobian matrix of the measurement model becomes singular and the analyst is forced to resume the equations solvability by heuristically tuning the algorithm parameters [10].

Another drawback of the application of these solution paradigms is the numerical conditioning of the measurement equations that could be sensibly affected by the following sources of ill-conditioning [11–13]:

- Large weighting factors aimed at enforcing the virtual measurements.
- Short and long lines connected at the same bus.
- A large number of injection measurements.

To overcome these limitations, more advanced solution paradigms based on factorizing techniques have been proposed in the literature [14, 15]. Although these techniques' results are numerically stable, especially those based on the orthogonal transformations, they can still suffer from divergence and oscillatory problems [12, 16].

A promising research direction aimed at overcoming this limitation is to rely on metaheuristic optimization algorithms (e.g. genetic algorithms [17], evolutionary programming [18], and fuzzy sets [19]). The application of these advanced paradigms allows the SE algorithm to improve its numerical stability further and to reduce the divergence probability. Despite these benefits, the mathematical analysis of SE based on metaheuristic algorithms lags behind. In particular, convergence analysis still remains almost unsolved, while efficiency analysis is equally challenging [20].

Consequently the research for alternative techniques aimed at solving the SE problem even in ill-conditioned cases is still an open problem and requires further investigation. In light of this, in this chapter we propose an alternative and comprehensive formalization of the SE problem based on the dynamic system theory.

The method is to formulate the SE problem by a set of ordinary differential equations, whose equilibrium points represent the problem solutions. According to this new solution paradigm, the power system state can be estimated by computing the quiescent state of an artificial dynamic model. Starting form the Lyapunov theory, we will show that this dynamical model can be designed to be stable with an asymptotical convergence to an equilibrium point and quite insensitive to many factors that can cause numerical instabilities to the traditional solution algorithms. These important features allow the analyst to overcome some of the inherent limitations of iterative minimization algorithms, which can fail to converge due to the highly non-linearities of the first-order conditions. Besides this, we will demonstrate that the proposed solution paradigm is characterized by an intrinsic filter capability that could be very useful in solving the SE problem in the presence of uncertain, noisy or redundant data.

In order to prove the effectiveness of the proposed methodology, simulation results obtained on IEEE test networks are presented and discussed.

5.2 Problem Formulation

Let's consider the following non-linear measurement model [16]:

$$\mathbf{z} = \mathbf{h}(\mathbf{x}) + \mathbf{e}, \tag{5.1}$$

where:

- $\mathbf{x} = [x_1, \ldots, x_n]$ is the state vector to be estimated.
- $\mathbf{z} = [z_1, \ldots, z_m]$ is the vector of the available measurements.
- $\mathbf{h}(\mathbf{x}) = [h_1(\mathbf{x}), \ldots, h_m(\mathbf{x})]$ is the vector of the functions relating the measurements to the power system state. They depend on the

power system admittance matrix and are in general non-linear, except when phasor measurement units (PMUs) measurements are available and complex quantities are expressed in rectangular coordinates [11].

- $\mathbf{e} = [e_1, \ldots, e_n]$ is the random noise vector capturing measurement errors and modeling uncertainty. We assumed that the components of the random noise vector are characterized by a normal distribution with zero mean and covariance matrix $\mathbf{R}$. If these components are statistically independent then $\mathbf{R}$ is a diagonal matrix and the ith diagonal element represents the variance of the noise associated to the ith measurement (namely σ_i^2).

In conventional bus-branch SE models, the state vector is composed of the voltage phasor (magnitude and phase) of the electrical buses, whereas the measurements vector typically includes bus power injections, branch power flows, and voltage magnitudes. Recently, the availability of phase measurement units has made it possible to incorporate direct measurements of the bus voltage angles into the SE process.

SE is typically formalized by the following WLS estimation problem:

$$\min_{\mathbf{x}} \sum_{i=1}^{m} \left(\frac{r_i(\mathbf{x})}{\sigma_i} \right)^2, \tag{5.2}$$

where $r_i(\mathbf{x}) = z_i(\mathbf{x}) - h_i(\mathbf{x})$ is the ith measurement residual.

The problem formalized in (5.2) can be adapted to model the effects of interconnecting buses (namely buses not connected to any load and/or generator). The latter can be considered as exact measurements (a.k.a. virtual measurements) and can be modeled by considering a proper set of equality constraints, namely [21]

$$\begin{cases} \min\limits_{\mathbf{x}} \sum\limits_{i=1}^{m} \left(\dfrac{r_i(\mathbf{x})}{\sigma_i} \right)^2 \\ \mathbf{c}(\mathbf{x}) = 0 \end{cases}. \tag{5.3}$$

According to this paradigm the SE problem formalized in (5.3) can be solved by the unconstrained minimization of the following scalar positive semidefinite function:

$$W(\mathbf{x}) = \frac{1}{2}\mathbf{r}(\mathbf{x})^T\mathbf{R}^{-1}\mathbf{r}(\mathbf{x}) + \frac{1}{2}\mathbf{c}(\mathbf{x})^T\mathbf{c}(\mathbf{x}), \tag{5.4}$$

where $\mathbf{r}(\mathbf{x})$ denotes the measurement residual vector.

In trying to address this issue, the traditional solution approaches aim at solving the first-order derivative condition,

$$\frac{dW(\mathbf{x})}{d\mathbf{x}} = 0. \tag{5.5}$$

That can be expanded as

$$\mathbf{H}_h^T(\mathbf{x})\mathbf{R}^{-1}(\mathbf{h}(\mathbf{x}) - \mathbf{z}) + \mathbf{H}_c^T(\mathbf{x})\mathbf{c}(\mathbf{x}) = 0, \tag{5.6}$$

where $\mathbf{H}_h(\mathbf{x}) = \frac{d\mathbf{h}(\mathbf{x})}{d\mathbf{x}}$ and $\mathbf{H}_c(\mathbf{x}) = \frac{d\mathbf{c}(\mathbf{x})}{d\mathbf{x}}$ represent the Jacobian matrix of $\mathbf{h}(\mathbf{x})$ and $\mathbf{c}(\mathbf{x})$ respectively. Solving (5.6) can be very complex due to the non-linear nature of the resulting set of equations, so iterative methods are employed in trying to obtain a solution that is within an acceptable tolerance. This could be obtained by applying an iterative scheme aimed at computing the corrections $\Delta\mathbf{x}$ at each iteration by solving the normal equations of the linear weighted least squares problem [12]

$$[\mathbf{H}_h^T(\mathbf{x})\mathbf{H}_h(\mathbf{x}) + r\mathbf{H}_c^T(\mathbf{x})\mathbf{H}_c(\mathbf{x})]\Delta\mathbf{x} = \mathbf{H}_h^T(\mathbf{x})\Delta\mathbf{z} + r\mathbf{H}_c^T(\mathbf{x})\Delta\mathbf{c}, \tag{5.7}$$

where r is the ratio between the weighting factors of the virtual and the telemetered measurements.

The solution of the normal equations could be very complex in several operating conditions. In detail, it has been observed that, for very large r, the matrix $r\mathbf{H}_c^T(\mathbf{x})\mathbf{H}_c(\mathbf{x})$ dominates. However, usually there are not enough virtual measurements to make the power system fully observable (namely to make the matrix $\mathbf{H}_c(\mathbf{x})$ full-rank). As a consequence, the matrix $[\mathbf{H}_h^T(\mathbf{x})\mathbf{H}_h(\mathbf{x}) + r\mathbf{H}_c^T(\mathbf{x})\mathbf{H}_c(\mathbf{x})]$ tends to be singular, causing ill-conditioning problems.

Other potential ill-conditioning sources have been identified in several studies [12]. In particular, it has been observed that a large number of injection measurements in the system and the presence of both long and short transmission lines could affect the numerical stability of the iterative solution algorithms [14].

As a consequence, many research efforts have been concentrated on proposing advanced solution techniques aimed at alleviating the ill-conditioning and the numerical instability problems in SE.

To address these issues, an alternative solution paradigm is proposed in this chapter.

5.3 A Dynamic Computing Paradigm for SE

To solve the SE problem, in this chapter we propose two computing paradigms based on the dynamic systems theory. The idea is to design stable artificial dynamic models whose equilibrium point represents the solution of the problem formalized in equation (5.3).

In detail, we assume that the components of the state vector $\mathbf{x}$ evolve according to dynamic trajectories $\mathbf{x}(t)$ (in this framework t represents an artificial parameter), and we aim at identifying a set of differential equations characterized by equilibrium points coincident with the SE problem solutions. Under these assumptions, the scalar positive-definite objective function $W(t)$ defined in (5.4) can be considered as a Lyapunov function [22, 23]. As a consequence, if we impose that the time derivative of $W(t)$ is negative-definite or negative-semidefinite along the trajectory $\mathbf{x}(t)$, then the Lyapunov theorem would assure the existence of an asymptotical stable equilibrium point which minimizes the objective function $W(t)$ and, consequently, solves to SE problem.

To demonstrate this statement, let's first express the objective function in equation (5.4) as

$$W(t) = \frac{1}{2}\mathbf{E}^T(t)\mathbf{E}(t), \tag{5.8}$$

where

$$\mathbf{E}(t) = [\mathbf{E}_1^T(t), \mathbf{E}_2^T(t)]^T = [(\mathbf{R}^{-1/2}\mathbf{r}(\mathbf{x}(t)))^T, (\mathbf{I}^{-1/2}\mathbf{c}(\mathbf{x}(t)))^T]^T. \tag{5.9}$$

Let's compute the time derivative of the function (5.8) as

$$\dot{W}(t) = \frac{d}{dt}W(t) = \mathbf{E}^T(t)\dot{\mathbf{E}}(t), \tag{5.10}$$

and, considering that

$$\dot{\mathbf{E}}(t) = \frac{d\mathbf{E}(t)}{d\mathbf{x}}\dot{\mathbf{x}}(t), \tag{5.11}$$

it follows that

$$\dot{W}(t) = \mathbf{E}^T(t)\frac{d\mathbf{E}(t)}{d\mathbf{x}}\dot{\mathbf{x}}(t). \tag{5.12}$$

Therefore, if $\mathbf{x}(t)$ evolves according to the gradient of $W(t)$, namely

$$\begin{aligned}\dot{\mathbf{x}}(t) &= -k\left(\frac{dW(t)}{d\mathbf{x}}\right)^T = -k\left(\frac{d\mathbf{E}(t)}{d\mathbf{x}}\right)^T \mathbf{E}(t) \\ &= -k[\mathbf{H}_h^T(\mathbf{x}(t))\mathbf{R}^{-1}(\mathbf{h}(\mathbf{x}(t)) - \mathbf{z}) + \mathbf{H}_c^T(\mathbf{x}(t))\mathbf{c}(\mathbf{x}(t))],\end{aligned} \tag{5.13}$$

where k is a positive constant, then by substituting (5.13) into (5.12) it follows that

$$\dot{W}(t) = -k\mathbf{E}^T(t)\frac{d\mathbf{E}(t)}{d\mathbf{x}}\left(\frac{d\mathbf{E}(t)}{d\mathbf{x}}\right)^T \mathbf{E}(t). \tag{5.14}$$

This is a quadratic form that is certainly negative-semidefinite. This important result allows us to conclude that the artificial dynamic system described in (5.13) is asymptotically stable with an exponential convergence ratio to its equilibrium points. Now we have to demonstrate that the quiescent states of this stable dynamic system coincide with the solutions of the problem in (5.3). This can be inferred by considering that if $\mathbf{x}^*$ is a generic equilibrium state of the system in (5.13), then it follows that $\dot{\mathbf{x}}(t*) = 0$ and

$$\left.\frac{dW(t)}{d\mathbf{x}}\right|_{\mathbf{x}=\mathbf{x}*} = 0. \tag{5.15}$$

The comparison of (5.15) with (5.5) allows us to conclude that the dynamic model converges to an equilibrium point which is a solution of the SE problem. Moreover, it is worth observing that this solution could be obtained without requiring any matrix inversion and/or manipulation. This important feature allows us to overcome the difficulties devolving from the ill-conditioning of the normal equations. Besides, it allows the solution algorithm to obtain stable results even when the power system is running at the edge of the voltage collapse points where the Jacobian matrix of the measurement equations is singular or close to being singular.

Furthermore, the proposed solution paradigm is characterized by an intrinsic data-filtering capability derived by the integral action of the computational process. To assess this benefit let's analyze the statistical characteristics of the obtained solution signal. To this aim let's decompose the dynamic trajectory $\mathbf{x}*(t)$ as

$$\mathbf{x}^*(t) = \mathbf{x}_m^* + \mathbf{v}(t), \tag{5.16}$$

where $\mathbf{v}(t)$ is a white noise random vector and $\mathbf{x}_m^*$ is the expected value of $\mathbf{x}*(t)$ that can be computed as

$$\mathbf{x}_m^* = \frac{1}{T}\int_{t_0}^{t_0+T} \mathbf{x}^*(t)dt, \tag{5.17}$$

where T is the integration range and to t_0 is the settling time.

By inverting (5.16) it is possible to estimate the noise vector as

$$\mathbf{v}(t) = \mathbf{x}^*(t) - \mathbf{x}_m^*. \tag{5.18}$$

Then the covariance matrix of the SE problem solution can be explicitly computed as

$$\mathrm{cov}(\mathbf{x}^*(t)) = E((\mathbf{x}^*(t) - \mathbf{x}_m^*)^T(\mathbf{x}^*(t) - \mathbf{x}_m^*)). \tag{5.19}$$

Moreover, by computing the corresponding calculated measurement vector $\mathbf{z}^*(t) = \mathbf{h}(\mathbf{x}^*(t))$ and its expected value $\mathbf{z}_m^* = \mathbf{h}(\mathbf{x}_m^*)$, it is possible to evaluate the covariance matrix of the calculated measurements as

$$\mathrm{cov}(\mathbf{z}^*(t)) = E((\mathbf{z}^*(t) - \mathbf{z}_m^*)^T(\mathbf{z}^*(t) - \mathbf{z}_m^*)). \tag{5.20}$$

The comparison of this value with the covariance matrix of the input measurements (namely $\mathrm{cov}(\mathbf{z}^*(t))$ versus $\mathrm{cov}(\mathbf{z}) = \mathbf{R}$) allows us to assess the filtering effect of the proposed paradigm. We conjectured that this feature allows the computing paradigm to effectively manage uncertainty and noisy data as far as redundant measurements.

The scheme of the proposed dynamic computation process is shown in Figure 5.1.

By analyzing this figure it is worth observing as the application of this scheme allows the analyst to solve the SE problem by requiring

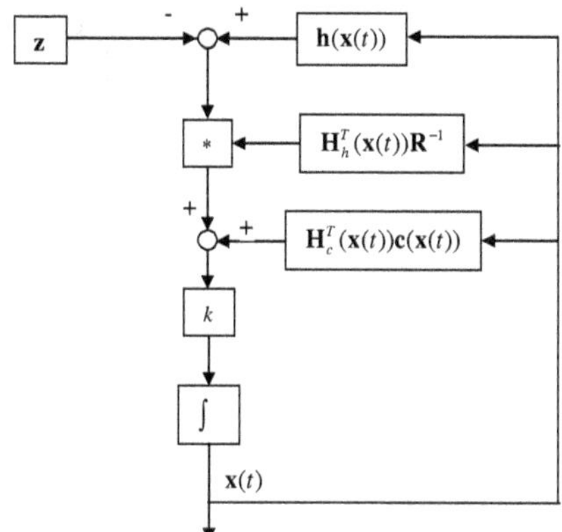

Figure 5.1. The "full dynamic" computing paradigm for SE.

only the time simulation of an artificial dynamic system. We use the term 'full dynamic' to describe the computing paradigm emerging from the application of this scheme.

The theoretical foundations presented in this chapter could be adopted to solve the SE problem according to a different perspective. The basic idea is to exploit the ability of the proposed dynamic computing paradigm to directly solve ill-conditioned linear algebraic systems:

$$\mathbf{A}\mathbf{x} = \mathbf{b}. \tag{5.21}$$

To solve this problem, let's define the following error function:

$$\mathbf{E}(t) = \mathbf{A}\mathbf{x}(t) - \mathbf{b}. \tag{5.22}$$

Then, according to the previously discussed theoretical results, it is easy to show that the dynamic model

$$\dot{\mathbf{x}}(t) = -k\mathbf{A}^T[\mathbf{A}\mathbf{x}(t) - \mathbf{b}] \tag{5.23}$$

is asymptotically stable and converges to equilibrium points that are solutions of the equations (5.21).

This can be inferred by considering that if $\mathbf{x}^*$ is a generic equilibrium state of the system (5.23), then it follows that

$$\mathbf{A}^T[\mathbf{A}\mathbf{x}^* - \mathbf{b}] = 0. \tag{5.24}$$

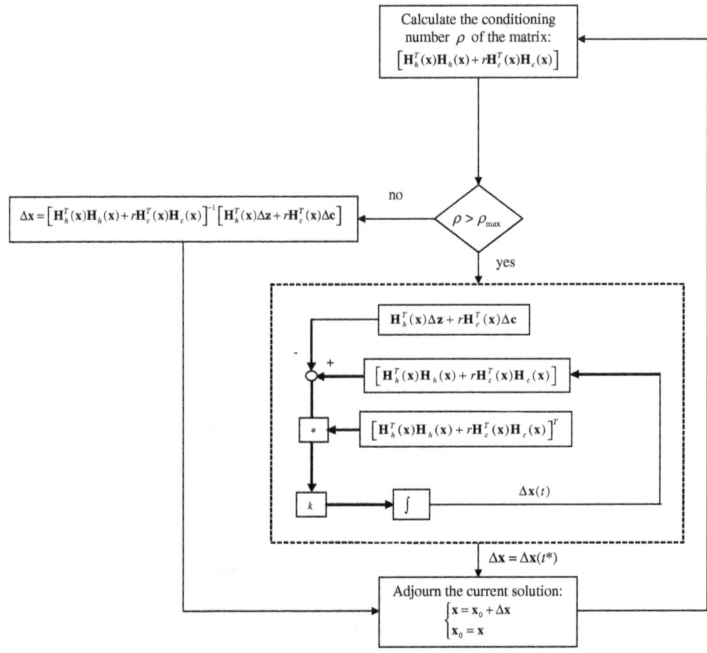

Figure 5.2. The "hybrid dynamic" computing paradigm for SE.

This important result allows us to solve the SE problem by deploying the hybrid solution paradigm depicted in Figure 5.2. As can be inferred from this figure, the idea is to enhance a state-of-the-art SE algorithm by the described dynamic based linear solver. The latter aims at solving the normal equations (5.7) only in the presence of ill-conditioning or numerical instability problems. We expect that the deployment of this solution paradigm sensibly improves both the efficiency and the reliability of the traditional SE algorithm since it increases the computing granularity (by employing a more detailed modelling technique) only when the system is singular or close to become singular, while it employs a state-of-the-art solver (which is certainly fastest) during well-defined operation states. The theoretical formalization of this concept according to the emerging paradigm of "granular computing" is currently under investigation by the authors.

5.4 Case Studies

The proposed dynamic computing paradigm has been applied to the task of solving the state estimation problem for two IEEE test networks in the presence of different operating scenarios.

The first case study analyzed deals with the application of the "full dynamic" computing paradigm for state estimation of the IEEE-30 bus test system. To this end a set of 93 measurements has been initially considered. The latter include one bus voltage magnitude ($\sigma_i^2 = 9 \times 10^{-4}$), 18 real and reactive bus power injections ($\sigma_i^2 = 10^{-4}$), and 28 real and reactive line power flow measurements ($\sigma_i^2 = 64 \times 10^{-6}$). The corresponding trajectories of the state variables are depicted in Figure 5.3. As expected, the artificial dynamic model converges with an exponential convergence ratio to an equilibrium point representing the obtained problem solution. In order to check the effectiveness of this solution we compared the dynamic evolution of the objective function (5.4) with the corresponding value obtained by applying a traditional state estimation algorithm based on the WLS method. The obtained results are reported in Figure 5.4. When analyzing this figure it is worth observing that for this operating condition, which is characterized by a well-defined normal matrix, the obtained solutions are coincident. This conclusion has been confirmed by further experiments and it can be considered rather general.

In order to assess the filtering capability of the dynamic computing paradigm, the previously described state estimation problem has been solved by corrupting the measurement signals with white noise. The corresponding trajectories of the state variables are depicted in Figure 5.5. By analyzing this figure it is worth noting that the proposed algorithm is characterized by an intrinsic filter capacity on input data mainly derived from the integral action deployed in the computational process. We conjecture that this feature could be particularly useful in reducing the number of redundant measurements required to solve the state estimation problem without significantly affecting the quality of the obtained solution.

This conclusion could be inferred by analyzing Figure 5.6, where the evolution of the performance index J_z (describing the global

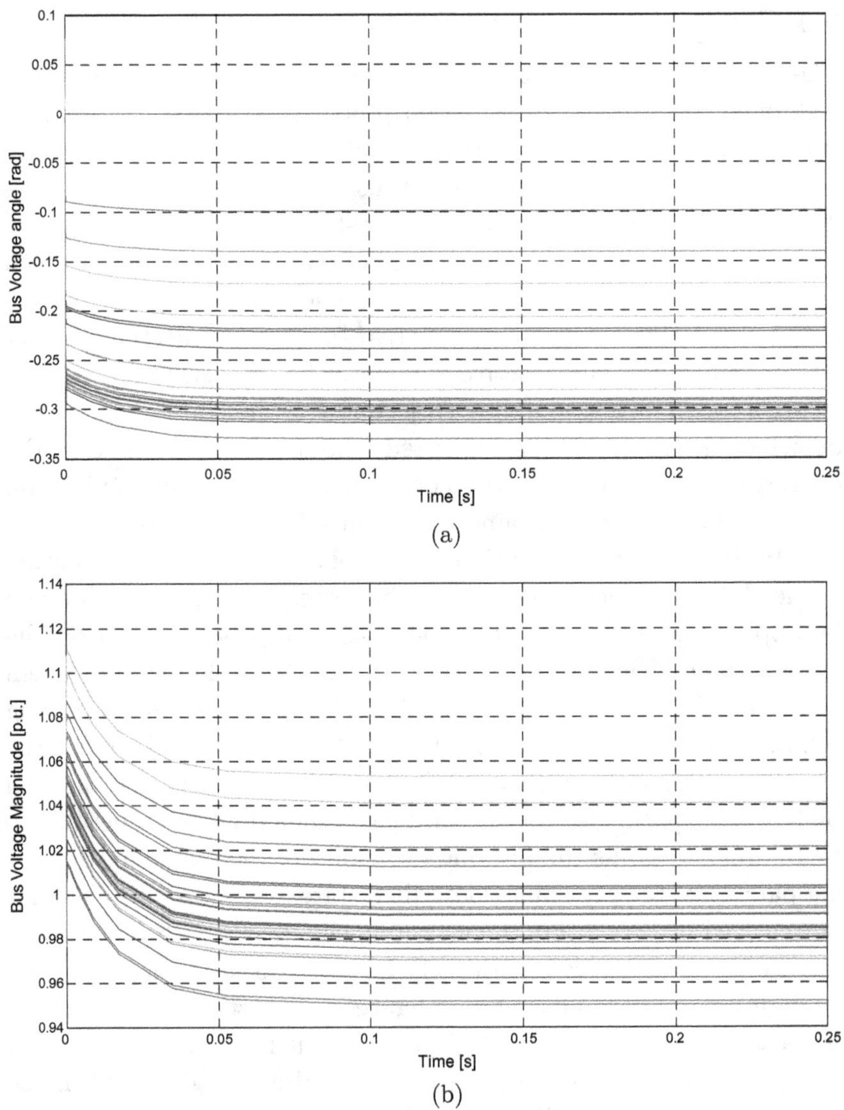

Figure 5.3. Trajectories of the state variables in the task of solving the state estimation problem for the IEEE-30 bus test system: a) bus voltage angle, b) bus voltage magnitude.

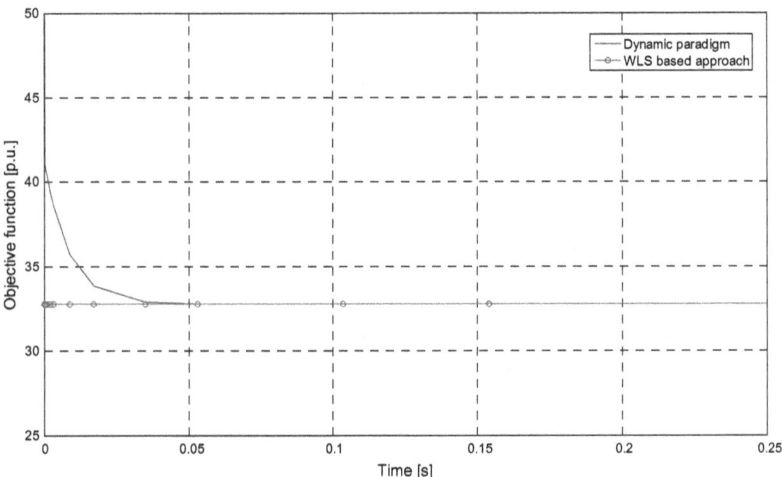

Figure 5.4. Dynamic evolution of the objective function (5.4).

uncertainty affecting the final solution)

$$J_z = \frac{\mathbf{z}_m^{*T} \operatorname{cov}(\mathbf{z}^*(t))^T \operatorname{cov}(\mathbf{z}^*(t))\mathbf{z}_m^*}{\mathbf{z}_m^{*T}\mathbf{z}_m^*} \tag{5.25}$$

as a function of the number of available measurements is depicted for both the dynamic and the traditional solution algorithms. By analyzing these results it can be observed that the application of the proposed paradigm allows the analyst to obtain lower values of J_z (of about one order of magnitude) in all the considered scenarios. As a consequence, to obtain a fixed performance index $\tilde{J}_z$, the proposed algorithm requires fewer measurements compared to the traditional solution algorithm.

Further benefits characterizing the proposed dynamic state estimation paradigm derive from its stable and widely convergent characteristics. These features could be extremely useful in solving the state estimation problem in the presence of ill-conditioning sources that could affect the stability and the convergence performance of the traditional solution algorithms.

To assess this feature we solved the state estimation problem for the analyzed power system in the presence of system singularities.

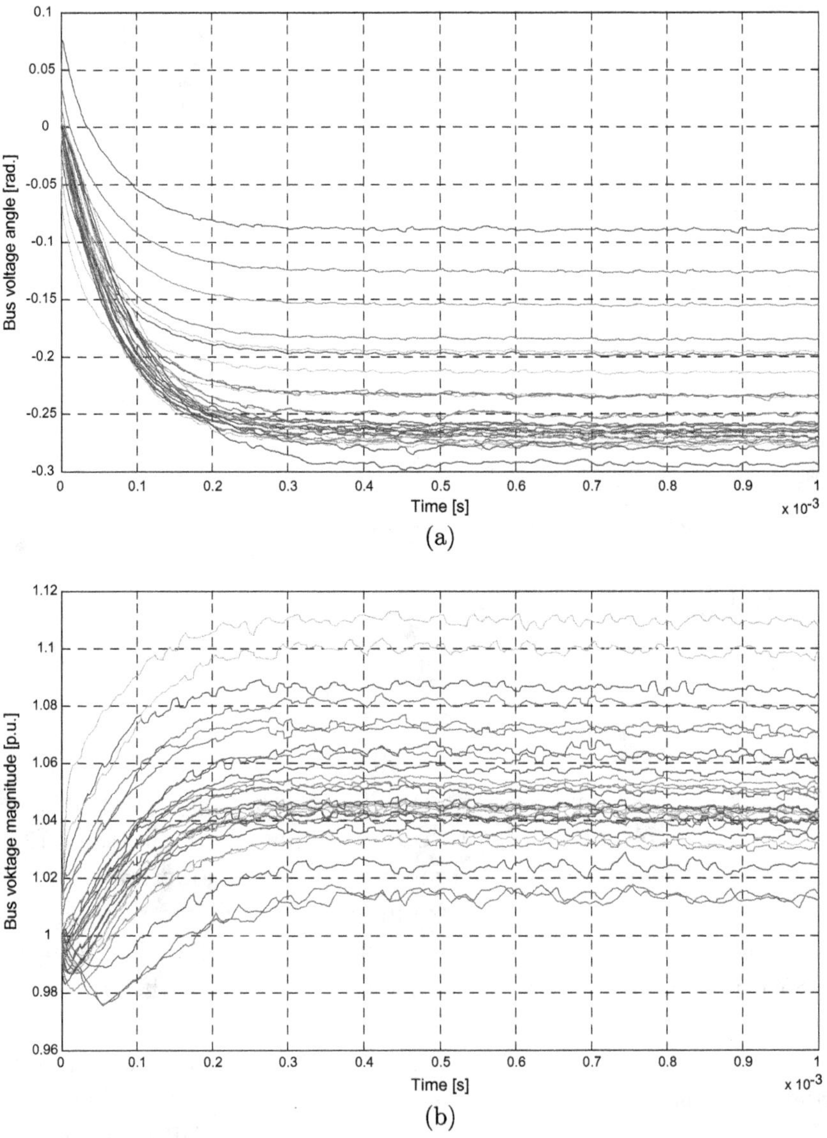

Figure 5.5. Trajectories of the state variables in the task of solving the state estimation problem for the IEEE-30 bus test system in the presence of noisy data: a) bus voltage angle, b) bus voltage magnitude.

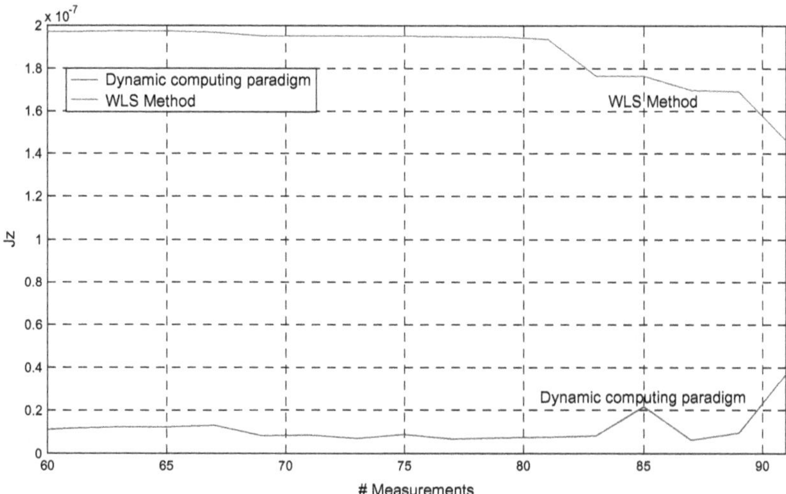

Figure 5.6. Evolution of the performance index J_z as a function of the number of available measurements.

The latter have been generated by reducing the number of available measurements and sensibly increasing the loading factor. Under these operating conditions the traditional solution algorithm failed to converge due to the singularity of the matrix $[\mathbf{H}_h^T(\mathbf{x})\mathbf{H}_h(\mathbf{x})+ r\mathbf{H}_c^T(\mathbf{x})\mathbf{H}_c(\mathbf{x})]$ and proper factorization techniques should be applied to face this issue. On the other hand, the convergence of the proposed algorithm was not affected by these ill-conditioning sources, as can be observed by analyzing Figures 5.7 and 5.8, where the dynamic trajectories of the state variables and of the objective function are depicted. As expected, in this case the artificial dynamic model also converges with an exponential convergence ratio to a stable equilibrium point.

The latter state estimation problem has also been solved by applying the "hybrid dynamic" computing paradigm. In this case the traditional solution algorithm has been equipped with a dynamic-based paradigm aimed at solving the normal equations (5.7) in the presence of system singularities. The dynamic trajectories of the state variables $\Delta\mathbf{x}(t)$ and the corresponding norm of the normal equation residuals for the first algorithm iteration are depicted

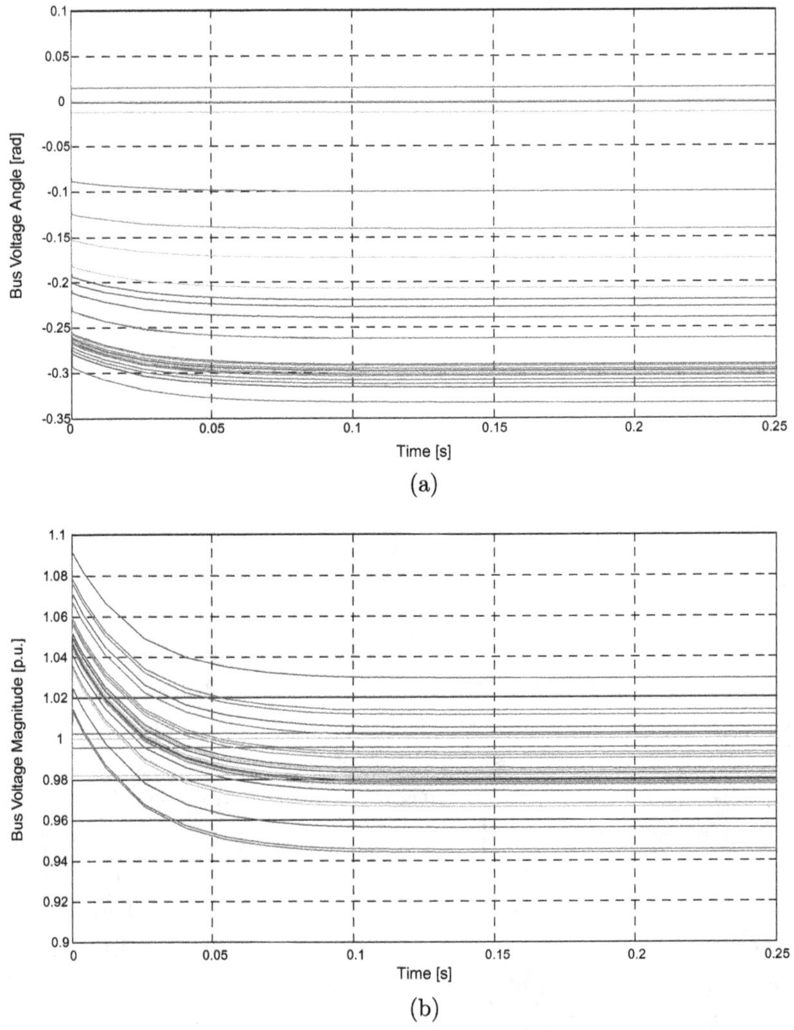

Figure 5.7. Trajectories of the state variables in the task of solving the state estimation problem for the IEEE-30 bus test system in the presence of ill-conditioning sources: a) bus voltage angle, b) bus voltage magnitude.

in Figures 5.9 and 5.10 respectively. This "dynamic solver" allows the traditional solution algorithm to converge to a feasible solution in four iterations and, consequently, to manage effectively the numerical instability problems induced by the ill-conditioning of the

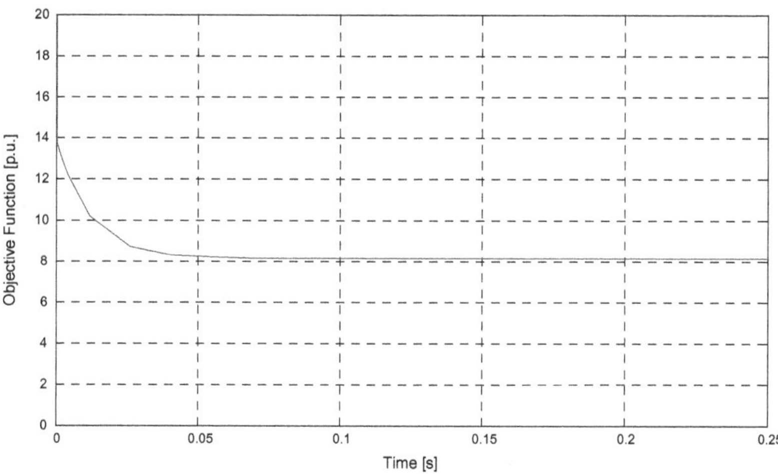

Figure 5.8. Dynamic evolution of the objective function (5.4) for the IEEE-30 bus test system in the presence of ill-conditioning sources.

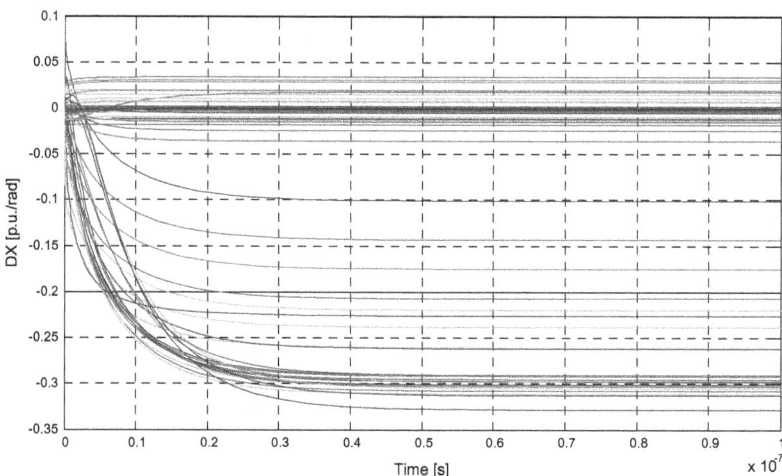

Figure 5.9. Trajectories of the state variables $\Delta x(t)$ in the task of solving the normal equations for the IEEE-30 bus test system in the presence of ill-conditioning sources (first iteration).

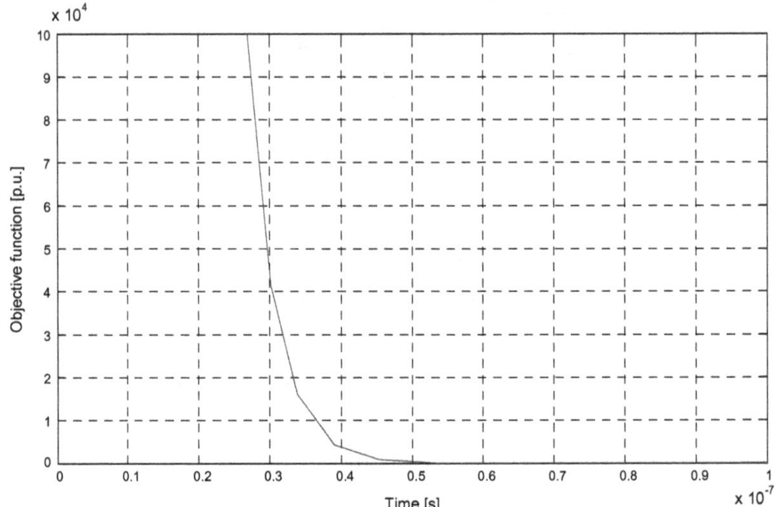

Figure 5.10. Dynamic evolution of the norm of the normal equations residuals for the IEEE-30 bus test system in the presence of ill-conditioning sources (first iteration).

system equations. Although the solutions obtained by applying the two dynamic paradigms coincide, we expect that the computational resources required by the "hybrid" approach are lower since it invokes the stable and widely convergent dynamic solver only in the presence of system singularities.

The effectiveness and robustness of the proposed dynamic computing paradigms on larger power systems have been confirmed by further simulation studies. In detail, Figures 5.11 and 5.12 summarize the results obtained by applying the "full dynamic" computing paradigm in the task of solving the state estimation of the IEEE-118 bus test network in the presence of ill-conditioning sources that affect the convergence of the traditional solution algorithm. In these figures the dynamic trajectories of the state variables and the corresponding evolution of the objective function have been depicted respectively. When analyzing these profiles it is worth observing that the dynamic model quickly converges to an equilibrium point, which represents a feasible solution of the state estimation problem. The same solution has been obtained by applying the "hybrid dynamic" paradigm. The corresponding results are depicted in Figure 5.13.

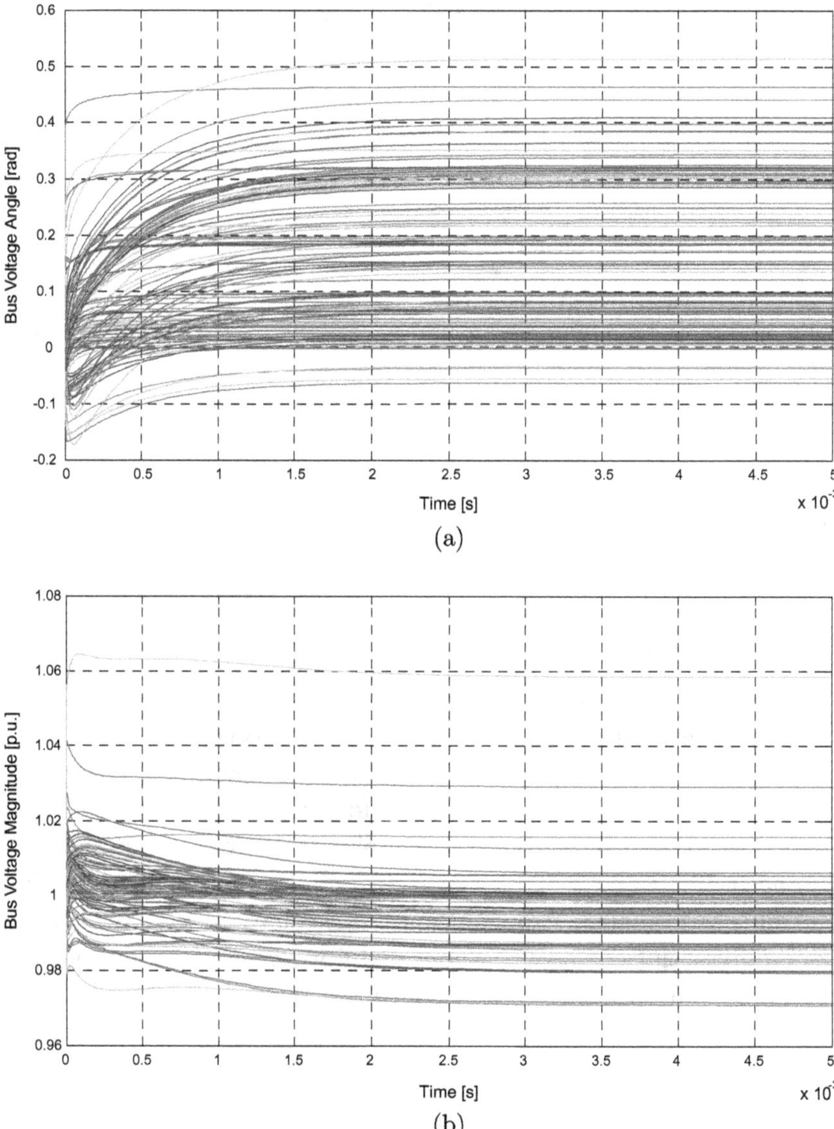

Figure 5.11. Trajectories of the state variables in the task of solving the state estimation problem for the IEEE-118 bus test system in the presence of ill-conditioning sources: a) bus voltage angle, b) bus voltage magnitude.

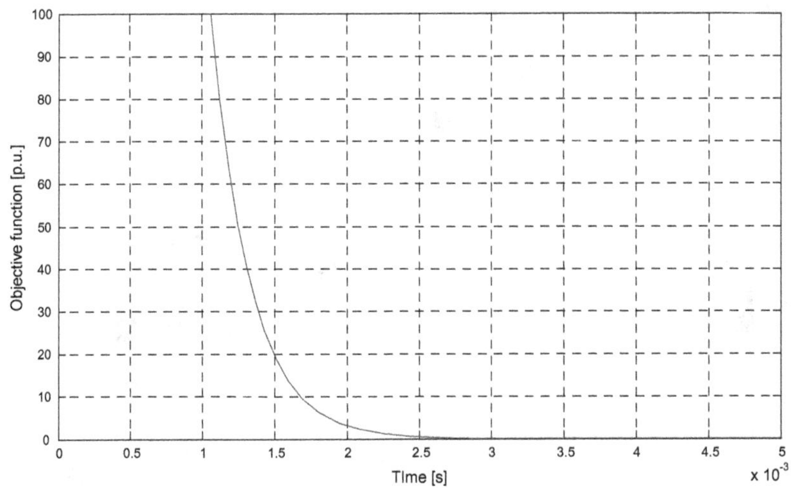

Figure 5.12. Dynamic evolution of the objective function (5.4) (IEEE-118 bus test system).

5.5 Conclusion

In this chapter a novel theoretical formalization of the power system state estimation problem has been proposed. The idea is to design stable artificial dynamic models that exponentially converge to the solutions of systems of linear and non-linear equations. These dynamic models can be deployed to solve the state estimation problem according to a "full" or a "hybrid" solution paradigm. The first one aims at formalizing the non-linear SE equations by a set of ordinary differential equations, whose equilibrium points represent the problem solutions. The second solution paradigm aims at enhancing a state-of-the-art solution algorithm by exploiting the ability of the proposed dynamic computing paradigm to directly solve ill-conditioned linear algebraic systems.

The numerical results obtained on two IEEE test power systems have shown that the proposed paradigms effectively solve the state estimation problem even in critical operating conditions when the Jacobian matrix of the system equations is singular or close to being singular. This important feature could be extremely useful in solving the state estimation problem in the presence

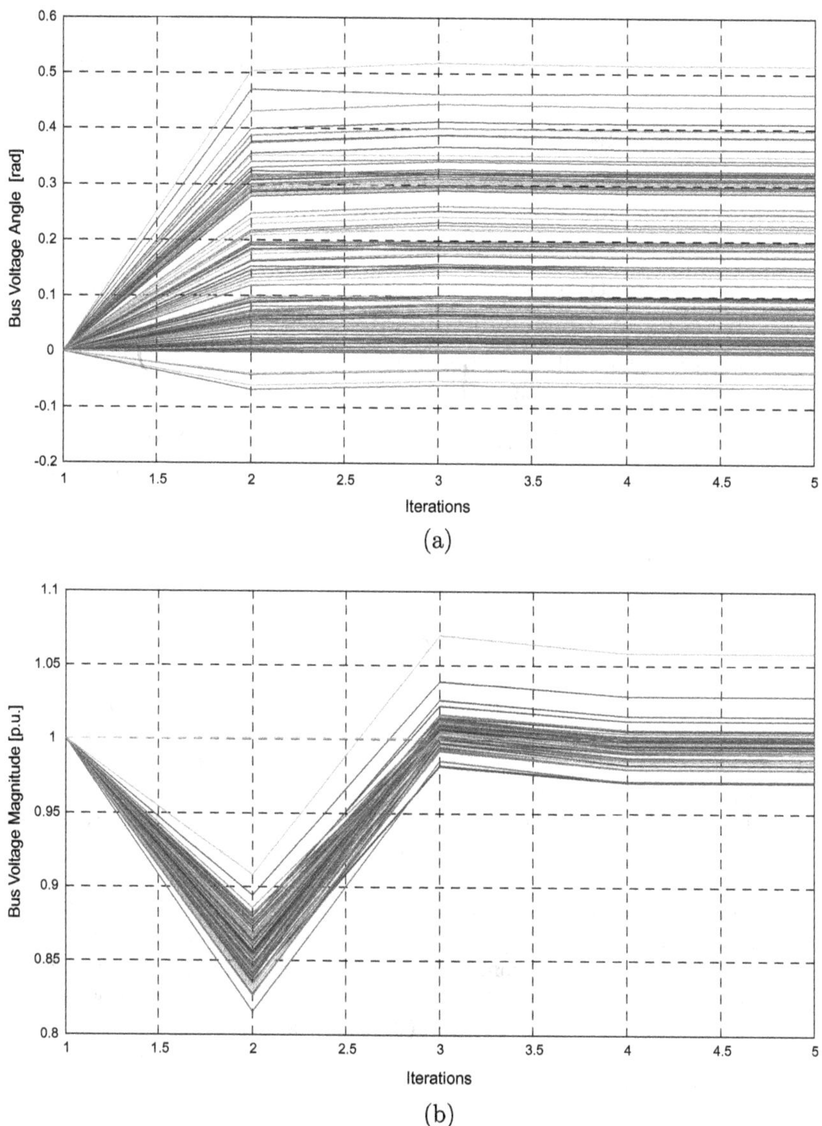

Figure 5.13. Solution of the state estimation problem for the IEEE-118 bus test system in the presence of ill-conditioning sources by the "hybrid dynamic" computing paradigm: a) bus voltage angle, b) bus voltage magnitude.

of ill-conditioning sources that could affect the stability and the convergence performance of the traditional solution algorithms. Another benefit of the proposed paradigms derives from their intrinsic filtering capacity, which could be particularly useful in reducing the number of redundant measurements required to solve the state estimation problem.

Finally, it is important to note that the application of the proposed state estimation paradigms for large-scale power systems could pose some computational difficulties. In addressing this flaw, it is possible to exploit the intrinsic parallelism characterizing the proposed algorithms. To accomplish this, the authors developed and tested a powerful parallelization algorithm aimed at effectively deploying the proposed dynamic architecture on a distributed computing environment.

References

[1] Abur, A. and Gómez-Expósito, A.G. (2004). *Power System State Estimation: Theory and Implementation*, CRC Press, Boca Raton, FL.

[2] Monticelli, A. (1999). *State Estimation in Electric Power Systems: a Generalized Approach*, Springer, New York.

[3] Kailath, T., Sayed, A.H. and Hassibi, B. (2000). *Linear Estimation*, Prentice Hall, Upper Saddle River, NJ.

[4] Schweppe, F.C. and Rom, D. (1970). Power system static-state estimation, part II: approximate model, *IEEE T. Power Ap. Syst.*, **89**, 125–130.

[5] Irving, M.R., Owen, R.C. and Sterling, M.J.H. (1978). Power system state estimation using linear programming, *IEEE Proc., Part C*, **125**, 879–885.

[6] Jabr, R.A.and Pal, B.C. (2004). Iteratively reweighted least absolute value method for state estimation, *IEE P-Gener Transm. D.*, **151(1)**, 103–108.

[7] Ebrahimian, R. and Baldick, R. (2001). State estimator condition number analysis, *IEEE T. Power Syst.*, **16(2)**, 273–279.

[8] Lin, C.E. and Huang, S.J. (1987). Integral state estimation for well-conditioned and ill-conditioned power systems, *Electr. Pow. Syst. Res.*, **12(3)**, 219–226.

[9] Gu, J.W., Clements, K.A., Krumpholz, G.R. *et al.* (1983). The solution of ill-conditioned power system state estimation problems via the method of Peters and Wilkinson, *IEEE T. Power Ap. Syst*, **102(10)**, 3473–3480.

[10] Torelli, F., Vaccaro, A. and Xie, N. (2013). A novel optimal power flow formulation based on the Lyapunov Theory, *IEEE T. Power Syst.*, **28(4)**, 4405–4415.

[11] Kekatos, V. and Giannakis, G.B. (2013). Distributed robust power system state estimation, *IEEE T. Power Syst.*, **28(2)**, 1617–1626.

[12] Holten, L., Gjelsvik, A., Aam, S. *et al.* (1988). Comparison of different methods for state estimation, *IEEE T. Power Syst.*, **3(4)**, 1798–1806.

[13] Gómez-Expósito, A., de la Villa Jaén, A., Gómez-Quiles, C. *et al.* (2011). A taxonomy of multi-area state estimation methods, *Electr. Pow. Syst. Res.*, **81(4)**, 1060–1069.

[14] Simoes-Costa, A. and Quintana, V.H. (1981). A robust numerical technique for power system state estimation, *IEEE T. Power Ap. Syst.*, **100**, 691–698.

[15] Monticelli, A., Murari, C.A.F. and Wu, F.F. (1985). A hybrid state estimator: solving normal equations by orthogonal transformations, *IEEE T. Power Ap. Syst.*, **105**, 3460–346.

[16] Monticelli, A. (2000). Electric power system state estimation, *Proc. IEEE*, **88(2)**, 262–282.

[17] Hossam-Eldin, A.A., Abdallah, E.N. and El-Nozahy, M.S. (2009). A modified genetic based technique for solving the power system state estimation problem, *World Academy of Science, Engineering & Technology*, **31**, 307–316.

[18] Contreras-Hernandez, E.J. and Cedeno-Maldonado, J.R. (2006). "A Self-Adaptive Evolutionary Programming Approach for Power System State Estimation", presented at 49th IEEE International Midwest Symposium on Circuits and Systems, San Juan, Puerto Rico, 6–9 August 2006.

[19] Shahidehpour, M. and Marwali, M. (2004). Role of fuzzy sets in power system state estimation, *Int.J. Emerging Electr. Power Syst.*, **1(1)**, available at: http://www.degruyter.com/view/j/ijeeps.2004.1.1/ijeeps.2004.1.1.1002/ijeeps.2004.1.1.1002.xml. Accessed May 2004.

[20] Yang, X.-S. (2011). Metaheuristic optimization: algorithm analysis and open problems, *Experimental Algorithms, Lecture Notes in Computer Science*, **6630**, 21–32.

[21] Abur, A. and Celik, M.K. (1993). Least absolute value state estimation with equality and inequality constraints, *IEEE T. Power Syst.*, **8(2)**, 680–686.

[22] Xie, N., Torelli, F., Bompard, E. *et al.* (2013). Dynamic computing paradigm for comprehensive power flow analysis, *IET Gener. Transm.Dis.*, **7(8)**, 832–842.

[23] Torelli, F. and Vaccaro, A. (2013). A generalized computing paradigm based on artificial dynamic models for mathematical programming, *Soft Computing*, **18(8)**, 1561–1573.

Chapter 6

Improving Voltage Regulation in Smart Grids through Adaptive Fuzzy Agents

Giovanni Acampora[a] and Autilia Vitiello[b]

[a]*School of Science and Technology, Nottingham Trent University, UK*

[b]*Department of Computer Science, University of Salerno, Italy*

6.1 Introduction

The electrical power system, built up over more than 100 years, is now one of the most relevant infrastructure components upon which modern society depends. It provides electrical energy to residential, commercial, and industrial consumers, trying to satisfy ever-growing demand. Most of today's generation capacity is based on fossil fuels, which contributes significantly to the increase of carbon dioxide in the world's atmosphere, with negative consequences for the climate and society in general.[1] Over the past 20 years, both the increasing demand for power and the need to reduce carbon dioxide emissions have led to the increasing development of the so-called *smart grids*, i.e., active, flexible, and self-healing web energy networks which marry information technology with the current electrical infrastructure.[2] In detail, the main benefits provided by smart grids are to: (1) drive significant grid efficiencies through network intelligence; (2) enable the integration of renewable energy resources (such as wind and solar) through the exploitation of distribution generation

[1]See http://new.abb.com/smartgrids/what-is-a-smart-grid.
[2]See http://www.itsyoursmartgrid.com/solutions/energy_internet.html.

(DG) units aimed at generating electrical energy on small scales as near as possible to the load centers, interchanging electric power with the network, with the two-fold advantage of meeting consumption in systems and saving the environment; (3) empower consumers to manage their energy usage and save money without compromising their lifestyle.

Unfortunately, the penetration of the DG units in smart grids increases the complexity of the electrical grids where new challenges in monitoring, metering, and controlling must be faced [20]. In particular, effective network voltage regulation is one of the main issues to address [7, 8]. Voltage regulation in electrical grids is normally achieved by the optimal coordination of a large set of regulating devices such as the on-load tap changer (OLTC), the line regulators, and the shunt capacitors. The presence of DG units in electrical grids increases the complexity of this regulation process since the power flow changes from unidirectional to bi-directional [21] and the power injections, intrinsically random for generators based on renewable sources, alter the voltage profiles on network buses. For this reason, it is necessary to design an adequate methodology aimed at assuring an efficient grid operation sequence through the optimal integration between DG units and traditional voltage-regulating devices. In order to address this need, the current trend is the use of multi-agent-based systems where each agent is equipped with fuzzy inference capabilities. Indeed, thanks to their features of autonomy, sociality, reactivity, and proactivity, multi-agent-based systems allow to overcome the drawbacks of a centralized approach such as low scalability levels, low flexibility, high network bandwidth, and large data storage resources. On the other hand, fuzzy logic allows the realization of effective voltage control strategies by handling imprecise and incomplete data simply, i.e., without the formulation of a complex mathematical model.

However, the solution to the voltage-regulation problem should be prompt, reliable, and accurate, but, above all, it should be highly adaptive in order to manage effectively the intrinsic time-varying phenomena affecting the smart grid operation [1]. For this reason, in this work, we propose a multi-agent-based approach where each agent is equipped with a novel fuzzy inference engine, named timed automata-based fuzzy controller (TAFC) [16], to regulate adaptively the reactive power flow injected by a DG unit into the electrical grid. Thanks to its high dynamic features, a TAFC is capable of modeling a system characterized by frequent changes over the time, and, consequently, its results are highly suitable for application in the electrical power systems context.

As shown in the experimental results section, where our proposal has been compared with a conventional fuzzy multi-agent approach, the proposed strategy results in an effective and suitable method to solve the voltage-regulation problem.

6.2 Related Works

In literature, the current trend to address the voltage-regulation problem in smart grids is based on multi-agent-based systems, fuzzy logic theory, and a combination of the two. In particular, Fakhan *et al.* [23] propose a decentralized approach based on a multi-agent system for addressing voltage regulation when wind generators are connected to a distribution network. Each agent has a local multi-objective optimization function and controls the voltage at its wind generator bus and participates in voltage regulation of the pilot bus. This one represents the voltage variations in all buses. All agents cooperate through the exploitation of several interaction protocols. On the other hand, Loia and Vaccaro [22] propose a decentralized approach based on the adoption of distributed fuzzy controllers with each one regulating the voltage magnitude of a specific smart grid bus equipped with a DG unit. In this system, each fuzzy controller knows both the variables characterizing the monitored bus (sensed by in-built sensors) and the global variables describing the actual performances of the entire smart grid (assessed by checking the current state of the system). Both local and global variables allow each controller to identify the proper control actions aimed at improving the grid voltage profile. Finally, Sajadi *et al.* [20] propose a combined approach consisting of a fuzzy multi-agent-based control for voltage regulation. In detail, this system comprises three kinds of agents: LTC (on-load tap changer) agent, DG agents, and load agents. The

LTC agent has two goals: the first one is keeping the voltage of feeders in a standard voltage range by changing the transformer tap, whereas the other one is minimizing the number of tap-changing operations to prevent excessive tap operation. As with the LTC agent, the DG agent has two goals. The first is to keep the voltage of its feeder in a standard voltage range. The second is to keep the generation of the DG unit at maximum. Finally, the main task of the load agent is the measurement of bus voltage at the load point. Each agent is based on the principle of fuzzy controller theory, and, as a consequence, it basically consists of a fuzzifier, an interference engine, a defuzzifier, and proper knowledge bases and rule bases.

However, all approaches in literature do not significantly take into account the dynamic nature which characterizes the modern power systems based on smart grids. In this work, we propose a fuzzy multi-agent system capable of adaptively regulating the power injected by the DG units belonging to a smart grid. The adaptive capability is provided through the exploitation of a novel fuzzy inference engine able to decide the most appropriate power level to be introduced in the electrical network by considering the current grid operational state.

6.3 Problem Formulation

The final aim of the voltage control process is to identify the optimal asset of voltage-regulating devices required to deliver higher service quality, in terms of voltage profile flattening and minimization of power losses. Therefore, the solution of the voltage-regulation problem requires the identification of the voltage-regulation devices asset that minimizes, for each grid state, a set of objectives subject to a number of inequality constraints.

As described in [22], the voltage-regulation devices asset is described by the following vector:

$$\mathbf{y} = [Q_{dg,1}, \ldots, Q_{dg,N_g}, \ldots, Q_{cap,1}, \ldots, Q_{cap,N_c}, V_{FTS,N_f}, m] \quad (6.1)$$

where $Q_{dg,i}$ is the reactive power injected by the ith $(i = 1, \ldots, N_g)$ DGS (distributed generation systems) connected to the smart grid and available for regulation; $Q_{cap,j}$ is the vector of the reactive power injected by the jth ($j = 1, \ldots, N_c$) capacitor bank; $V_{FTS,k}$ is the set point of the kth ($k = 1, \ldots, N_f$) flexible AC transmission system (FACTS) and m is the tap position of the HV/MV (high voltage/medium voltage) line tap-changing transformer. Note that the vector $\mathbf{y}$ takes values in the solution space $\mathbf{\Omega}$:

$$\mathbf{y} \in \mathbf{\Omega} \Leftrightarrow \begin{cases} Q_{dg,min,i} \leq Q_{dg,i} \leq Q_{dg,max,i} & i = 1, \ldots, N_g \\ Q_{cap,min,j} \leq Q_{cap,j} \leq Q_{cap,max,j} & j = 1, \ldots, N_c \\ V_{FTS,min,k} \leq V_{FTS,k} \leq V_{FTS,max,k} & k = 1, \ldots, N_f \\ tap_{min} \leq m \leq tap_{max} \end{cases} \tag{6.2}$$

When solving the voltage-regulation problem, several constraints must be satisfied. They include the technical constraints for correct system operation in terms of allowed voltage ranges for the network buses (i.e. $V_{min,i} \leq V_i \leq V_{max,i}$ $i = 1 : n$) and maximum allowable currents for the n_l power lines (i.e. $I_l \leq I_{max,l}$ $l = 1 : n_l$).

The objectives to be minimized in identifying the optimal voltage-regulating devices asset takes into account both technical and economic aspects (i.e. power losses, reactive power costs, voltage magnitude). Since the design objectives are in competition, the voltage-regulation problem has no unique solution and a suitable trade-off between objectives has to be identified.

6.4 An Adaptive Fuzzy Multi-Agent System for Voltage Regulation

In this section, we present our proposal to address the voltage-regulation problem in a smart grid based on an adaptive fuzzy multi-agent system. The architecture of our system is presented in Figure 6.1. This architecture is based on a network of cooperative agents, each one regulating the voltage magnitude of a specific smart grid unit. Each one of these agents accomplishes the following tasks:

(1) Acquisition of local bus measurements, i.e., measuring voltage magnitude, active and reactive bus power, through a set of sensors.

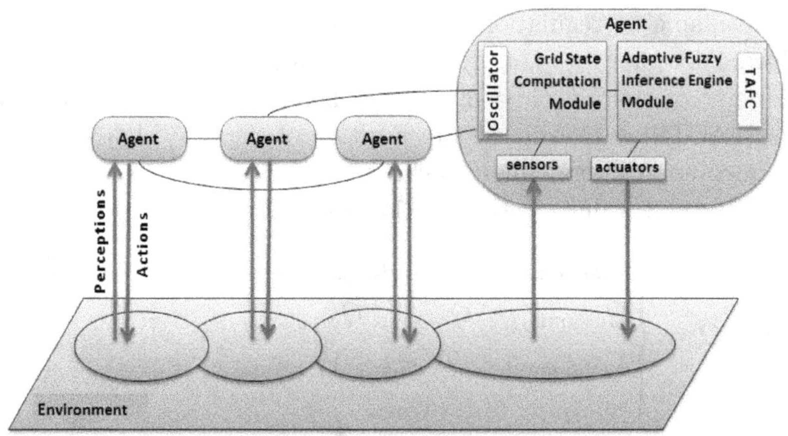

Figure 6.1. The architecture of our adaptive fuzzy multi-agent system for voltage regulation in smart grids.

(2) Estimation of the state of the grid by considering local and global variables.
(3) Computation of the appropriate power level to be injected in the network through an adaptive fuzzy inference engine.
(4) Management of the voltage control through a set of actuators.

In order to achieve these goals, apart from sensors and actuators, each agent is composed of two modules: the *grid state computation module* and the *adaptive fuzzy inference engine module.*

Hereafter, more details about these two key modules in our architecture are given.

6.4.1 *Grid state computation module*

This module is aimed at estimating the current grid state by processing the global variables characterizing the current operation of the smart grid. These variables are estimated by adopting a bio-inspired paradigm as described by Loia and Vaccaro [22]. In detail, each agent is equipped with an oscillator initialized by the local sensor measurements. The oscillators of nearby agents are mutually coupled by proper local coupling strategies derived from the mathematics of populations of mutually coupled oscillators [26, 27]. This bio-inspired paradigm allows oscillators to reach a consensus on the weighted average of the variables sensed by all of the agents. Thanks to this paradigm, each agent can assess, in a totally decentralized way, the many important variables characterizing the operation of the global smart grid, such as the mean grid voltage magnitude and the power losses. On the basis of the agreed mean grid voltage magnitude, the possible states the module can compute are the following ones:

(1) *Grid voltage low*: this state is characterized by high load demand. As a result, high power line loading and, consequently, high power losses and a very low value of the mean grid voltage magnitude are expected on the grid.
(2) *Grid voltage high*: this state is characterized by low load demand. As a result, low power line loading and, consequently, low power losses and a very high value of the mean grid voltage magnitude are expected on the grid.
(3) *Normal operation*: this state represents the nominal operating point of the electrical grid. Both the power losses and the value of the mean grid voltage magnitude lie within permissable intervals.

6.4.2 *Adaptive fuzzy inference engine module*

Once the current smart grid state has been assessed by using the *grid state computation module*, the *adaptive fuzzy inference engine module* processes both local and global variables to decide the voltage control strategy to be followed. In the following, for sake of understandability, the possible strategies to be taken by each agent are described by the following control rules:

- If the smart grid state is classified as *grid voltage low* (respectively as *grid voltage high*), then the control objective is to raise (respectively reduce) the mean grid voltage magnitude V_m by properly increasing (respectively decreasing) the reactive power injected by the DG units into the grid. In order to obtain a uniform rise in voltage magnitude, the ith controller compares the local bus voltage magnitude (V_i) with the mean grid voltage magnitude (V_M) and:

(1) If $V_i < V_M$, it increases (respectively decreases) the injected reactive power $Q_{dg,i}$ by a quantity directly (respectively inversely) proportional to $|V_M - V_i|$, namely:

$$\Delta Q_{dg,i} = \alpha_i(V_i) \cdot (V_M - V_i)$$

respectively

$$\Delta Q_{dg,i} = \frac{\alpha_i(V_i)}{V_i - V_M}$$

(2) Otherwise, it increases (respectively decreases) the injected reactive power $Q_{dg,i}$ by a quantity inversely (respectively directly) proportional to $|V_M - V_i|$, namely:

$$\Delta Q_{dg,i} = \frac{\alpha_i(V_i)}{(V_i - V_M)}$$

respectively

$$\Delta Q_{dg,i} = \alpha_i(V_i) \cdot (V_M - V_i)$$

- If the smart grid state is classified as *normal operation*, then the control objective is to improve the voltage profile (namely to reduce the voltage magnitude deviation). To address this issue, the ith controller compares the local bus voltage magnitude (V_i) with the mean grid voltage magnitude (V_M) and:

  (1) If $V_i < V_M$, it increases the injected reactive power $Q_{dg,i}$ by a quantity directly proportional to $|V_M - V_i|$, namely:

  $$\Delta Q_{dg,i} = \alpha_i(V_i) \cdot (V_M - V_i)$$

  (2) Otherwise, it decreases the injected reactive power $Q_{dg,i}$ by a quantity directly proportional to $|V_M - V_i|$, namely:

  $$\Delta Q_{dg,i} = \alpha_i(V_i) \cdot (V_M - V_i)$$

  where $\alpha_i(V_i)$ is a monotonically increasing function of the actual value of the voltage magnitude of the ith bus.

These user-supplied human language rules are effectively implemented by an adaptive fuzzy inference engine, the TAFC. In detail, the exploitation of a fuzzy inference engine allows the conversion of these linguistic rules into their mathematical equivalents, and, as a consequence, simplifies the job of the system designer, resulting in much more accurate representations of the way systems behave in the real world. However, since the solution to the voltage-regulation problem should be highly adaptive in order to manage the intrinsic time-varying phenomena affecting the smart grid operation effectively, we propose the exploitation of a novel fuzzy inference engine, TAFC, capable of facing the dynamic changes that characterize power systems.

TAFCs are evolvable fuzzy systems which extend standard fuzzy controllers (Mamdani or TSK) by using three additional concepts: *control eras*, *control configurations*, and *control time*. By means of these concepts, the life cycle of a given system can be considered as composed of a sequence of disjointed time intervals, i.e., the control eras. Each control era is characterized by a specific *control configuration* which is formed by: (1) the number and typology of fuzzy variables and (2) the number and structure of relationships between variables. Finally, the control time is the mechanism that allows the system to switch between adjacent control eras; in other words, the control time sets the current control configuration of the system and the duration of the control eras.

In order to extend the conventional fuzzy control vision with the above concepts, a modified version of timed automata [18] has been used. A timed automaton is a standard finite-state automaton extended with a finite collection of real-valued *clocks* providing a straightforward way to represent time-related events, whereas automata-based approaches cannot offer this feature. The clocks can be reset to 0 (independently of each other) with the transitions of the automaton, and keep track of the time elapsed since the last reset. The transitions of a timed automaton are labeled with a *guard* (a condition on clocks), an *action* or *symbol* on alphabet Σ, and a *clock reset* (a subset of clocks to be reset). Intuitively, a timed automaton starts execution with all clocks set to zero. Clocks increase uniformly with time while the automaton is within a node. A transition may be taken only if the current values of the clocks satisfy the associated constraints. By taking the transition, all clocks in the clock reset will be set to zero, while the remaining keep their values

[28]. A precise definition of timed transition table, which determines the timed automaton behavior, is given below.

Definition 6.1. A *timed transition table* $\mathcal{A}$ is a tuple $\langle \Sigma, S, S_0, C, E \rangle$, where

- Σ is a finite alphabet,
- S is a finite set of states,
- $S_0 \subseteq S$ is a set of start states,
- C is finite set of clocks, and
- $E \subseteq S \times S \times \Sigma \times 2^C \times \Phi(C)$ gives the set of transitions. An edge $\langle s, s', a, \lambda, \delta \rangle$ represents a transition from state s to state s' on input symbol a. The set $\lambda \subseteq C$ gives the clocks to be reset with this transition, and δ is a clock constraint over C. ■

A simple example [18] of a timed automaton is reported in Figure 6.2. The start state of the automaton is S_1. There is a single clock, named x. The annotation $x := 0$ on an edge corresponds to the action of resetting the clock x when the edge is traversed. Instead, the annotation $(x < 2)$? represents a clock constraint which means that the edge can be traversed only if the value of the clock x is less than 2. In general, the behavior of the automaton is as follows. The automaton starts in the state S_1 and moves to state S_2 reading the symbol input a. The clock x gets set to 0 along with this transition. While in state S_2, the value of the clock x shows the time elapsed since the occurrence of the last symbol a. The transition from the state S_1 to state S_2 is enabled only if the value of the clock x is less than 2. The whole cycle repeats when the automaton moves back to state S_1.

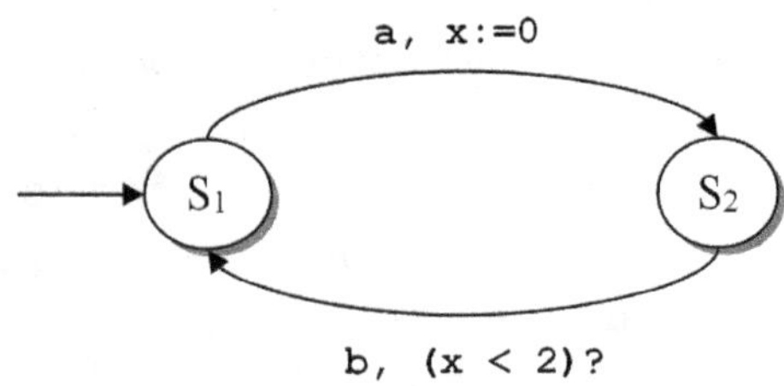

Figure 6.2. A timed automaton.

The set of behaviors expressed by a system modeled by means of a timed automaton is defined by a *timed language*, i.e., a collection of *timed words*. A timed word is a pair (σ, τ), where $\sigma = \sigma_1\sigma_2\ldots$ is an infinite word and $\tau = \tau_1\tau_2\ldots$ is an infinite sequence of time values $\tau_i \in \mathbb{R}$ with $\tau_i > 0$, satisfying constraints of *monotonicity* and *progress* (see Alur [18]). In detail, if a timed word $w = (\sigma, \tau)$, it presents the symbol σ_i at time τ_i. Therefore, if σ_i is an event occurrence then the corresponding component τ_i is interpreted as the time of occurrence of σ_i.

As for the timed automaton presented in Figure 6.2, the timed language is represented by all words in which a and b alternate and the delay between a and the following b is always less than 2. Therefore, a possible word is $w = (\sigma, \tau)$, where $\sigma = abab$ and $\tau = 0.0, 1.8, 2.2, 3.7$. Given the word $w = (a, 0.0) \rightarrow (b, 1.8) \rightarrow (a, 2.2) \rightarrow (b, 3.7)$, the automaton starts in the state S_1 and moves to state S_2 reading the symbol input a at time 0.0. The clock x gets set to 0 along with this transition. While in state S_2, the value of the clock x increases. When the symbol b is read at time 1.8, the automaton moves from the state S_2 to state S_1 since the clock x has the value 1.8 which satisfies the guard present on the edge. The automaton moves again to the state S_2 when the second symbol a is read at time 2.2. Finally, the automaton moves to state S_1, when the final symbol b is read at time 3.7. Indeed, at time 3.7, the x value is 1.5, and then, the clock satisfies again the guard.

Theoretically, this timed behavior is captured by introducing the *run* concept. Intuitively, a run is a collection of sequential discrete transitions, where each transition denotes an event releasing a task and the guard on the transition (i.e. a temporal constraint) specifies all the possible arriving times of the event. Formally, a run is defined as follows.

Definition 6.2. A run r, denoted by $(\bar{s}, \bar{\nu})$, of a timed transition table $\langle \Sigma, S, S_0, C, E \rangle$ over a timed word (σ, τ) is an infinite sequence of the form

$$r : \langle s_0, \nu_0 \rangle \xrightarrow[\tau_1]{\sigma_1} \langle s_1, \nu_1 \rangle \xrightarrow[\tau_2]{\sigma_2} \langle s_2, \nu_2 \rangle \xrightarrow[\tau_3]{\sigma_3} \ldots$$

with $s_i \in S$ and $\nu_i \in [C \to \mathbb{R}]$, for all $i \geq 0$, satisfying the following requirements:

- *Initiation*: $s_0 \in S_0$ and $\nu_0(x) = 0$ for all $x \in C$.
- *Consecution*: for all $i \geq 1$, there is an edge in E of the form $\langle s_{i-1}, s_i, \sigma_i, \lambda_i, \delta_i \rangle$ such that $(\nu_{i-1} + \tau_i - \tau_{i-1})$ satisfies δ_i and ν_i equals $[\lambda_i \mapsto 0](\nu_{i-1} + \tau_i - \tau_{i-1})$. ■

Therefore, by considering the automaton in Figure 6.2, the run which corresponds to word $w = (a, 0.0) \to (b, 1.8) \to (a, 2.2) \to (b, 3.7)$ is as follows:

$$r : \langle S_1, [0] \rangle \xrightarrow[0]{a} \langle S_2, [0] \rangle \xrightarrow[1.8]{b} \langle S_1, [1.8] \rangle \xrightarrow[2.2]{a} \langle S_2, [0] \rangle \xrightarrow[3.7]{b} \langle S_1, [1.5] \rangle.$$

The timed transition table together with the run concept are the main notions used in TAFC for extending the standard fuzzy controller definition. Indeed, TAFCs are able to manage the control configurations by associating each of them with a state in the timed automaton and the control eras progression by using the *run* concept (Definition 6.2) where the ith transition moves the system from the ith control era to the $(i+1)^{\text{th}}$ one. In this vision, a timed word determines how and when to execute the switching among successive control eras. Therefore, a timed word coincides with the control time concept.

More in detail, when a TAFC transits from a state S_1 to a state S_2 through a transition T_1, an opportune control configuration (or fuzzy controller) C is activated to manage the system until a successive transition T_2 will be taken. The time that elapses between the two transitions is the duration of the control era related to the control configuration C. The control configuration C is obtained by transforming a previous control configuration related to the state S_1 by means of particular *transformation operators* that are related to the transition T_1. All possible transformation operators compose the set C_{op} defined as follows:

$$C_{op} = \{\oplus, \ominus, \boxplus^k, \boxminus^k, \boxdot^k, \sim, \ltimes, \rtimes, \bowtie, \circledast, \oslash, \circledcirc, \divideontimes, \propto\}$$

where $\oplus$ and $\ominus$, respectively, adds and deletes a fuzzy variable from the current configuration; $\boxplus^k$, $\boxminus^k$, and $\boxdot^k$, respectively, adds, removes, and modifies k fuzzy rules related to the current configuration; $\sim$ changes the fuzzy implication method of the rule base related to the current configuration; $\circledast$, $\oslash$, and $\circledcirc$, respectively, adds, deletes, and modifies a term to a fuzzy variable in the current configuration; $\propto$ modifies the defuzzify method of configuration; $\bowtie$ modifies the fuzzy aggregation method; $\divideontimes$ changes default value of an output variable in the current configuration; $\ltimes$ and $\rtimes$ change, respectively, the lower bound and upper bound of the universe of discourse of a fuzzy variable in the current configuration.

Therefore, TAFCs exploit a novel kind of transition edges capable of changing the control configuration of the modeled system through the exploitation of transformation operators. Formally, TAFCs extend the timed automaton definition by means of a so-called timed control transition table (see Definition 6.3).

Definition 6.3. A *timed control transition table* $\mathcal{A}_C$ is a tuple $\langle \Sigma \cup \{\epsilon\}, S, S_0, C, E_C \rangle$, where

- Σ is a finite alphabet;
- ϵ represents the empty event, that is, when it is on a transition, the crossing of this transition depends only by temporal constraints;
- S is a finite set of states;
- $S_0 \subseteq S$ is a set of start states;
- C is finite set of clocks; and
- $E_C \subseteq S \times S \times \Sigma \times 2^C \times \Phi(C) \times C^*_{op}$ gives the set of transitions, where C^*_{op} represents the set of all possible sequences of transformation operators. An edge $\langle s, s', a, \lambda, \delta, o^n \rangle$ represents a transition from state s to state s' on input symbol a which can be also the empty event. The set $\lambda \subseteq C$ gives the clocks to be reset with this transition, δ is a clock constraint over C and $o^n \in C^*_{op}$ is a sequence of n transformation operators, with $n \geq 1$, defined in order to change the current control configuration of modeled system. ■

It is worth to noting that in each sequence of transformation operators an operator can be repeated in order to execute the same task on different arguments. Besides, it is important to establish that the operators are executed in the same order of their definition in the sequence.

As a consequence of the extension of the timed automaton table definition, also the run concept (see Definition 6.2) is extended by the concept of *control run* defined as:

Definition 6.4. A control run r_c, denoted by $(\bar{s}, \bar{\nu})$, of a timed transition table $\langle \Sigma \cup \{\epsilon\}, S, S_0, C, E_C \rangle$ over a timed word (σ, τ) and a collection of sequences of transformation operators $\Omega = \{n_1, n_2, \ldots, n_{|\Omega|}\} \subseteq C^*_{op}$, is an infinite sequence of the form

$$r_c : \langle s^0, \nu_0 \rangle \xrightarrow[\tau_1]{\sigma_1, n_1} \langle s^1, \nu_1 \rangle \xrightarrow[\tau_2]{\sigma_2, n_2} \langle s^2, \nu_2 \rangle \xrightarrow[\tau_3]{\sigma_3, n_3} \ldots$$

with $s^i \in S$ and $\nu_i \in [C \to \mathbb{R}]$, for all $i \geq 0$, and $n_i \in C^*_{op}$, for all $i \geq 1$, satisfying the following requirements:

- *Initiation*: $s^0 \in S_0$ and $\nu_0(x) = 0$ for all $x \in C$.
- *Consecution*: for all $i \geq 1$, there is an edge in E_C of the form $\langle s^{i-1}, s^i, \sigma_i, \lambda_i, \delta_i, n_i \rangle$ such that $(\nu_{i-1} + \tau_i - \tau_{i-1})$ satisfies δ_i and ν_i equals $[\lambda_i \mapsto 0](\nu_{i-1} + \tau_i - \tau_{i-1})$.
- *Atomicity*: the operators of sequence $n_i \in C^*_{op}$ are atomic operations and their computation time is equals to 0, i.e, they do not modify the duration of permanence in the automaton state s^i, $(\tau_i - \tau_{i-1})$.
- *Evolution*: each state s^i of a pair $\langle s^i, \nu_i \rangle$ in r_c is mapped on a fuzzy controller F^i. ■

At this point, it is possible to give a formal definition of a TAFC.

Definition 6.5. A TAFC T is an ordered pair composed by an initial control configuration, represented by a fuzzy controller named F^0, modeling the control behavior of system during first phase of its existence and a timed control transition table T_C describing the dynamic evolution of the system. Formally:

$$T = (F^0, T_C).$$ ■

6.5 Case Study and Experimental Results

This section discusses the application of the proposed methodology to the task of voltage regulation for the IEEE 30-bus test system depicted in Figure 6.3.

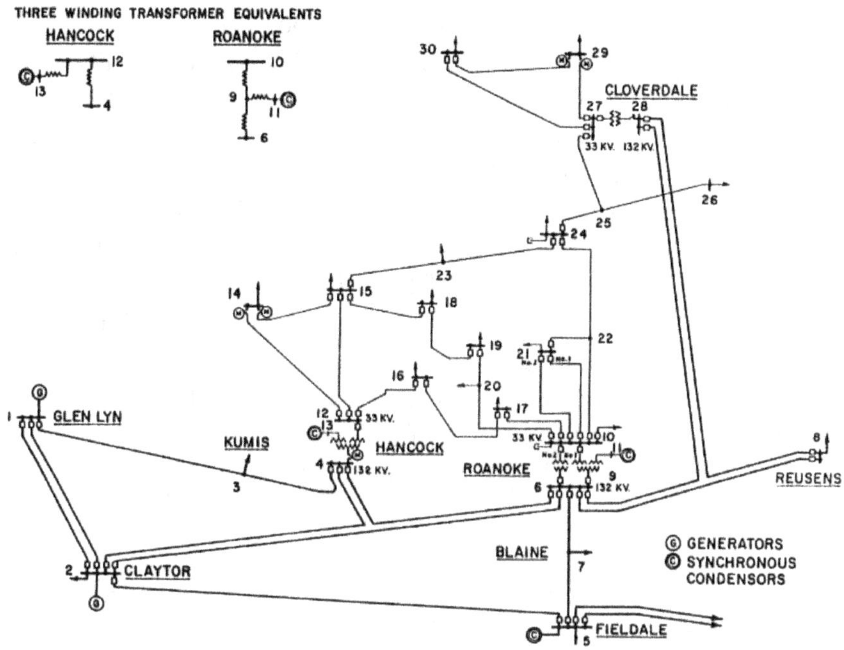

Figure 6.3. The IEEE 30-bus test system.

Six dispatchable DG units have been considered in our experiments. The regulating devices asset is, therefore, identified by six variables:

$$\mathbf{y} = [Q_{dg,1}, Q_{dg,2}, Q_{dg,3}, Q_{dg,4}, Q_{dg,5}, Q_{dg,6}] \tag{6.3}$$

In our experiment, each variable $Q_{dg,i}$ with $i = 1, \ldots, 6$ is regulated by an identical voltage TAFC $T = (C, T_A)$. As far as the regulation performances are concerned, detailed simulation analyses that consider highly variable load patterns have been developed.

In particular, the TAFC $T = (C, T_A)$ is exploited for regulating the reactive power flows injected by the DG units where C is a fuzzy logic controller representing the initial configuration of T and modeling the control behavior of each variable during the first phase of its existence, whereas, T_A is the extended timed automaton that describes the dynamic evolution. In particular, the timed automata T_A regulates the reactive power flows injected by the DG units during a simulation run over a time equal to 150 minutes.

In detail, the fuzzy controller C is composed of two input variables, the mean grid voltage magnitude (V_M) and the difference between the mean grid voltage magnitude and the local bus voltage magnitude (DV_i) and an output one, the reactive power flow (DQ). The variable V_M is characterized by three fuzzy sets, named *very_low*, *zero*, and *very_high*, whereas, both variables DV_i and DQ are characterized by five fuzzy sets, named *negative big* (NB), *negative small* (NS), *zero error* (ZE), *positive small* (PS), and *positive big* (PB). The rule base is composed of 11 rules defined by a domain expert. The designed fuzzy inference engine computes the conventional Mamdani's inference method [24] consisting of min-max operations, whereas, the process of defuzzification uses the mean of maxima method [25]. As for the timed automaton T_A, it is composed by seven states $S_1, S_2, \ldots, S_7$. Each state stores a control configuration capable of regulating the reactive power flows during the corresponding control era. For the sake of simplicity, in Figure 6.4, the description of the transformation operators is replaced by a function $\phi_{i,j}$ capable of calculating the set of operators needed to transform the control configuration related to the state S_i in the control configuration related to the state S_j. For example, Figure 6.4 shows the behavior held by the TAFC T in the state S_1 (Figure 6.4(a)) and the behavior held in the state S_2 (Figure 6.4(b)) because of the transformation provided by the function $\phi_{1,2}$ over the control configuration.

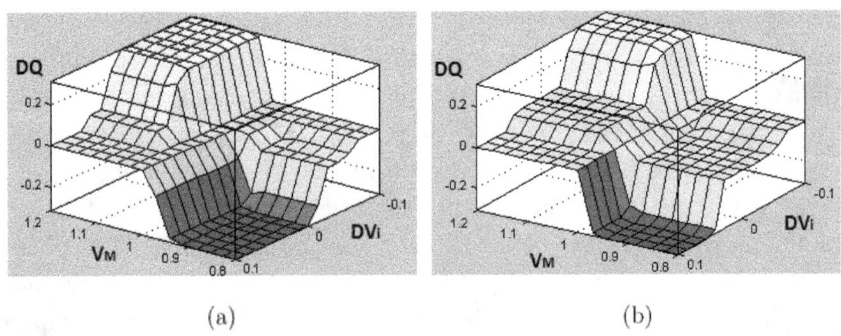

(a) (b)

Figure 6.4. Behavior held by the TAFC T in the state S_1 in (a) and in the state S_2 in (b).

The events described through the letters a, b, c, d, e, f on the automaton transitions correspond to the following conditions related to the voltage magnitude M:

- $a \Leftrightarrow M < 0.99$
- $b \Leftrightarrow M > 1.01$
- $c \Leftrightarrow M > 0.99$
- $d \Leftrightarrow M < 1.01$
- $e \Leftrightarrow M < 0.97$
- $f \Leftrightarrow M > 1.03$

In order to show the better performances provided by our strategy, the proposed TAFC T has been compared with a standard fuzzy controller F. The evaluation of the provided performances has been based on technical and economic aspects, and in particular on the power losses (see Figure 6.5), reactive power costs (see Figure 6.6), and voltage magnitude (see Figure 6.7).

In order to measure the superiority of the strategy effectively, the mean absolute errors (MAEs) regarding the considered performance aspects have been computed for the compared controllers, T and F.

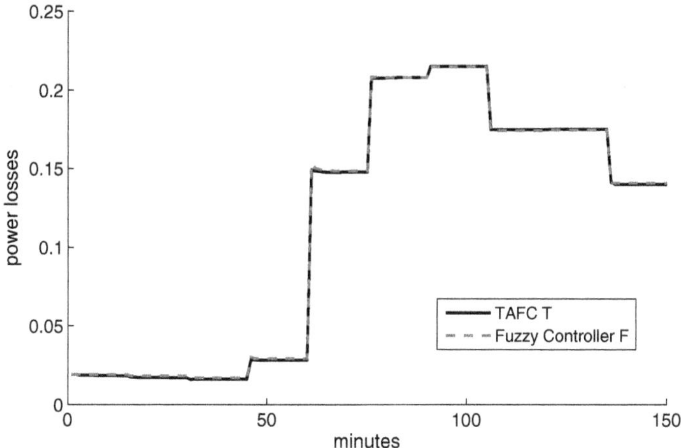

Figure 6.5. The power losses values for the TAFC T and the conventional fuzzy controller F.

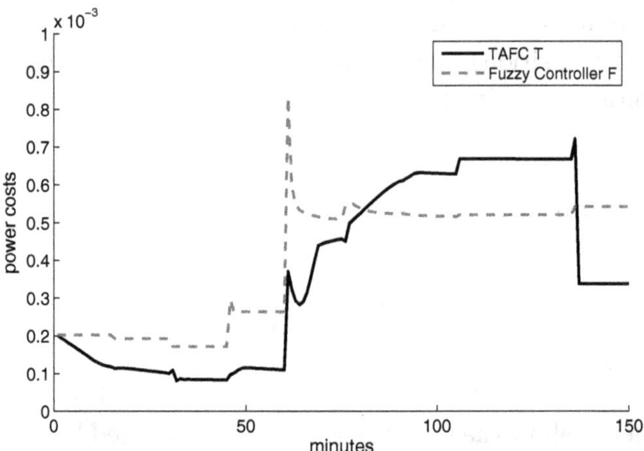

Figure 6.6. The reactive power costs values for the TAFC T and the conventional fuzzy controller F.

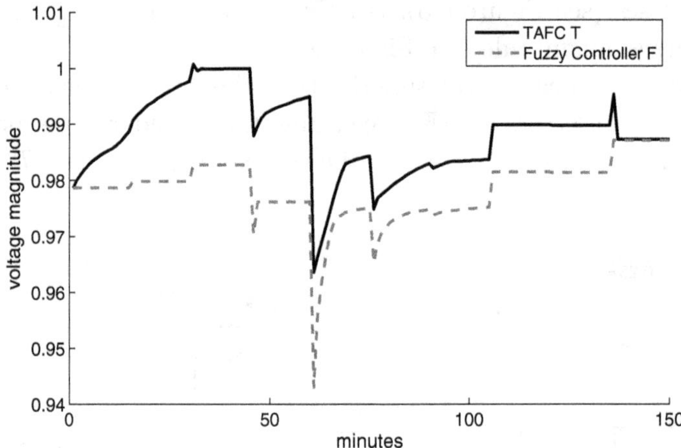

Figure 6.7. The voltage magnitude values for the TAFC T and the conventional fuzzy controller F.

More precisely, the MAE for each aspect has been calculated as:

$$MAE = \frac{1}{N} \cdot \sum_{i=1}^{N} |G(i) - T(i)| \tag{6.4}$$

where N is the number of iterations of the simulation (equal to the number of minutes of simulation) and $G(i)$ and $T(i)$ are the guessed

Table 6.1. MAEs of our controller T and the standard F for all performance aspects. In the last column are reported the relative improvements.

Performance Aspect	MAE of T_A	MAE of F	Rel. impr.
Power losses	0,1142	0,1146	0,35%
Reactive power costs	3,7245E-4	4,0137E-4	7,2%
Magnitude Voltage	0,0119	0,0216	44,9%

and the desired value for the performance aspect (power losses, reactive power costs, and magnitude voltage) in the ith iteration, respectively. In particular, the value 0 has been considered as the desired value for the power losses and reactive power costs, whereas 1 has been considered as the desired value for the magnitude voltage.

Table 6.1 shows the computed MAEs concerning the performance aspects for our proposal and the compared conventional fuzzy controller. As highlighted by the perceptual improvement shown in the last column of Table 6.1, the exploited TAFC T provides better performances than a conventional fuzzy controller.

6.6 Conclusions

The current trend to regulate efficiently the voltage in smart grid platforms is represented by the exploitation of multi-agent-based systems where each agent is equipped with fuzzy inference capabilities. However, the solution to the voltage-regulation problem should be prompt, reliable, and accurate, but, above all, it should be highly adaptive in order to manage effectively the intrinsic time-varying phenomena affecting the smart grid operation. For this reason, in this work, we propose a multi-agent-based approach where each agent is equipped with a novel fuzzy inference engine, TAFC, capable of adaptively regulating the reactive power flows injected by a DG unit into the electrical grid. In our architecture, each agent employs traditional sensors to acquire local bus variables and mutually coupled oscillators to assess the main variables that characterize the operation of the global smart grid. These variables are then amalgamated by an adaptive module held by each agent and composed mainly of a TAFC capable of identifying proper control actions aimed at improving the grid voltage profile and reducing power losses. As for the regulation performances, the developed simulation studies confirm the effectiveness of the proposed strategy in solving the voltage-regulation problem also in the presence of highly variable load patterns.

References

[1] Acampora, G., Loia, V. and Vitiello, A. (2011). "Exploiting timed automata based fuzzy controllers for voltage regulation in smart grids", presented at 2011 IEEE International Conference on Fuzzy Systems, 27–30 June 2011.

[2] Cecati, C., Mokryani, G., Siano, P. *et al.* (2010). An overview of the smart grid concept, *Proceedings of the 36th IEEE Annual Conference of the Industrial Electronics Society*, 3316–3321.

[3] Madani, V. and King, R.L. (2008). Strategies to meet grid challenges for safety and reliability, *International Journal of Reliability and Safety*, **2(1,2)**, 146–165.

[4] Amin, S.M. and Wollenberg, B.F. (2005). Toward a smart grid, *IEEE Power and Energy Magazine*, **3(5)**, 34–38.

[5] Schroder, A., Laresgotti, I., Werlen, K. *et al.* (2009). Intelligent self-describing power grids, *Proceedings of the 20th International Conference and Exhibition on Electricity Distribution, 2009*, 1–4.

[6] King, R.L. (2008). Information services for smart grids, *Proceedings of 2008 IEEE Power and Energy Society General Meeting — Conversion and Delivery of Electrical Energy in the 21st Century*, 1–5.

[7] Joos, G., Ooi, B.T., Gillis, D. *et al.* (2000). The potential of distributed generation to provide ancillary services, *Proceedings of IEEE Power Engineering Society Summer Meeting 2000*, 1762–1767.

[8] Bontempi, G., Vaccaro, A. and Villacci, D. (2006). An adaptive local learning based methodology for voltage regulation in distribution networks with dispersed generation, *IEEE Transactions on Power Systems*, **21(3)**, 1131–1140.

[9] Tomsovich, K. and Hiyama, T. (2001). Intelligent control methods for systems with dispersed generation, *Proceedings of IEEE Power Engineering Society Winter Meeting 2001*, **2**, 913–917.

[10] Marel, M.I., El-Saadany, E.F. and Salama, M.M.A. (2002). Flexible distributed generation, *Proceedings of IEEE Power Engineering Society Summer Meeting 2002*, **1**, 49–53.

[11] Spatti, D.H., da Silva, I.N., Usida, W.F. *et al.* (2010). Fuzzy control system for voltage regulation in power transformers, *Latin America Transactions,*

IEEE (Revista IEEE America Latina), **8(1)**, 51–57.

[12] Hassan, A.R and Sadrul Ula, A.H.M (1994). Design and implementation of a fuzzy controller based automatic voltage regulator for a synchronous generator, *IEEE Transactions on Energy Conversion*, **9(3)**, 550–557.

[13] Pipattanasomporn, M., Feroze, H. and Rahman, S. (2009). "Multi-agent systems in a distributed smart grid: Design and Implementation", presented at IEEE PES 2009.

[14] Higgins, N., Vyatkin, V., Nair, N.-K. *et al.* (2008). Concept of intelligent decentralised power distribution automation with IEC 61850, IEC 61499 and holonic control, *Proceedings of IEEE Conference on Systems, Machine and Cybernetics*, 1–9.

[15] P. Siano, P., Citro, C., Cecati, C. *et al.* (2011). Smart operation of wind turbines and diesel generators according to economic criteria, *IEEE Transactions on Industrial Electronics*, **58(10)**, 1–12.

[16] Acampora, G., Loia, V. and Vitiello, A. (2010). "Hybridizing fuzzy control and timed automata for modeling variable structure fuzzy systems", presented at 2010 IEEE International Conference on Fuzzy Systems, July 2010.

[17] Mi, Z. and Wang, F. (2009). "Substation reactive power and voltage control using fuzzy control theory", presented at 2009 International Conference on Industrial and Information Systems, Haikou, China, April 2009.

[18] Alur, R. (1994). A theory of timed automata, *Theoretical Computer Science*, **126**, 183–235.

[19] Ricalde., L.J., Ordonez, E., Gamez, M. *et al.* (2011). Design of a smart grid management system with renewable energy generation, *Proc. IEEE Symposium on Computational Intelligence Applications in Smart Grid(CIASG)*, 1–4.

[20] Sajadi, A., Farag, H.E., Biczel, P. *et al.* (2012). Voltage regulation based on fuzzy multi-agent control scheme in smart grids, *Energytech, 2012 IEEE* , 29–31 May, 1–5.

[21] Tengku Hashim, T.J., Mohamed, A. and Shareef, H. (2012). A review on voltage control methods for active distribution networks, Electrical Review, **6**, 304–312.

[22] Loia, V. and Vaccaro, A. (2011). "A decentralized architecture for voltage regulation in smart grids," presented at 2011 IEEE International Symposium on Industrial Electronics (ISIE), 27–30 June 2011.

[23] Fakham, H., Ahmidi, A., Colas F. *et al.* (2010).Multi-agent system for distributed voltage regulation of wind generators connected to distribution network, *Proceedings of IEEE PES Innovative Smart Grid Technologies Conference Europe (ISGT Europe)*, 1–6.

[24] Mamdani, E.H., and Assilian, S. (1975). An experiment in linguistic synthesis with a fuzzy logic controller, *International Journal of Man-Machine Studies*, **17(1)**, 1–13.

[25] Lee, C.C. (1990). Fuzzy logic in control system: Fuzzy logic controller — Part 19, *IEEE Transactions on Systems, Man, and Cybernetics*, **20(2)**, 404–435.

[26] Delvenne, J.-C. and Carli, R. (2007). Optimal strategies in the average consensus problem, *Proceedings of 46th IEEE Conf. Decision Control*, pp. 2498–2503.

[27] Barbarossa, S. (2005). Self-organizing sensor networks with information propagation based on mutual coupling of dynamic systems, *Proceedings of International Workshop of Wireless ad hoc Networks*, 1–6.

[28] Acampora, G., (2011). "A TSK neuro-fuzzy approach for modeling highly dynamic systems", presented at 2011 IEEE International Conference on Fuzzy Systems, 27–30 June 2011.

Chapter 7

Smart Metering

Daniele Gallo[a], Carmine Landi[a], Marco Landi[b] and Mario Luiso[a]

[a] *Dipartimento di Ingegneria e dell' Informazione, Seconda Universitá degli Studi di Napoli, Caserta, Italy*
[b]*Department of Industrial Engineering University of Salerno, Fisciano, Italy*

7.1 Introduction

7.1.1 *Introduction to smart meters*

In the smart grid arena, measurement systems play a primary role no longer related only to energy billing but also to the on-line monitoring of the network. As the source of the data for the functioning of the network, these measurement systems constitute a fundamental element of the "smart" architecture. Typically, we refer to the metering system as the "smart meter". The smart meters are required to perform accurate and real-time bi-directional power and energy measurements. Indeed, the Directive 2006/32/EC states that customers must be billed for their actual consumption; such specification may only be met through reliance upon real-time metering devices that monitor the actual state of the network. Moreover, the possibility for a user to act both as a customer and as an energy supplier poses the need for bi-directional metering devices.

The smart meter must also perform another essential task to achieve higher energy efficiency: it should help the customers in building up better awareness regarding their consumption and, eventually, open up the path to better energy utilization.

7.1.2 *Evolution of electricity meters*

Electricity meters are devices used to measure the quantity of electricity supplied to a customer, essentially to bill and to calculate transmission and distribution costs for grid operators. The most common type of meter is the accumulation one, which integrates the power absorption over a period of time, generally coinciding with the billing period. Then an operator carries out the reading of the measurements manually. More recently, meters that record energy usage over shorter intervals have been adopted; they allow for better customer profiling and therefore the design of tariffs that reflect demand, and for the customers to better understand their consumption.

However, it must be noted that manual reading of customers' consumption represents a relevant cost for utility companies. For this reason, systems that allow for users' consumption reading and correct billing without the need for a human operator have been of great interest in research and industry fields. Consequently, several automatic meter reading (AMR) programs have been developed; in this case digital measurement data is obtained and transmitted to the utility company via a one-way communication network.

Although AMR allows for a better monitoring of the distribution network, it is still limited in the services it can provide to customers and utilities.

As an evolution of the metering devices and architecture, a two-way communication infrastructure has been introduced. The so-called advanced metering infrastructure (AMI), and the meters interfacing with it, can bring significant advantages to all the stakeholders of the power grid (see Table 7.1). First of all, the customers can be directly informed about their consumptions, leading in the long run to better electricity utilization and, ultimately, to energy savings. In addition, customer service is improved and suppliers can apply variable pricing schemes. Finally demand response resource management and distribution control can be attained.

The idea of a smart grid is in direct continuity with the automation brought about with the AMI (see Figure 7.1). In fact, relying on the metering and communication infrastructure, the "smart" evolution of the power grid consists of developing new applications,

Table 7.1. Advantages of smart metering.

	Energy suppliers and network operators benefits	Customer benefits	Overall benefits
Short-term	Lower metering costs and more accurate readings	Improved information determines energy savings	Better customer service
	Easier detection of frauds and theft	More frequent and accurate billing	Variable pricing schemes
	Reducing peak demand via demand response (DR)	Integration with home area automation	Better energy utilization through better management of DR and DG (distributed generation)
Long-term	Better planing of generation, network, and maintenance	Enablement to sell ancillary services to the grid (DR, DG, V2G; vehicle-to-grid)	Easier integration of new technologies such as EVs (electric vehicles)
	Support real-time system operation		

favoring the interactions of new and old actors on the grid, and providing new and innovative services to the customers. The smart grid fully encompasses the capability for two-way communication of the network, supporting advanced grid applications such as load management, distribution automation, power quality monitoring, negotiations, and bidding on the open energy market.

7.1.3 *Current developments*

The metering infrastructure represents a key enabler for the realization of the vision of a smart grid. Thus, devices to measure electricity consumption and provide advanced features compatible with new grid applications are the object of much regulatory effort, many investments, and multiple research projects.

Due to the regulatory push by the EU, many member states have implemented, or are about to implement, some legal framework for the installation of smart meters. In some of them, electronic meters

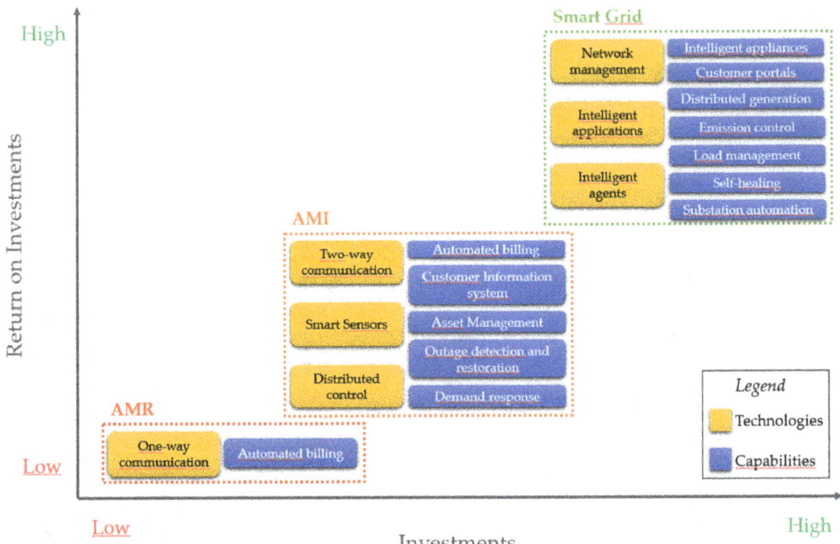

Figure 7.1. Comparison of return on investments vs. investments between AMR, AMI and smart grids.

have already been widely installed, even in the absence of specific legal requirements [1].

Reports assess that, as of 2011, 45 million smart meters have already been installed in the EU [2] and forecasts are for 180 million to 240 million installations by 2020, with customer penetration of about 70% [2, 3] (see Figure 7.2). Significant investments have already been mobilized and a few countries have already proceeded to full smart metering rollout. A conservative estimate is that at least €5 billion has been spent to date on smart metering pilot projects and rollouts. Considering the member states which, at the date of publication, have already committed themselves to, or shown strong interest in, a full smart metering rollout, we can estimate that the total investment in smart metering will be at least €30 billion by 2020.

Several research projects currently in place in EU member states highlight that three communication infrastructure options are typically available for smart metering purposes: communication via the electricity grid (power line carrier), communication via telephone

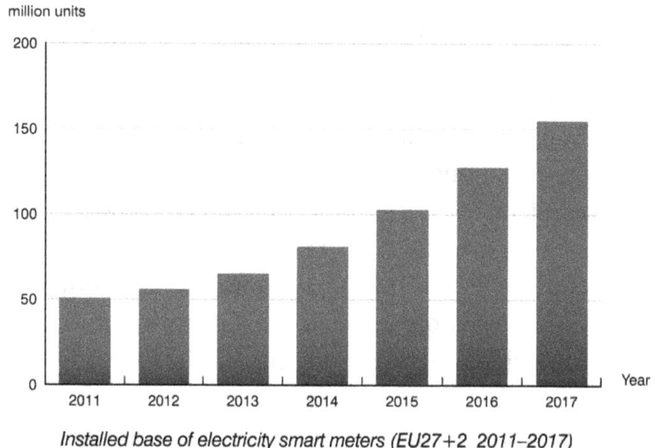

Figure 7.2. Berg Insight — smart metering in Europe (Nov. 2012).

lines and the cable infrastructure (ADSL, TV distribution cable), and wireless communication (mobile telephony, radio frequency (RF)). The choice of a particular communication option strongly depends on the local conditions. However, according to available information, the most widespread communication option is the combined use of power line carrier (PLC) for the connection of the smart meter with the concentrator in a secondary substation and the use of GSM/GPRS for the concentrator/management system connection [2, 4]. In this regard, it is worth citing the open public extended network (OPEN) meter project [5, 7], which aims at providing a set of widely accepted open standards to guarantee interoperability of systems and devices to be adopted in the automated metering infrastructure.

Germany and Italy have proven to be two of the most active European countries in the development and adoption of automated metering infrastructures. Interoperability and coordination are the main drivers in the German E-Energy framework. It encompasses six different and complementary projects related to the implementation of a smart ICT-based power grid, integrating all the actors of the future grid. The Smart Watts project aims at realizing active customer participation in a demand response framework; the smart meters are needed to provide near-time consumption data, used to adjust energy prices dynamically, and offer economic incentives for customers to shift their consumptions to off-peak (cheaper) periods. A similar approach is followed by the MeRegio project, aiming at in-house appliance optimization according to energy price signals for better energy use and energy savings.

With a budget of over €2 billion, Italy accounts for almost half of the total spending related to smart meter projects in the EU. The great majority of this budget is, however, attributable to only one project, the Telegestore project by generation and distribution operator ENEL, which consisted of the national roll out of smart meters in Italy [2].

From the several projects of this type in place, a common trait emerged: the main barriers to the adoption of smart metering technologies and infrastructures in Europe are policy-related, social, or regulatory, rather than technical. They range from lack of interoperability standards to regulatory uncertainty regarding roles and responsibilities in the new smart grid applications, from consumer resistance against new technologies and habits to limited repeatability of pilot projects due to different local policies. To overcome such problems and reach coordination throughout the EU, projects like the Meter-ON were born, aiming to provide any grid stakeholder with clear recommendations on how to tackle the technical barriers and regulatory obstacles endangering the uptake of smart metering technologies and solutions in Europe [8].

The thrust towards the adoption of smart grid and smart metering technologies in North America is also great. In the US 38 million smart meters are currently installed, and the Federal Energy Regulatory Commission (FERC) forecasts there will be 65 million by 2015. From the point of view of providing better customer service, the industry is working to favor interoperability and clearer information for customers; toward this aim, the Green Button initiative focuses on the adoption of a common and standardized format for energy data coming from smart meters and AMR meters. Efforts to standardize the format of energy usage information and protect customer privacy have fostered the rapid development of new applications to further engage and inform customers.

The widespread adoption of smart meters also helps in managing a now aging power grid, allowing for quicker identification of outages and potential problems on the grid. However it must be pointed out that there is not uniformity in the regulations throughout the US states, leading in some cases to local regulations hindering the realization of an all-automated metering infrastructure (e.g. in the case of "opt-out" programs, which give individual customers the opportunity to forgo advanced meter installations). Nonetheless, fueled by industry-led adoption projects, penetration of smart meters and AMI is growing.

7.1.4 *The OPEN meter project*

One of the main projects that aims at laying a common ground for the requirements and solutions of smart meter implementations is the OPEN meter project. Its main objective is to specify a comprehensive set of open and public standards for AMI, supporting electricity, gas, water, and heat metering, based on the agreement of all the relevant stakeholders in this area, and taking into account the real conditions of the utility networks so as to allow full implementation. The scope of the project is to address knowledge gaps for the adoption of open standards for smart multi-metering equipment and all relevant aspects — regulatory environments, smart metering functions, communication media, protocols, and data formats — are considered within the project. The result of the project will be a set of draft standards, based on already existing and accepted standards wherever possible. These standards include the IEC 61334 series PLC standards, the IEC 62056 DLMS/COSEM standards for electricity metering, the EN 13757 series of standards for utility metering other than electricity using M-Bus and other media. These existing standards will be complemented with new standards, based on innovative solutions developed within the project, to form the new body of AM/smart metering standards. The resulting draft standards will be fed into the European and international standardization process.

The project is strongly coordinated with the smart metering standardization mandate given by the European Commission to the

European standardization organizations, the Commission for European Normalization (CEN), the Comité Européen de Normalisation Electrotechnique (CENELEC), and the European Telecommunications Standards Institute (ETSI). The OPEN meter project should remove a perceived barrier to the wide-scale adoption of smart metering in Europe, by ensuring that the requirements for smart metering can be met by products and systems based on open, international standards to ensure interoperability, and which are accepted and supported by the widest possible circle of stakeholders. The OPEN meter project is financed by the European Commission within the Seventh Framework Programme, Area 7/1: Smart Energy Networks/Interactive distribution energy networks, Topic 7/1/1: Open-Access Standard for Smart Multi- Metering Services.

7.2 Research and Industrial Development

7.2.1 *Metering infrastructure and smart meter requirements*

The smart meter needs a supportive communication infrastructure to deliver all the benefits associated with its adoption. Therefore, the design of a meter requires meeting the broader challenge of integrating into an existing infrastructure, or designing and implementing a new one.

To illustrate the main requirements and specifications related to a smart meter, we refer to the advanced metering infrastructure scheme described in the following. The AMI under consideration assumes that the smart meter is not only a measurement device, but also the interface for connecting customers to all the other actors of the grid. In particular, its goal is being able not only to convey measurement data to a management center, but also to allow the reception of price signals from the market and signals for demand response resource management, enabling remote load and generation management for the customers who agreed to participate in demand response (DR) programs. In this scheme, the meter constitutes the hub for all energy consumption in the customers' premises.

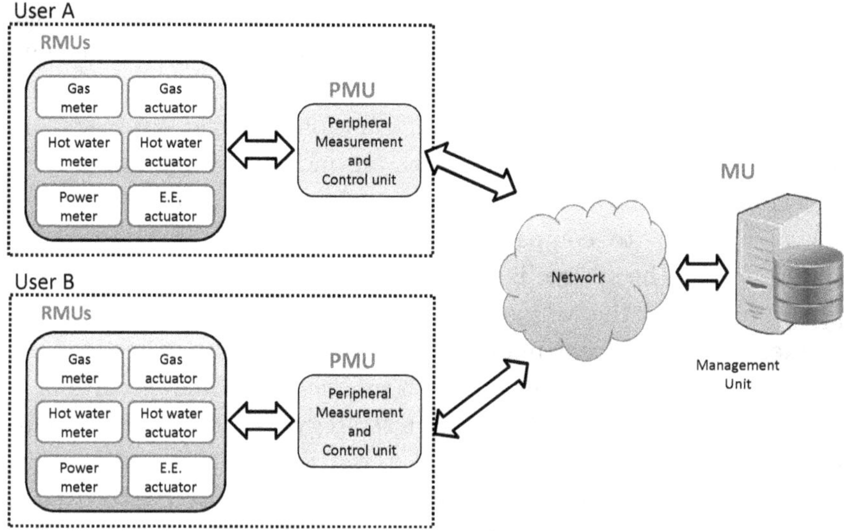

Figure 7.3. Architecture of an AMI.

The AMI, shown in Figure 7.3, is composed of three main parts: the remote measuring units (RMUs), the peripheral measurement units (PMUs) and a management unit (MU). The RMUs are the actual sensing devices; they execute measurements regarding electrical energy, gas, and hot water consumption and, using a data bus, can transmit such data to a PMU. A PMU has the task of collecting measurements from the RMUs, performing data elaboration if required (for example, regarding electricity consumption, usage statistics related to a specific customer can be computed or quality metrics may be calculated) and sending the information to the MU. In fact, the PMUs act just like gateways between RMUs and the MU. Moreover, it is often not important to send upstream the complete measurement data; some aggregated synthetic data may suffice. In this case, the PMUs also have the task of computing synthetic information starting from the measurement data from the RMUs.

This network could also be made of several PMU levels. Typical examples of applications where the network can be sectioned in different branches are a university campus, a large business, or a hospital with different departments connected to different lines.

The MU represents the interface of the AMI with the system operator (SO); it communicates data regarding loads and consumption statistics related to an aggregation of customers. Therefore it provides the SO with relevant information for grid management. Moreover, it provides the users with an informative picture of their own consumptions, allowing them to analyze not only current energy usage, but also to compare it to historical data. In addition, as stated before, the system is designed with the ability to manage DR programs. Thus, the MU is also the interface with the open energy market: it can receive information regarding line congestion and availability of energy; it also receives market prices and, according to the received data, can put in place a strategy to administer load curtailments to customers who agreed to participate in such programs.

The commands are then conveyed through the PMUs to the RMUs. From a functional point of view, the realization of load curtailment procedures needs the presence of actuators, which have to be integrated in the scheme now depicted. In particular, they are placed at the same level as the RMUs, requiring the communication bus (to the PMU) to be bi-directional, thus communicating upwards the measurement results and receiving the actuation commands.

The MU can also provide support for distributed generation, allowing each user to sell his energy on the market. In an ideal configuration, the MU may provide the cheaper solution to the user and at the same time allow the SO to cut down absorption peaks.

Without loss of generality, we can hypothesize that a smart meter prototype may integrate all the functions of an RMU and of a PMU: executing, collecting measurements, capturing usage statistics, and performing customer profiling. In the following the specifications for the design of a smart electricity meter are described. Considering the electricity meter works as a hub for all energy consumptions, the underlying assumption is that other meters perform their own measurements independently, with the smart meter acting only as gateway for the data they provide.

The first and main purpose of a smart meter is to obtain accurate and timely bi-directional electric energy measurements. In particular, it must be pointed out that the meter has to perform its measurements on distorted voltage and current waveforms, and therefore it has to resort to advanced measurement techniques and power metrics. In fact, traditional measurement techniques are limited in the sense that they have been developed referring to sinusoidal conditions, while the real waveforms measureable on the power grid are far from sinusoidal. The traditional metrics for the computation of active and reactive power and energy lose their meaning, since there is not a univocal definition of the measurand. Therefore, both the hardware (sensors, A/D converters, architecture of the microcontroller) and the software implemented on the meter should be designed for the application of advanced power measurement techniques and to perform power quality measurements. Some hints of power quality measurements and power metrics are reported in the next paragraphs.

Being part of a more complex infrastructure, the smart meter must be equipped with communication devices that allow it to send its data to a control center and, at the same time, receive information and commands. Moreover, it might be able to interface with meters in charge of measuring other energy consumptions, such as hot water and gas.

Naturally, the ability to receive commands is based on the assumption that the meter has onboard proper actuators that can translate digital command signals into actions on the related grid branches. In particular, to cover all possible application scenarios, two different kind of actuators are considered in the following: proportional, which can regulate their output in the continuous domain, and binary, which can only be set to an on or an off position.

7.2.2 *Hints of power quality problem and indices*

The increasing diffusion of non-linear loads, such as switching power supplies, determines a relevant distortion of the waveforms on the power grid. In fact, such loads represent a source of current harmonics and inter-harmonics: as their concentration increases, the interaction with other devices installed in the same environment increases too, determining a bigger influence on the electricity distribution system.

The current harmonics and inter-harmonics interact with the distribution system impedance, causing as a consequence even deformations in voltage waveforms. The distorted waveforms can be the cause of a wide array of problems, ranging from over-heating in distribution transformers and in electric motors to malfunctions in electronic equipment. Given the implications of electricity being a service and a product, the supplier must meet some degree of quality in the power supply. The power quality (PQ), in its most general form, represents the evaluation and the analysis of the distortion in voltage and current waveforms, with respect to their nominal values on the power grid, with the aim of containing their negative side effects.

The reference standards for power quality are CEI EN 50160 and IEC 61000-4-30. Certainly, the most relevant form of low power quality is represented by outages (see Figure 7.4). In fact, the continuity of service, being the fundamental type of service provided to customers, has the priority over every other factor that may deteriorate the quality of the supply. Eight different main phenomena that deteriorate power quality may be listed:

- Alteration of RMS value.
- Short-duration alterations (interruption/voltage sags/voltage swells).
- Long-duration alterations (extended interruption/over-voltages/under-voltages).
- Supply voltage imbalance.
- Harmonic distortion.
- Inter-harmonic distortion.
- Voltage fluctuations (flicker).
- Transient disturbances.

In addition to these, fluctuation of the fundamental frequency should be taken into consideration. In fact, the frequency of the fundamental keeps steady if there is exact parity between generation and demand. However, even in the case that the power balance condition is met exactly, random increase or decrease in loads disrupts the balance. Frequency variations are extremely important, since many users are extremely sensitive to such phenomena. The CEI EN 50160 sets as a

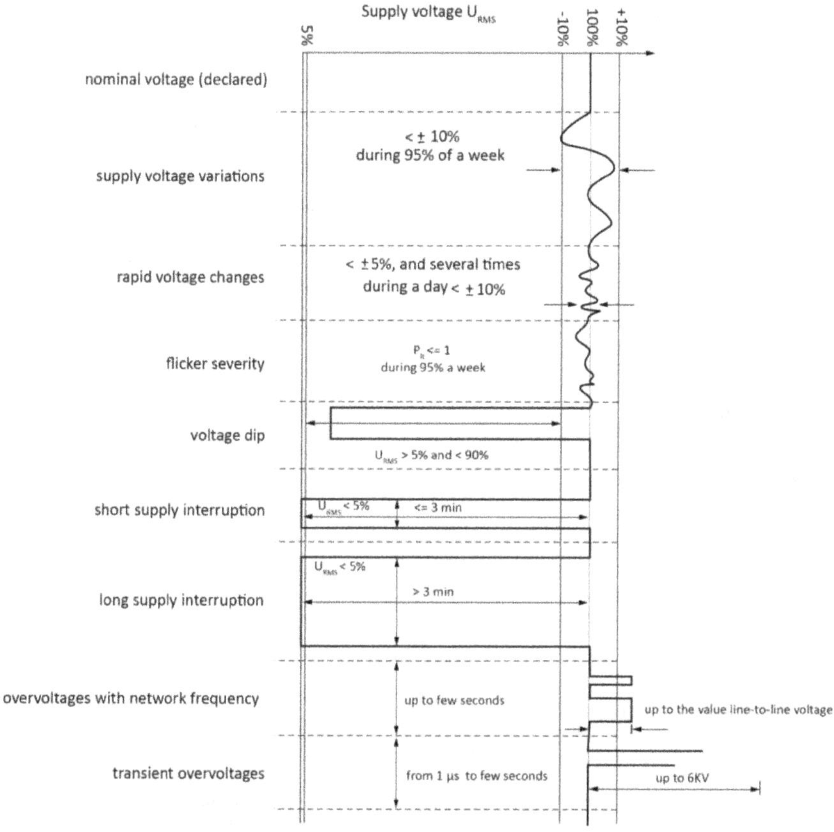

Figure 7.4. EN50160 requirements in graphical form.

PQ requirement that the fundamental frequency must be contained in the range of $\pm 1\%$ around the nominal value, 95% of the time.

There are numerous algorithms and definitions of indices of power quality that analyze different aspects of disturbances conducted on the power system [9]. Some of these are reported below:

The ***root mean square* (RMS) value** for a continuous signal $f(t)$, over the interval $[T_1, T_2]$ is given by:

$$\text{RMS} = \sqrt{\frac{1}{T_2 - T_1} \int_{T_1}^{T_2} [f(t)]^2 \, dt}.$$

The ***root mean square* (RMS) value** for a sequence of N discrete samples $\{x_1, x_2, \ldots, x_N\}$ is given by:

$$\text{RMS} = \sqrt{\frac{1}{N} \sum_{i=1}^{N} x_i^2}.$$

The ***current harmonic distortion*** **(ITHD)** is given by:

$$\text{ITHD} = \frac{\sqrt{\sum_{h=2}^{\infty} I_h^2}}{I_1} \cdot 100 \quad (\%),$$

where I_1 represents the current at the fundamental frequency and I_h is the hth current harmonic.

The ***voltage harmonic distortion*** **(VTHD)** is given by:

$$\text{VTHD} = \frac{\sqrt{\sum_{h=2}^{\infty} V_h^2}}{V_1} \cdot 100 \quad (\%),$$

where V_1 represents the voltage at the fundamental frequency and V_h is the hth voltage harmonic.

The ***short-term flicker severity*** $(\boldsymbol{P_{ST}})$ is calculated over a period of ten minutes according to a standardized formula which takes into account the response of the human eye and brain. Given d_{max} the maximum relative voltage change, and F the shape factor associated with the voltage change, P_{ST} is computed as follows:

$$t_f = 2.3(F d_{\max})^{3.2} \rightarrow P_{ST} = \left(\sum t_f / T_p\right)^{1/3.2}$$

with T_p the observation period. The value of P_{ST}shall not be greater than 1.

The ***long-term flicker severity*** $(\boldsymbol{P_{LT}})$ is calculated from a sequence of 12 P_{ST} values over a twelve hour interval, according to the following formula: $P_{LT} = \sqrt[3]{\sum_{i=1}^{N} \frac{P_{STi}^3}{12}}$. The value of P_{LT} shall not be greater than 0.65.

7.2.3 *Power metrics*

In sinusoidal conditions, the instantaneous power $p(t)$, which is the product of the voltage and current waveforms, is composed of a constant term (the active power) plus a time-dependent term. If $v(t)$ and $i(t)$ represent voltage and current waveforms, then

$$v(t) = \sqrt{2}\,V cos(\omega_1 t) \tag{7.1}$$

and

$$i(t) = \sqrt{2}\,I cos(\omega_1 t - \varphi). \tag{7.2}$$

The instantaneous power $p(t)$ is given by

$$p(t) = v(t)i(t) = VI[\cos(\varphi) + cos(2\omega_1 t - \varphi)] \tag{7.3}$$

$$\begin{aligned} p(t) &= VI\cos(\varphi)[1 + \cos(2\omega_1 t)] + VI\sin(\varphi)\sin(2\omega_1 t) \\ &= P[1 + \cos(2\omega_1 t)] + Q\sin(2\omega_1 t). \end{aligned} \tag{7.4}$$

P represents the active power, a uni-directional component that is responsible for the energy exchange. Reactive power Q accounts for power fluctuations in AC (alternating current) circuits, which do not result in a net transfer of energy. Active and reactive power can be related via the apparent power S:

$$S = VI = \sqrt{P^2 + Q^2}. \tag{7.5}$$

However, the situation changes when harmonics and inter-harmonics are present in the current and voltage waveforms; their multiple interactions give rise to several products, not representative of the energy exchange, but whose correct interpretation would be needed for a correct management of the electrical system. In the following an example of a signal with only one additional harmonic for both current and voltage is reported.

$$v_d(t) = \sqrt{2}V_1 cos(\omega_1 t) + \sqrt{2}V_2 cos(\omega_2 t), \tag{7.6}$$

$$i_d(t) = \sqrt{2}\, I_1 cos(\omega_1 t - \varphi_1) + \sqrt{2}\, I_2 cos(\omega_2 t - \varphi_2). \tag{7.7}$$

In this case the instantaneous power $p(t)$ is given by

$$\begin{aligned} p_d(t) = v_d(t) i_d(t) = {} & [V_1 I_1 \cos(\varphi_1) + V_2 I_2 \cos(\varphi_2)] \\ & + [V_1 I_1 \cos(2\omega_1 t - \varphi_1) + V_2 I_2 \cos(2\omega_2 t - \varphi_2)] \\ & + \{V_1 I_2 \cos[(\omega_1 - \omega_2)t + \varphi_2] \\ & + V_1 I_2 \cos[(\omega_1 + \omega_2)t - \varphi_2] \\ & + V_2 I_1 \cos[(\omega_2 - \omega_1)t + \varphi_1] \\ & + V_2 I_1 \cos[(\omega_1 + \omega_2)t - \varphi_1]\}. \end{aligned} \tag{7.8}$$

While the definitions of active and reactive power in sinusoidal conditions are clear and there is unanimous agreement on the physical significance of such terms, the interpretation of the additional terms present in non-sinusoidal conditions is still the subject of much debate in the literature. Several authors have proposed different definitions for electrical power quantities in non-sinusoidal conditions, trying to extend to this domain the properties that active, apparent, or reactive power have in the sinusoidal domain. In general, different schools of thought resort to different approaches regarding the measurement algorithms (identified as *metrics*) to compute the electrical power quantities of interest. The main ones are:

(1) Theories in the frequency domain.
(2) Theories in the time domain.
(3) Theories at instantaneous values.

The theories in the frequency domain apply to periodic waveforms and are based on the decomposition of the signals with the Fourier series. These approaches originate from Budeanu's theory. While preserving the same definition for apparent power, a kind of superposition of effects is considered, adopting in non-sinusoidal conditions the same definitions for active and reactive power defined in sinusoidal conditions. Their expressions are:

$$\begin{array}{ll} \text{Active power:} & \text{Reactive power:} \\ P = \sum_{n \in N} V_n I_n \cos \varphi_n. & Q_B = \sum_{n \in N} V_n I_n \sin \varphi_n. \end{array} \tag{7.9}$$

As is clear when comparing these expressions to equation (7.8), they do not include all the power terms. The same inconsistency is obtained when considering the apparent power; in fact, it can be proven that $S^2 > P^2 + Q_B^2$. To make up for the inconsistencies Budeanu introduces an additional power term, the distortion power, defined as

$$D_B = \sqrt{S^2 - P^2 - Q_B^2}. \tag{7.10}$$

Other theories following the same school of thought, such as the ones by Shepherd and Zakikhani or by Sharon, arise from criticism and corrections to Budeanu's theory.

The theories in the time domain arise from the current-splitting principle and are born from the one developed by Fryze. Considering a system with an applied voltage $v(t)$ and a current $i(t)$ flowing into it, having the same periodicity, the current can be divided into two terms:

$$i(t) = i_a(t) + i_r(t), \tag{7.11}$$

where

$$i_a(t) = \frac{\frac{1}{T}\int_0^T vi\,dt}{\frac{1}{T}\int_0^T v^2\,dt} v(t) = \frac{P}{V^2} v(t). \tag{7.12}$$

The $i_a(t)$ is called active current, and has the same shape as the voltage waveform. The second current term $i_r(t)$, orthogonal to $i_a(t)$, is the non-active current, representing the difference between total and active current:

$$i_r(t) = i(t) - i_a(t). \tag{7.13}$$

This approach preserves the definition of apparent power S. The active power P is dependent only on the current component $i_a(t)$, and the non-active power N is obtained from the apparent and active ones:

$$P = \frac{1}{T}\int_0^T vi\,dt = \frac{1}{T}\int_0^T vi_a\,dt, \tag{7.14}$$

$$N = \sqrt{S^2 - P^2}. \tag{7.15}$$

Basically the foundation of Fryze's theory is considering non-active all the power components that cannot be considered active. The theories of Kusters and Moore, Page, and Czarnescki extend Fryze's approach, decomposing the non-active current and relating its components to physical properties of the considered load.

The theories at instantaneous values rely on power definitions that include time-dependent terms instead of constant quantities like RMS and average values. Such approaches, like the ones from Ferrero and Superti-Furga, are becoming increasingly widespread thanks to developments in power electronics and control techniques, which enable them to be applied in active systems for harmonic compensation.

With the scientific debate still open, up to now the only standard regarding the power measurements in sinusoidal and non-sinusoidal conditions is the IEEE 1459-2010 [10]. It partly adopts some definitions from the theories introduced in the previous paragraphs and partly introduces new ones. The aim of the standard, even if not reaching univocal definitions, is to provide a means to characterize the quality of the electrical supply and to help the design and use of instrumentation for power measurements.

The standard does not specify method of analysis for the waveforms, recurring implicitly to the FFT. The fundamental idea expressed in the IEEE 1459 is the decomposition of voltages and currents into one component representing the signal at the fundamental frequency and another component including all the harmonics and inter-harmonics (considered harmful for the electrical system).

In the following the most relevant formulations introduced in the standard are reported.

Voltage:
$$V^2 = V_1^2 + V_H^2 = V_1^2 + \sum_{h \neq 1} V_h^2$$

Current:
$$I^2 = I_1^2 + I_H^2 = I_1^2 + \sum_{h \neq 1} I_h^2$$

Active power:
$$P = \frac{1}{T}\int_0^T p(t)dt = P_1 + P_H$$

Apparent power:
$$S^2 = (VI)^2 = (V_1I_1)^2 + (V_HI_1)^2 + (V_1I_H)^2 + (V_HI_H)^2$$

Fundamental apparent power:
$$(V_1I_1)^2 = S_1^2 = P_1^2 + Q_1^2 = (V_1I_1cos\varphi_1)^2 + (V_1I_1sin\varphi_1)^2$$

Non-fundamental apparent power:
$$S_N^2 = (V_HI_1)^2 + (V_1I_H)^2 + (V_HI_H)^2 = S^2 - S_1^2$$

Non-active power:
$$N = \sqrt{S^2 - P^2}$$

7.3 Industrial Products

Some manufacturers, such as Echelon and GE Digital Energy, produce smart meter solutions for smart grids.

7.3.1 *Networked Energy Services (NES) smart grid system from Echelon*

The Networked Energy Services (NES) [11] is a software-driven smart grid solution that incorporates smart meters, grid connectors and concentrators, and system software. The meters are deployed in a meshed network and communicate with each other and with the concentrator via power line communication (PLC). Communication with the utility's management system is based on an IP connection. Optional modules allow connection over ZigBee.

The main component of NES smart grid systems is the IEC single phase smart meter, designed for residential and small commercial energy consumers. Each meter provides a set of different energy services when operating within the NES system. Some of these services are: automated two-way meter reading, power quality measurements and analysis, remote electronic disconnect and local physical reconnect, distribution system asset optimization, outage detection and restoration management, blackout detection, real-time direct load control, load profiling, billing for time-of-use, prepay, optional max demand, display of energy consumptions, and relevant energy usage parameters.

The main metrological characteristics are reported in the following:

- Active: Class 1 certified to IEC 62053-21, Class B certified to EN 50470-3 (MID).
- Reactive: Class 2 certified to IEC 62053-23.
- Operating temperature: −40°C to +70°C.
- Voltage:
  - 220V to 240V phase-to-neutral, range −20% to +15% (MTR 1000 Series).
  - 230V phase-to-neutral, range −20% to +20% (MTR 0600 Series).
- Frequency: 50 Hz +5%.
- Service type: one-phase, two-wire.
- Optional CNX modules:
  - CNX 2000: Compliant with ZigBee Smart Energy 1.0.
  - CNX 3000: Power line communications on CENELEC C-band spectrum, compatible with both ZigBee Smart Energy profile and the open LonWorks®control networking standard.

7.3.2 *The Grid IQ AMI P2MP Solution from GE Digital Energy*

The Grid IQ AMI P2MP Solution [12] is a metering and communication infrastructure, which makes use of a point-to-multipoint or RF "Star" architecture. The Smart Meter SGM1100 adopts PLC communications with the DLMS/COSEM protocol to interact with the access point. The access point is designed for indoor or outdoor operation and can be easily deployed on buildings, utility poles, or communication towers enabling low-cost pervasive coverage in the most challenging environments. The smart meter operating system (SMOS) provides visibility to data retrieved from network management services. SMOS also provides the back-office integration functions that deliver data from across the network to core operational systems, such as outage management systems and other applications. SMOS supports various industry standard interfaces and protocols.

The smart meter allows time-of-use billing measures, multiple load profile recording and multi-energy recording; in addition monitors power quality parameters and stores statistical and historical load data with up to one minute resolution. Finally, it allows for remote firmware update.

From a metrological point of view, the meter main characteristics are:

- Active: Class B certified to EN 50470-3 (MID).
- Reactive: Class 2 certified to IEC 62053-23.
- Operating temperature: $-25°$ to $+70°$C.
- Nominal voltage: 230 V $\pm$ 20%.
- Configuration: Single-phase single-element direct connect.

7.3.3 *Other products*

Some other industrial manufacturers, such as Texas Instruments and Accent [13, 14], provide integrated circuits, systems-on-chips, printed circuit boards, etc. for the development of smart metering solutions. These could be used by manufacturers of smart meter solutions to produce industrial implementations.

7.4 Custom Solutions

7.4.1 *Network architecture*

In Figure 7.5, the simplified scheme of the proposed smart meter network is shown [16, 17]. It includes a master data aggregator and

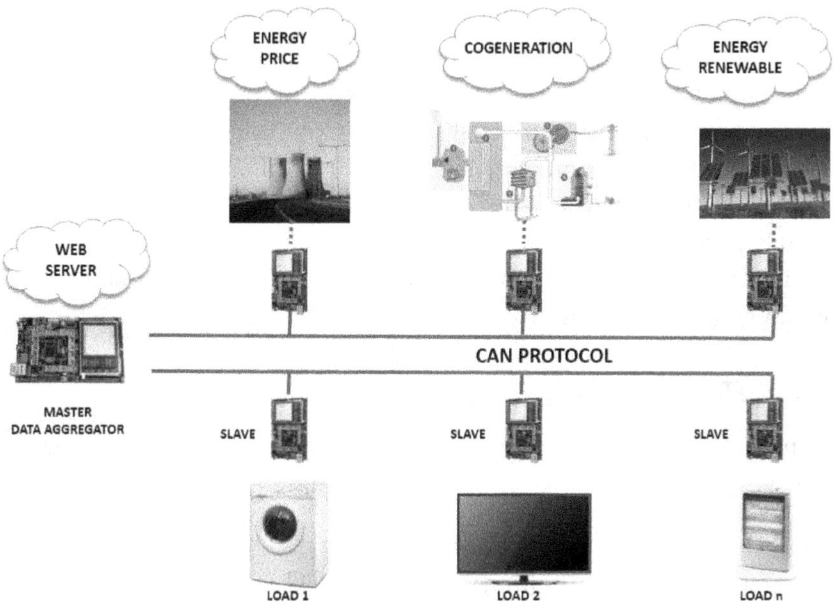

Figure 7.5. Architecture of the proposed smart metering network.

several slave devices. The data aggregator, thanks to the implemented web server provides information regarding:

- Renewable source availability.
- Co-generator status.
- Actual energy prices.

The availability of renewable sources is key information for effective management of the power system. In fact, the high uncertainty related to wind patterns makes it impossible to consider the allocation of a predefined wind-related capacity. For this reason the renewable sources are often used jointly with storage systems. Monitoring of the charge level of storage systems could be an additional feature of the smart meter network; while it is not treated in the described system, it is one of the enhancements to be implemented in the near future. For an integrated management some information regarding the co-generators is needed, such as their status and the thermal energy requirement. Finally the data aggregator needs to know the energy price, which can be updated daily or even hourly.

The slave smart meters are connected to the single node of the power network. Each device continuously acquires voltages and currents and calculates power and energy consumption/generation and several power quality parameters. Moreover, each slave meter controls, by means of actuators, loads on three different sub-branches.

In addition, the master microcontroller acquires information about energy pricing and therefore it is able to make decisions for efficient use of the energy, such as whether to disconnect a single load or the time of use of a load.

7.4.2 *Hardware implementation*

From a functional point of view, the meter consists of the following blocks:

(1) A metering unit that tracks the energy usage of the customer and processes the billing.
(2) A communication unit that enables two-way digital communication with the energy company.
(3) An actuation unit that starts and shuts down the energy supply.

From a physical point of view, each meter consists of:

(1) A transduction section composed by voltage and current sensors and level adapters.
(2) An elaboration section that acquires the output of the sensors and processes the acquired samples.
(3) A display monitoring several types of information.
(4) A memory section that stores the billing value in an EEPROM [18].
(5) Communication drivers and interfaces.

The transduction stage and the elaboration section are described in the following subsections.

7.4.2.1 *Meter architecture*

The hardware implementation is built around a STM32F107VCT6 microcontroller, which incorporates the high-performance ARM®

Cortex^{TM}-M3 32-bit RISC core operating at a 72 MHz frequency. Its main features are:

(1) 256 KB of Flash memory and 64 KB of general-purpose SRAM.
(2) Low power: Sleep, Stop and Standby modes.
(3) 2 × 12-bit, 1 μs A/D converters (16 channels) with conversion range from 0 V to 3.6 V and up to 2 MHz in interleaved mode.
(4) 2 × 12-bit D/A converters.
(5) 12-channel DMA controller.
(6) Up to 80 fast I/O ports.
(7) CRC calculation unit, 96-bit unique ID.
(8) Up to four 16-bit timers, one 16-bit motor control PWM timer, and two watchdog timers.
(9) Up to two I2C, five USARTs, two CAN interfaces (2.0B Active) with 512 bytes of dedicated SRAM, USB 2.0 full-speed device/host/OTG controller, 10/100 Ethernet MAC with dedicated DMA and SRAM (4 KB) and with IEEE1588 hardware support.

7.4.2.2 *Voltage and current sensing*

Measurements on high-medium-voltage power networks involve issues not faced in measurements applied to other types of systems. First of all, they require precise means for scaling currents and voltages down to usable metering levels. For most practical purposes, this role has been adequately filled by magnetic core instrument transformers, i.e. voltage transformers (VT) and current transformers (CT). Another requirement regards their linearity over a wide frequency range, so as to be able to analyze the whole spectrum of voltage and current waveforms. However, instrument transformers currently available for measuring harmonics are characterized by a parasitic capacitance, which causes resonance problems. In addition, the transformers have a non-linear magnetization characteristic; this property causes the transformer core to saturate in some cases and to inject harmonics of its own into the measurements. Moreover, the inductive and capacitive effects they exhibit strongly limit their dynamic performance. Typically, commercial instrument transformers are usable in the narrow 50–400 Hz frequency range.

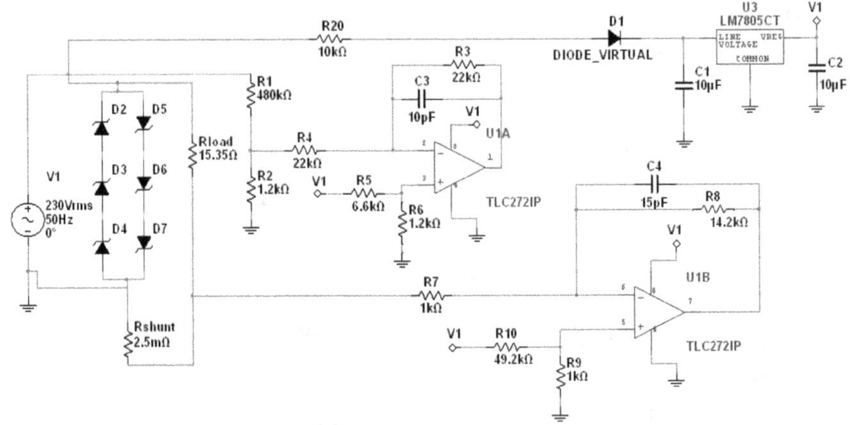

Figure 7.6. Circuit diagram of the CVCT.

Obviously those limits make VT and CT unusable for the analyses of high-frequency harmonic and of low-frequency inter-harmonic components. Therefore, new types of voltage and current transducers were developed to make the smart meter able to measure power quality disturbances in a wide frequency range. Voltage and current sensing sections coexist in a prototype of a combined voltage and current transducer (CVCT) [19, 20]. The block scheme is shown in Figure 7.6 and a photo is produced in Figure 7.7. As can be seen, it is made of simple electrical and electronic components and thus represents a low-cost solution. Over-voltages protection is realized by employing a Zenes diode barrier, symbolically represented in the scheme by three diodes in series. The two sections of the CVCT are powered from the input voltage waveform: a simple half-wave rectifier and a linear regulator obtain a $5\,\mathrm{V_{DC}}$ single supply from $230\,\mathrm{V_{AC}}$. The voltage transducer is a high impedance resistive divider with a differential operational amplifier; the current transducer is a low-resistance resistive shunt with a differential operational amplifier. Input voltage is in the range $[-460\sqrt{2}, 460\sqrt{2}]$ V, which corresponds to an RMS value equal to $460\,\mathrm{V_{RMS}}$, in order to make the meter able to measure power quality parameters such as voltage swells. Current input is in the range $[-30\sqrt{2}, 30\sqrt{2}]$ A, which corresponds to an RMS value equal to $30\,\mathrm{A_{RMS}}$. Both the outputs are in the range

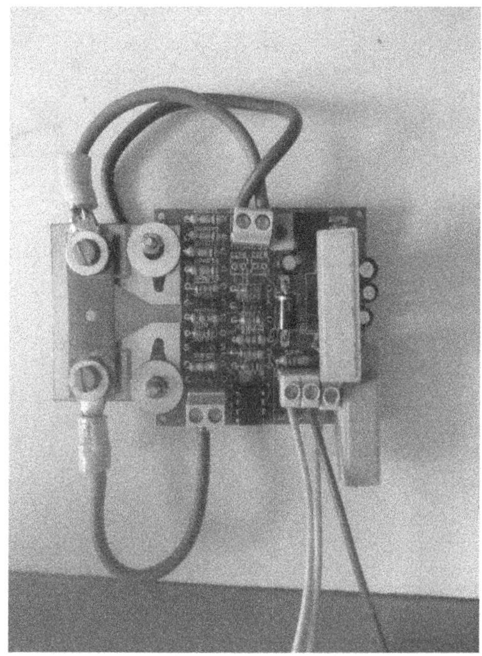

Figure 7.7. A photo of the realized CVCT.

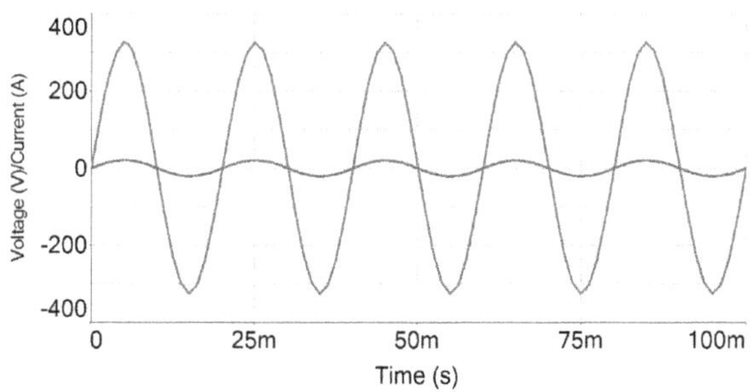

Figure 7.8. Voltage and current at the input of CVCT.

$[0, 3]$ V, in order to be suitable for microcontroller analog inputs; with inputs equal to zero the outputs correspond to $1.5\,V_{DC}$. The realized CVCT has been simulated in Multisim environment. Figures 7.8 and 7.9 show, respectively, inputs ($230\,V_{RMS}$ and $15\,A_{RMS}$) and outputs of the CVCT.

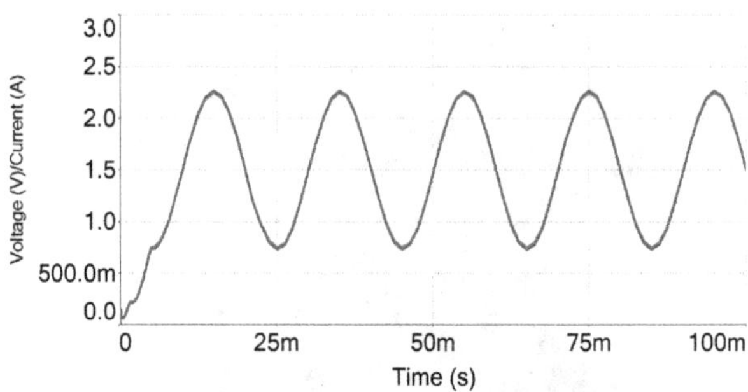

Figure 7.9. Outputs of CVCT.

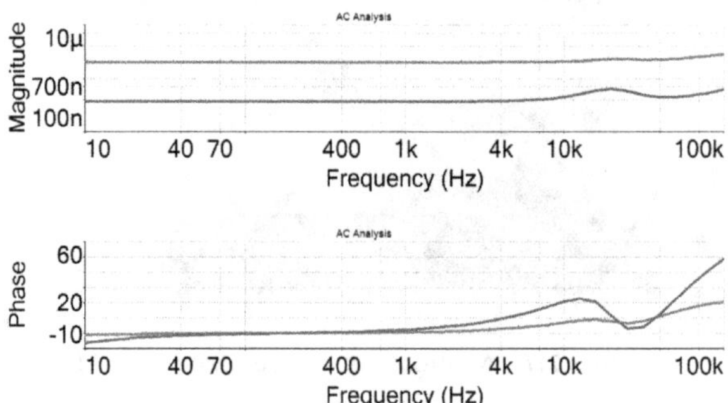

Figure 7.10. AC analysis of the realized CVCT: magnitudes and phases of the outputs.

From Figure 7.9 it can be seen that:

(1) Outputs are inverted with respect to inputs.
(2) The signal becomes stationary after a small transient due to stabilization of supply voltage by the linear regulator.
(3) Mean values are 1.5 V for both outputs.

In Figure 7.10 the magnitude and phases of the outputs, from the AC analysis simulation, are shown; it can be seen that in the range of interest for power quality analysis (i.e. until 10 kHz), the frequency bandwidth of the CVCT is suitable for power quality analysis applications.

7.4.2.3 *Actuators*

The prototype meter is equipped with two different kinds of actuators: a proportional one and three binary ones. For the proportional one, a BTA16-800BRG TRIAC and the respective control module ZAX27A have been considered. With this solution, electric loads of up to 400 V and 3 A can be powered. The binary actuators are essentially a latching relay, specifically the Omron G2R. They act like an on/off switch for the load connected to them. The presence of a three latching relays allows for the sectioning of the circuit that the meter has to monitor into three branches, each of which can be powered separately.

7.4.3 *Software implementation*

7.4.3.1 *Measurement software implementation*

In the slave meter, the elaboration section is able to compute the following parameters:

(i) Voltage and current RMS values.
(ii) Active power (P) and power factor (PF).
(iii) Energy consumption.
(iv) Power consumption profile.
(v) Frequency.
(vi) Voltage and current total harmonic distortion (VTHD and ITHD).
(vii) Voltage dip events.

As for the implemented software, it adopts on-line data processing to obtain the desired quantities. To this aim, an accurate synchronization is essential because most parameters depend on the actual fundamental frequency; frequency deviation from the nominal value should be continuously monitored. The synchronization of the input sequence is implemented through:

(i) A hysteresis block that selects a number of samples between the first and second zero crossing.

(ii) A least squares linear regression block that rebuilds the real index position of the input samples zero crossing.

By defining the fundamental and the sampling frequencies as f_0 and f_c respectively, the index values for the first and second zero crossing as $x(1)$ and $x(0)$ respectively, and their residuals, $\Delta x(1)$ and $\Delta x(0)$, and adopting the mathematical relation (7.16), it is possible to obtain the fundamental frequency value:

$$f_0 = f_c \frac{1}{x(1) + \Delta x(1) - x(0) + \Delta x(0)}. \tag{7.16}$$

A section monitors dip events through RMS continuous processing. Considering N, the ratio between the sampling rate and the input signal frequency, the relations (7.17), based on the Eulero's equation, calculate the RMS values:

$$\begin{aligned} V_{RMS}^2 &= \frac{1}{N} \sum_{k=0}^{N-1} v_k^2, \\ I_{RMS}^2 &= \frac{1}{N} \sum_{k=0}^{N-1} i_k^2. \end{aligned} \tag{7.17}$$

The algorithm adopts a sliding window technique and this leads to (7.18):

$$\begin{aligned} V_{RMS}^2(k) &= V_{RMS}^2(k-1) + \frac{v_k^2 - v_{k-N+1}^2}{N}, \\ I_{RMS}^2(k) &= I_{RMS}^2(k-1) + \frac{i_k^2 - i_{k-N+1}^2}{N}. \end{aligned} \tag{7.18}$$

The active power is calculated as in (7.19):

$$P(k) = P(k-1) + \frac{v_k i_k - v_{k-N+1} i_{k-N+1}}{N}. \tag{7.19}$$

The power factor is calculated with (7.20):

$$PF = \frac{P}{S}, \tag{7.20}$$

where P is the active power and S the apparent power.

Subsequently a digital resampling is made to obtain in exactly ten cycles of the fundamental a number of samples that is a power of two. The results of all the measurement sections are validated using flag control: flagged results are not accounted for in subsequent analysis, unflagged data are grouped with reference to absolute time in order to obtain a measurement with a 10 minute clock boundary. VTHD and ITHD are evaluated through fast Fourier transform (FFT) of voltage and current signals, after a resampling process to obtain a number of samples equal to 256 for each signal, i.e. a power of four [21]. The new samples are taken at a non-integer index corresponding to (7.21):

$$k\alpha = k\frac{T_{10cycles}f_s}{2^n} = m_k + d_k \quad \forall\, k = 1, \ldots, 2^n. \tag{7.21}$$

The integer and decimal part of the index corresponding to the kth new sample $y_R(k)$ are respectively m_k and d_k.

The value of new samples can be calculated as in (7.22):

$$y_R(k) = y(m_k) + \Delta y = y(m_k) + \frac{d_k(y(m_k+1) - y(m_k))}{10}, \tag{7.22}$$

where $y(m_k)$ and $y(m_k+1)$ are two consecutive samples adopted to calculate $y_R(k)$, and finally the distance between $y_R(k)$ and $y(m_k)$ is Δy.

7.4.3.2 *Communication protocol*

In order to realize a hierarchical architecture, two-level communication is realized. At the lower level, smart meters communicate with the data concentrator through CAN protocol; at a higher level, the data concentrator exchanges data with the user, through TCP/IP protocol.

7.4.3.2.1 CAN protocol

The implemented smart meter network requires a reliable low-level communication interface. The main required features are:

(i) Low-cost implementation.
(ii) Noise immunity.

(iii) Easy configuration.
(iv) Multicast network.

For these reasons, the CAN protocol [22] is adopted. It was specifically designed to operate seamlessly even in the presence of high electromagnetic disturbances thanks to the adoption of transmission signals with a balanced difference of potential. The immunity to electromagnetic interference can be further increased by using a twisted pair cable type. The bit rate can be up to 1 Mbit/s in nets shorter than 40 m. Slower speeds allow for communication over greater distances (125 kbit/s to 500 m) as in the considered case. The CAN communication protocol is standardized in ISO 11898-1 [23]. A priority-based bus arbitration allows to transfer first messages with higher priorities: if the bus is idle, any node may begin to transmit; however, if two or more nodes begin to send messages at the same time, the message with the higher id (which has more dominant bits, i.e., zeroes) will overwrite other nodes lower ids, so that eventually (after this arbitration on the id) only the dominant message remains and it is received by all nodes. Messages with numerically smaller values of id have higher priority and they are transmitted first. The CAN communication is implemented by the STM32F107VCT6, in order to efficiently manage a large number of incoming messages [24]. The simplified architecture of the STM32 CAN interface is shown in Figure 7.11.

7.4.3.2.2 Protocol utilization of CAN architecture

The master data aggregator (see Figure 7.5) sends a message with a "remote frame". It is a message without information content, whose aim is to request a data frame from the slaves. Three transmit mailboxes are provided to the software for setting up messages. The transmission scheduler decides which mailbox has to be transmitted first, for example the energy consumption of a single load. The message is converted by a parallel–serial converter and it is sent to the CAN TX Pin. The master receives the remote frame through the CAN RX Pin. Then, the message is converted in parallel through a serial–parallel converter. The frame is sent to an acceptance filter that is composed

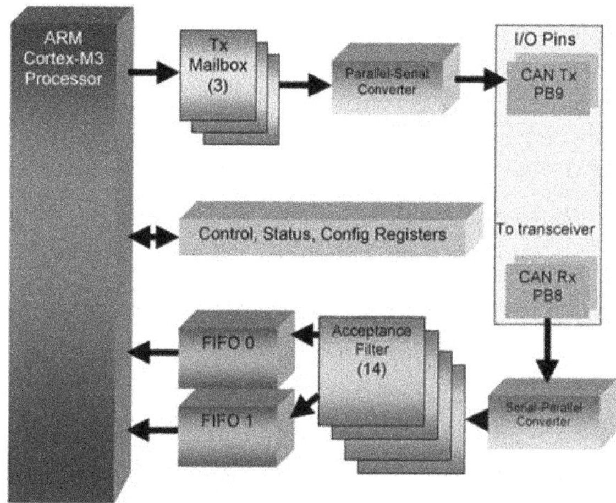

Figure 7.11. CAN communication device architecture.

of 14 configurable identifier filter banks for selecting the incoming messages that the software needs and discarding the others. Two reception FIFO (first in first out) buffers are used by the hardware to store the incoming messages. Three complete messages can be stored in each FIFO. The FIFOs are completely managed by hardware. When a remote frame is received, the device sets up a response message — a data frame corresponding to the remote frame — and sends it to the other device, which previously sent the remote frame. The structure of the data and remote frame is as follows. The start of frame denotes the start of the frame transmission. The id is the identifier for the data and also represents the message priority. The remote transmission request is set to dominant (0). The identifier extension bit and reserved bit must be dominant (0). The data length code consists of four bits and indicates the number of data bytes (0–8 bytes). The data field denotes the data to be transmitted (0–8 bytes) and it only is in the data frame. The cyclic redundancy check, composed by 15 bits, is an error-detecting code used to detect accidental changes to raw data. The ACK slot is sent recessive (1) from the transmitter and any receiver can assert a dominant (0); the end of frame must be recessive (1).

7.4.4 *Smart metering network management*

7.4.4.1 *Operating system*

A real-time operating system has been implemented, both on the slave meter and the master data aggregator, to support the different operations of the smart meter. There is a main task that enables and disables all the four tasks implemented [25, 26]. They are:

- **CAN manage** to manage locally slave microcontrollers.
- **UIP Server** to manage the communication over TCP/IP protocol.
- **Measure** to measure the parameters reported in Section 7.4.3.1.
- **User Interface** to show the power and energy profile consumption and manage the touch screen.

In Figures 7.12 and 7.13, respectively, the display of a smart meter with all tasks and the power consumption, through the task user interface, are shown.

7.4.4.2 *Communication over TCP/IP*

In the data aggregator, a web server collects the statistics of each household and extracts other information [26]. Through the web server, the user can remotely monitor the power profile of a single

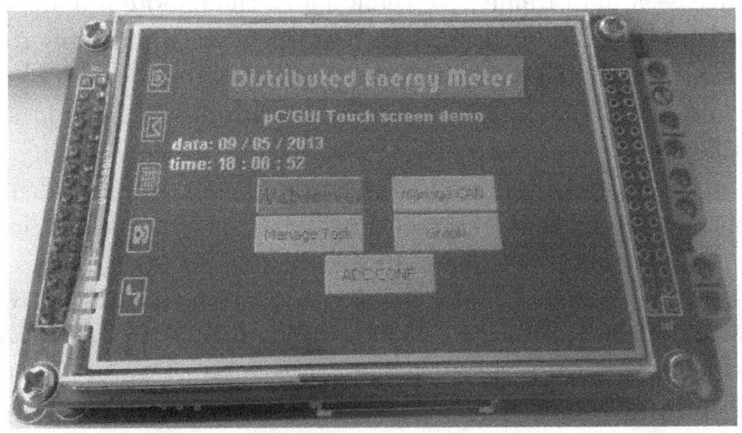

Figure 7.12. User interface for accessing the implemented tasks.

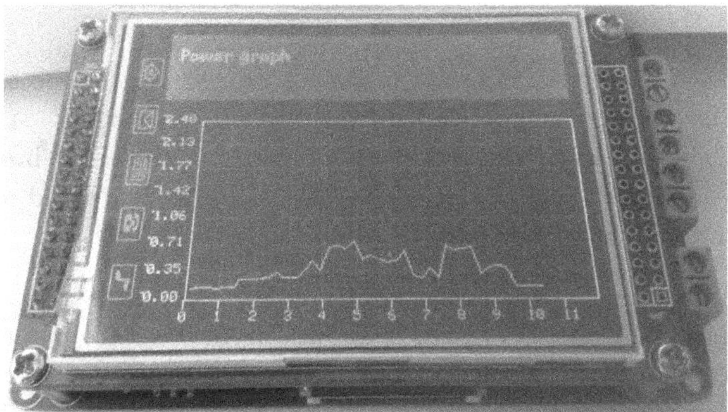

Figure 7.13. Graphical representation of the results from the executed task.

load. For these reasons, an HTTP web server has been implemented. It can serve dynamic web pages and files from a read-only ROM file system, and provides several scripting languages. We report an example for the power consumption request. The steps of the CGI (common gateway interface) are the following:

(i) The user clicks the power graph.
(ii) The client browser is shown.
(iii) A request is sent to the web server.

The web server:

(i) Loads the UIP packet management routine.
(ii) Checks the UIP packet.
(iii) Starts the routine httpd_add_call.
Checks the request (power graph).

The service procedure of the script is the following:

(i) Sends the file header.html.
(ii) Writes the text "Load Power Profile".
Calls the function Create Graph.
(iii) Terminates the script.

In the development of the web server application, HTML protocol is used to provide static web pages to the client. The concrete steps are:

(i) Users, in the client browser, make a request to the web server.
(ii) The web server makes a judgment on the request.
(iii) The web server transfers the file directly to the client browser.
(iv) The header part contains the title of the website and several links to view other pages.
(v) The body contains the linked pages.

In Figure 7.14 the web page is shown. It is possible to remotely monitor the instantaneous power consumption of a specific load, as shown in Figure 7.15.

7.4.4.3 *Cyber-security*

Security becomes a fundamental issue in a smart grid environment. To maintain the steady operation of a smart power grid, the grid must be thoroughly monitored by widespread use of sensors and measurement devices [27, 28]. In addition, the heavy reliance on ICT, not only to monitor, but also to control the power grid, determines the risk of exposure to cyber attacks, which can determine direct

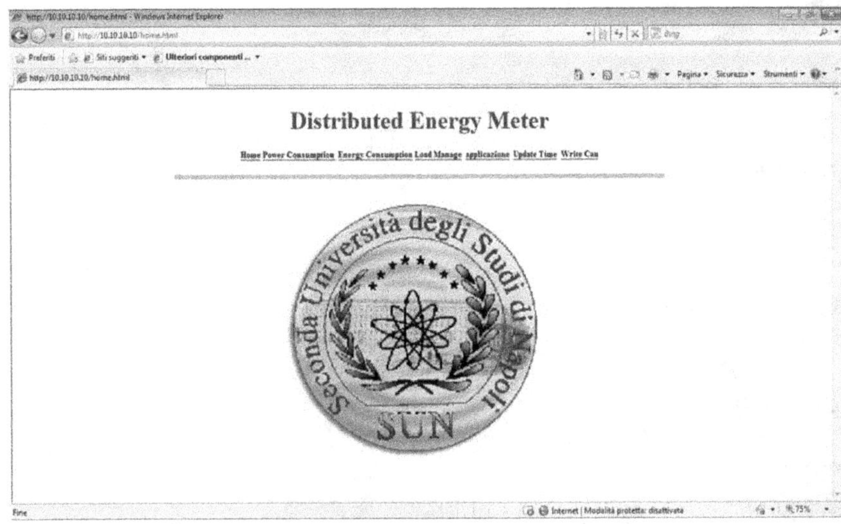

Figure 7.14. The web page.

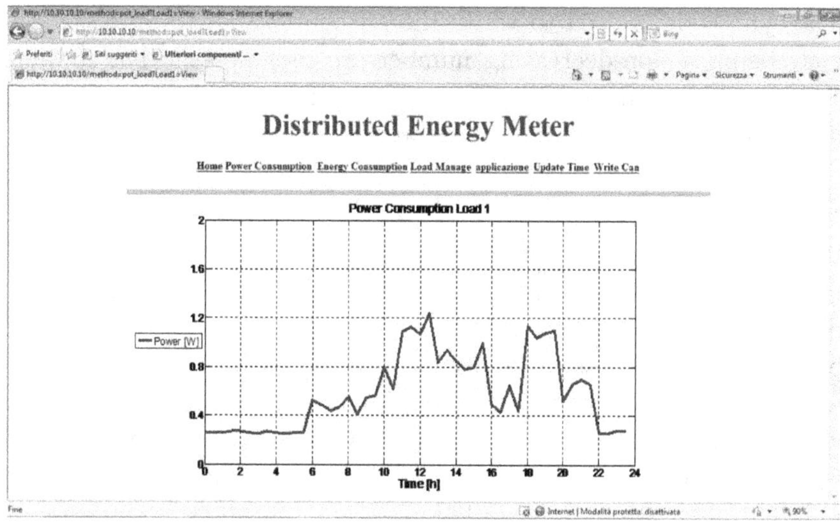

Figure 7.15. Power graph of a specific load.

effects on the electrical grid. It can create several problems, such as: billing frauds; theft of personal data; and connection/disconnection of loads and sources, with risks for power system stability and safety. For these reasons, it becomes fundamental to develop system control algorithms to improve cybersecurity of the communication network. Here is presented an algorithm, applicable to the proposed metering infrastructure, which does not use any encryption system. The idea is to use a MAC (message authentication code) to check the message and the authenticity of the sender. The steps for the message authentication are:

- The sender adds a sync code, a non-decreasing number, and a secret key, shared with the receiver, to the original message.
- The MAC is calculated with a hash function that the sender replaces with the secret key.
- The receiver, using the secret key shared with the sender, computes the MAC. If the computed MAC and the reference one are the same, the message is considered true.
- If the receiver notes that the two MACs are the same, it states that the message is the original one.

The sync code is used to verify the authenticity of the message; in fact, being a non-decreasing number, an old message has a value that should be smaller than that of a new message. If the values are different, it is assumed that there were not any external attacks.

7.4.4.4 *Load management strategy*

In general, demand response techniques can help to reduce the need for new power plants by displacing some loads from peak hours. In the described system, a strategy for automatic load management based on a user-defined cost threshold has been implemented. Considering a number of users N, each of them having M different branches to which loads are connected, the total absorbed power at the instant t is given by the sum of the power for all the branches:

$$P_{TOT}(t) = \sum_{i=1}^{N} \sum_{j=1}^{M} P_{ij}(t). \tag{7.23}$$

Assuming that each branch is equipped with a switch that can turn off the associated branch or can power it up again, and that the state of the branch is represented by the binary variable σ_{ij} ($\sigma_{ij} = 1$ if the branch ij is powered up and $\sigma_{ij} = 0$ if the corresponding switch is open), then equation (7.23) becomes:

$$P_{TOT}(t) = \sum_{i=1}^{N} \sum_{j=1}^{M} \sigma_{ij} P_{ij}(t). \tag{7.24}$$

As said before, the goal of the system is to implement automatic load management. Introducing a power threshold Λ, the problem configures as a non-linear optimization

$$\min[\aleph(\boldsymbol{\sigma}, t)], \tag{7.25}$$

where the cost function is

$$\aleph(\boldsymbol{\sigma}, t) = \Lambda - P_{TOT}(t) = \Lambda - \sum_{i=1}^{N} \sum_{j=1}^{M} \sigma_{ij} P_{ij}(t) \tag{7.26}$$

and $\boldsymbol{\sigma}$ represents the matrix containing the binary of the different branches, which represent the decision variables. If the absorbed power tends to be greater than the threshold, one or more branches will be disconnected (the corresponding decision variable is set to 0); similarly, when the threshold increases, more branches can be powered up again, until $\aleph$ is minimized. The optimization configures as a constrained problem; in fact, because Λ is the power value not to be overcome, it must be guaranteed that

$$\aleph(\boldsymbol{\sigma}, t) \geq 0. \tag{7.27}$$

Additional constraints may be determined by assigning a priority to each circuit branch (see Figure 7.16); naming λ_{ij} the priority level of the ij^{th} branch, it can be imposed that, while managing the load disconnecting or reconnecting branches, this is done according to the order defined by the set priorities. Therefore, the constraint may be formalized as

$$\sigma_{ij} \leq \sigma_{lk} \quad \text{if } \lambda_{ij} \leq \lambda_{lk}. \tag{7.28}$$

Naturally, it might be the case that two different branches have the same priority level; in this case the adopted policy is to disconnect first the loads that are absorbing more power. In a similar manner, while powering back up the loads, in the case of equal priority, precedence is given to the ones which were absorbing less power prior to the disconnection. This strategy allows to serve the largest possible number of loads, rather than supplying fewer loads but with higher absorptions. This policy, briefly summarized in the block diagram

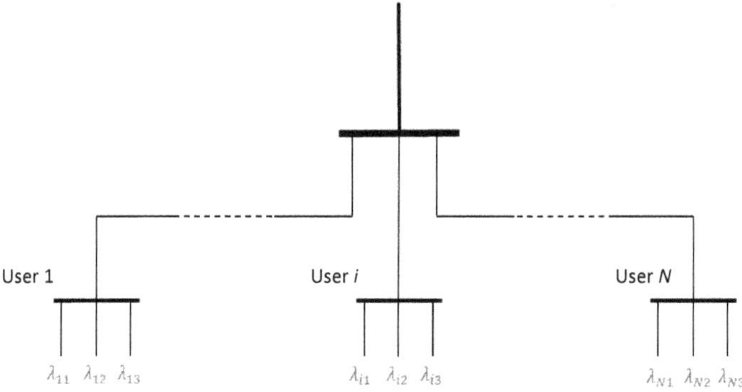

Figure 7.16. Considered electrical branches.

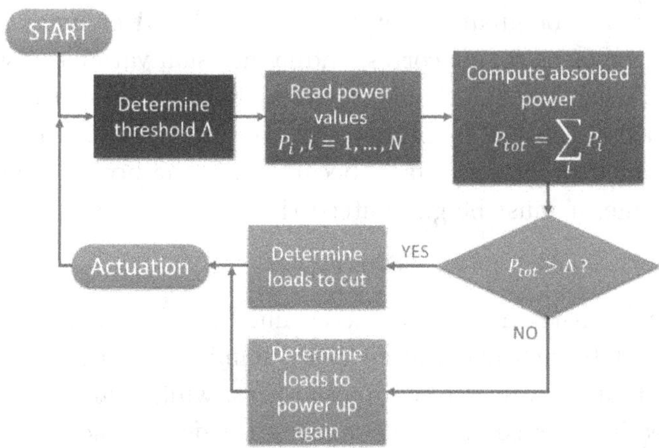

Figure 7.17. Block scheme of the load management algorithm.

in Figure 7.17, may obviously be easily changed, to adapt the load management system to the specific context of the application.

An additional note regarding how to set the priorities: they are user-defined, and can be static or the user can set a rule according to which the same branch assumes a different priority level over time. For example, a rule can be set so as to keep the priority level of the branch feeding the air conditioning system high during the period of the day the user is in the building, and lower it otherwise.

Finally, the system may easily include the availability of locally produced electricity. Its effect can be seen as a positive contribution to the power threshold level or, equally, as a lowering of the power demand the grid has to supply. In this case the cost function introduced in equation (7.26) becomes

$$\aleph(\boldsymbol{\sigma}, t) = \Lambda - P_{TOT}(t) = \Lambda - \sum_{i=1}^{N} \sum_{j=1}^{M} \sigma_{ij} P_{ij}(t) + \sum_{h=1}^{Ngen} P_h(t), \tag{7.29}$$

with $Ngen$ the number of local power sources.

7.4.4.5 *Load curtailments threshold setup*

The power threshold Λ is determined dynamically according to the cost of energy. Setting Λ_{min} as a minimum level of power that must

Table 7.2. Prices of electricity.

Class	Description	Price €/MWh
F1	Peak	93.23
F2	Mid-level	88.97
F3	Off-peak	65.47

be supplied, Λ is determined as

$$\Lambda = MAX[\Lambda(C(t), \Lambda_{min}], \tag{7.30}$$

where $C(t)$ represents the cost of electricity provided by the GME (the Italian electricity market operator).

For the prototype system the threshold has been calculated considering a tariff plan with different prices of electricity for peak, mid-level, and off-peak hours. The average prices for December 2011 are reported as an example in Table 7.2.

The user or the energy manager can set a power threshold setting a limit for the cost of electricity considering as reference the class F2. Then, the system adjusts the so determined power level according to the prices of energy, raising it during off-peak hours and lowering during peak hours, by weighting the power level with the price of energy in the current class versus the reference one.

7.4.5 *Characterization of the smart meter and of the metering infrastructure*

The realized smart meter network has been characterized in terms of measurement accuracy and communication performance. Characterization results are reported in the following subsections.

7.4.5.1 *Issues related to the characterization of smart meters*

The presence of non-linear and time-variant loads in the network causes the distortion of voltages and currents. The main problems related to these disturbances stem from the flow of non-active energy caused not only by non-sinusoidal currents and voltages but also by the energy dissipated in the neutral path due to the zero-sequence current components, which has economic significance. These flows consume energy and someone has to pay for it, so the utility companies are vitally concerned with energy loss in the network because generators cover this loss, and the distributing company has to pay for it at the high-voltage revenue metering points. In a certain way, they should make the polluting customers pay an adequate penalty; otherwise, these costs are charged on all the actors of the energy market. Penalties are applied for absorptions with a low-power factor that are verified through reactive-energy metering.

This gives great importance to both active- and reactive-energy metering in non-sinusoidal conditions. The IEC standard [29] for characterization of the accuracy of static active meters takes as reference sinusoidal conditions, and some power quality phenomena are only accounted as influence quantities that change the accuracy of meters. The IEC standard for characterization of the accuracy of static reactive meters applies for sinusoidal currents and voltages containing the fundamental frequency only [30]; no reference is made to what should be measured in situations with harmonic distortion.

In this way, commercial instruments, built according to the IEC approach, are designed and tested mainly for sinusoidal waveforms, and, at most, additional tests are performed in specific non-sinusoidal conditions but accounting for larger accuracy tolerance. Moreover, since there is no clear reference as to which algorithm should be used for digital metering, different manufacturers adopt different implementations, which are equivalent in sinusoidal conditions, but provide very different results when utilized with distorted current and voltage waveforms.

In order to fully define the product energy in generation, transmission, and distribution stages and to economically regulate how energy is sold by electrical utilities and bought by final users, proper metering in non-sinusoidal conditions is required.

Starting from all these considerations, from a metrological point of view, the verification of energy meters becomes a strong need but, at the same time, a very complex task. In fact, a full analysis of all the influence parameters that lead to non-sinusoidal conditions, and all their combinations, requires a huge number of tests. Here, the results

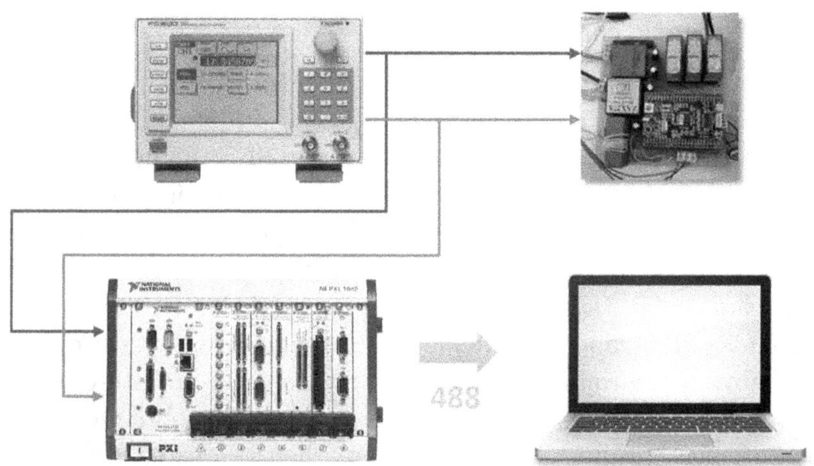

Figure 7.18. Experimental set-up for static characterization.

of the characterization of the implemented smart meter in static and dynamic conditions are presented; to provide the test signal for non-sinusoidal conditions, sinusoidal waveforms were artificially distorted.

7.4.5.2 *Characterization of measurement accuracy*

In order to prove the reliability of the implemented instrument, a thorough characterization, in static and dynamic conditions, has been performed [25, 31]. To this end, the following instruments, shown in Figure 7.18, were used:

- Function Generator Yokogawa FG320 (Features: dual channel output; frequencies range from 1 μHz to 15 MHz; amplitude range $\pm$10 V; AC Amplitude accuracy $\pm$ (0.8% of setting +14 mV); DC (direct current) output accuracy $\pm$ (0.3% of setting +20 mV).
- PXI 1042 chassis with a PXI-DAQ 6123 (Features: 16-Bit; 500 kHz/ch; simultaneous sampling).
- Pacific Power Source 3120 AMX (Features: maximum power of 12 kVA; frequency range of 20 Hz to 50 kHz; line regulation of 0.027 mV; load regulation of 0.00135 mV; THD of 0.1%; voltage ripple and noise of $-$70 dB).

7.4.5.2.1 Static characterization

For static characterization, only the behavior of the A/D conversion systems of the microcontroller is taken into account. The tests are executed according to the set-up reported in Figure 7.18. The adopted function generator has two independent output channels that can be separately configured with proper values of amplitude and phase. These signals are acquired at the same time by the two A/D channels of the microcontroller and by the A/D channels of a PXI-DAQ 6123 adopted as reference. Through software developed in the Labview environment, it is possible to monitor and store continuously the values supplied by the generator and to obtain expected measurement results. These values are then compared with those shown on the display of the power meter. In the first set of tests a DC voltage is generated at different levels, with steps of 10% of the full scale range. Each test is repeated ten times. A systematic deviation is found for each input level with a value that is within the range 0.1%–0.8 %. Starting from the obtained results it is possible to evaluate, recurring to the least squares method, gain and offset correction parameters for each input channel. After the compensation the mean error is lower than 0.05% and the standard deviation is lower than 0.03%.

7.4.5.2.2 Dynamic characterization

For dynamic characterization, the signals provided by the function generator are amplified by the power amplifier, the Pacific Source 3120 AMX, and the PXI measurement system is again adopted as the reference value; a simplified scheme of the testing station is shown in Figure 7.19. The test sets are chosen according to considerations reported in [25, 31]. The tests were performed in sinusoidal and non-sinusoidal conditions. In sinusoidal conditions the effects of frequency deviation and phase angle variation on active and reactive power were evaluated. The sinusoidal tests have been performed varying input parameters around rated values: frequency (50 Hz ± 15%); input voltage amplitude (50% to 100%); input current amplitude (0% to 100%); and finally the phase displacement between $-\pi/4$ and

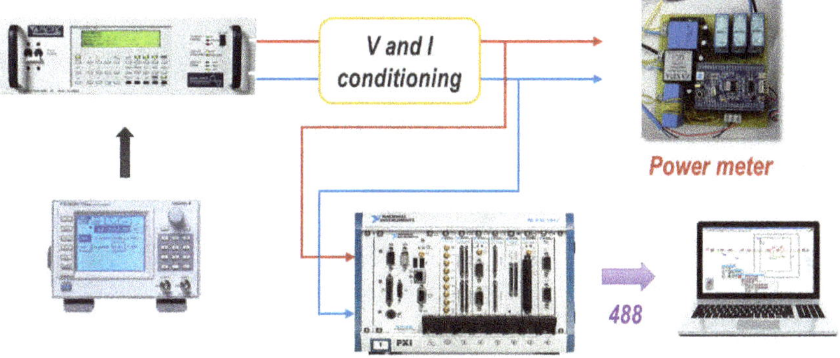

Figure 7.19. Experimental set-up for dynamic characterization.

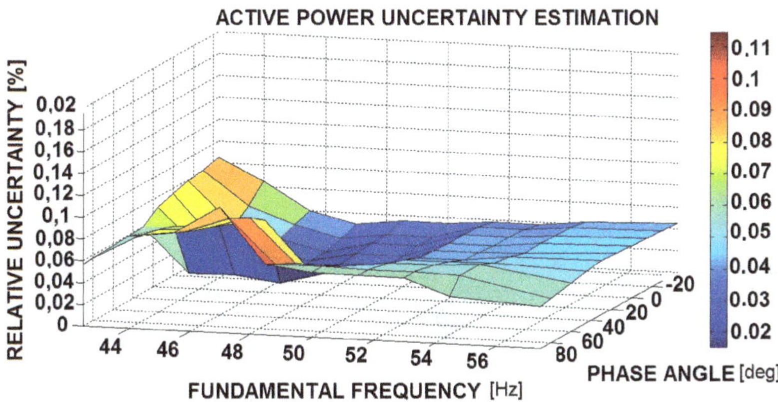

Figure 7.20. Active power uncertainty estimation vs. phase angle and fundamental frequency.

$\pi/2$. In Figures 7.20 and 7.21 the percentage relative uncertainties for active and reactive powers in sinusoidal conditions are reported.

In non-sinusoidal conditions, the effects of the fundamental phase angle and the harmonic order variation on active and non-active power are evaluated. For the non-sinusoidal tests, according to [32], a fixed THD of 8% is adopted. For each test, five harmonic components spanning between the 3rd and the 39th harmonic order are superimposed to the fundamental tone, with fixed THD. The testing procedures is better detailed in [25, 31, 33, 34]. In Figures 7.22

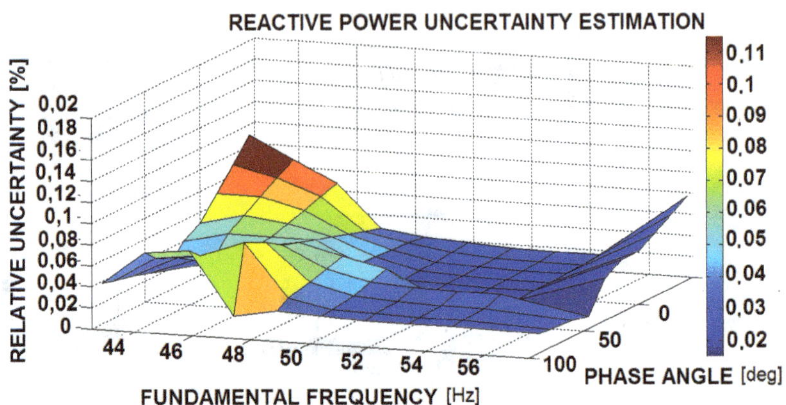

Figure 7.21. Reactive power uncertainty estimation vs. phase angle and fundamental frequency.

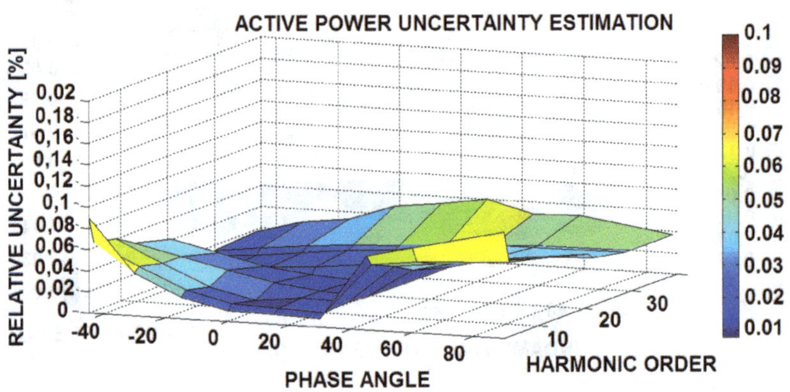

Figure 7.22. Active power uncertainty estimation vs. harmonic order and phase angle.

and 7.23 the percentage relative uncertainties for active and non-active power in non-sinusoidal conditions are reported.

7.4.5.3 *Case study for load management*

To test the load management algorithm we set up a test case and simulated it in the MATLAB environment. Considering the case of ten different users, a total power demand profile can be obtained from their individual consumptions. Each user accounts for three different

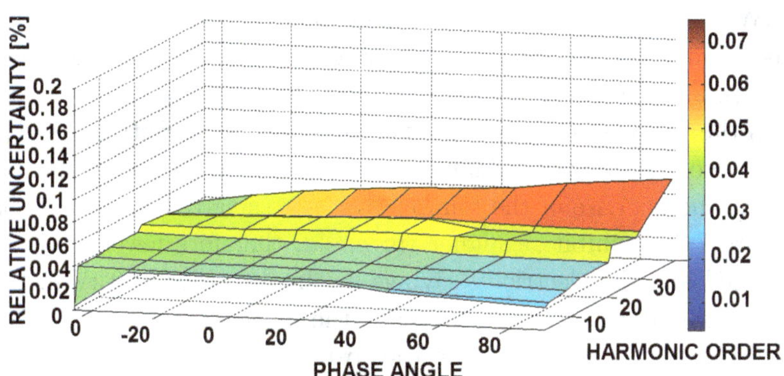

Figure 7.23. Non-active power uncertainty estimation vs. harmonic order and fundamental frequency.

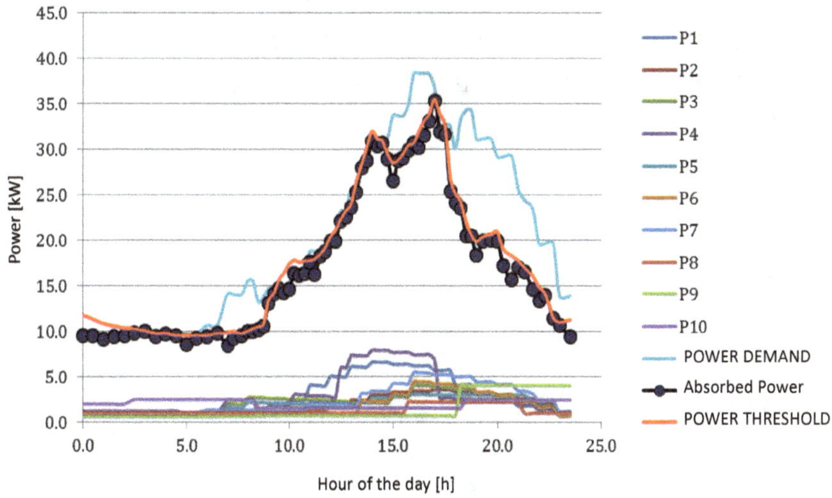

Figure 7.24. Simulation example of the load management algorithm.

branches, each one with its own priority level. Figure 7.24 shows the load curves, together with the graph of the threshold defined for the system. As can be seen, the algorithm successfully manages to contain power absorption below the threshold level. In this case, the load management algorithm allows for energy savings of around 80 kWh, with respect to the original demand. Naturally the threshold may be modified for higher or lower electricity (and therefore cost) savings, as underlined in the following two examples.

In the first case (Figure 7.25) the amount of electricity saved with respect to the original demand reaches 170 kWh, doubling the savings at the expense of the number of loads served. The second case (Figure 7.26) exhibits a higher threshold, therefore fewer loads are curtailed and the electricity savings are in the order of 9 kWh. It is worth remembering that, in this case, the choice of the threshold falls upon the user, who can decide the costs he wants to incur for electricity and rest assured that he will not to go beyond that amount. This strategy, however simple, has proven the physical feasibility and functionality of the prototype AMI architecture. Naturally, for a full realization of a demand response program, the threshold may be determined through a negotiation between users and the market. Moreover, the availability of reserve capacity to the grid system operator may be warranted by opportunely modifying the threshold. In any case, once the value of Λ has been determined, proper action

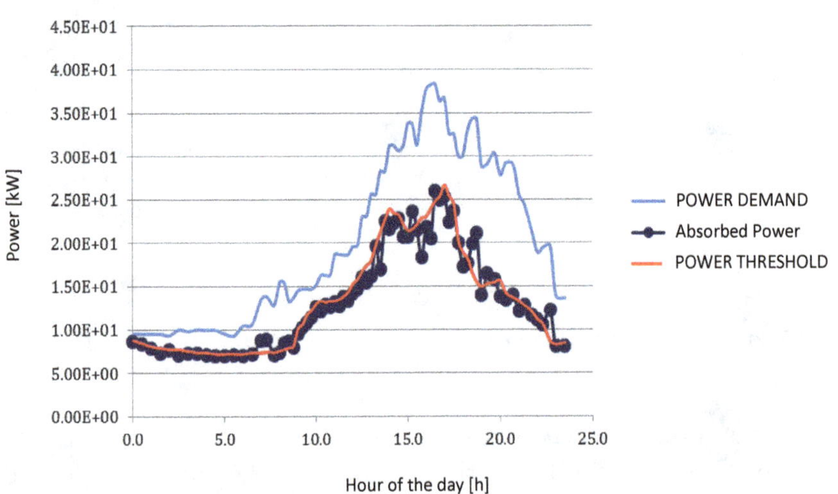

Figure 7.25. Case with lower savings.

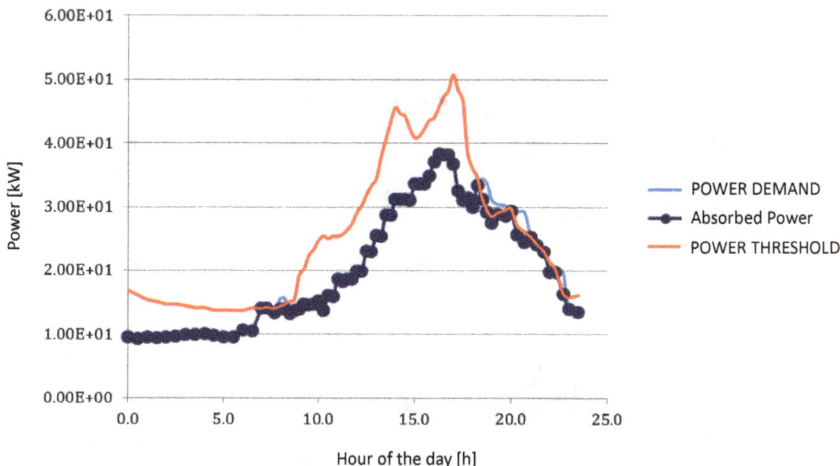

Figure 7.26. Case with higher savings.

will be undertaken to reduce the absorbed power below this amount. The algorithm is implemented on the master data aggregator, which after finding the optimal solution sends the commands to the smart meter that realizes the load curtailments through its actuators.

7.4.5.4 *Network communication characterization*

Distributed energy meters transfer measurement results to the data aggregator through CAN protocol. In Figure 7.27 an example with two slave microcontrollers that communicate with a data aggregator is reported. They continuously acquire voltage and current and calculate several parameters, which are shown on the display.

Several tests have been performed to evaluate the transmission time. The time measurements required for these tests are performed through a Tektronix TDS3012B oscilloscope. In order to check the time latency, an output bit of the DAC is used to generate a square wave as a signal to acknowledge the microcontroller operation. A first test is made to calculate the delay between the instant when the master microcontroller sends the request and the instant when a slave detects an interrupt for the reception of the request. The estimated time is approximately 3.6 ms (Figure 7.28 (a)). In the second test, the

Figure 7.27. Example of device connection for data transmission.

data aggregator requires data related to the active power from both slaves with two different priority levels. It receives the data from the slave with the highest priority after approximately 25 ms (Figure 7.28 (b)) and the data from the lower priority slave after approximately 60 ms (Figure 7.28 (c)). A complete analysis of the utilized protocol, in terms of communication capabilities depending on the number of units in the network and the units' throughput, has been performed in [7]. Regarding the throughput, it is shown that it slightly increases when the number of devices increases from 5 to 20; when the number of devices is higher than 20 the throughput remains constant. Furthermore, in [35] a correlation is reported between number of devices, latency time, throughput, and payload, i.e. the length of the message. In particular, it is observed that the latency time remains practically constant with a payload equal to 8 bytes, i.e. the length used in the smart meter network and the number of devices.

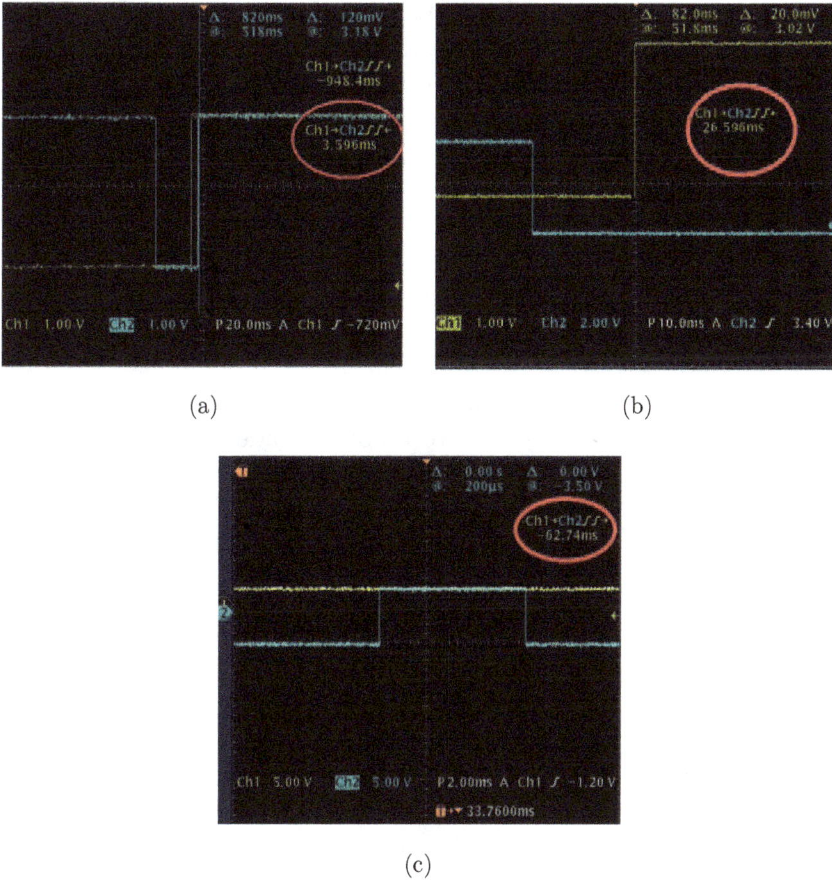

(a) (b)

(c)

Figure 7.28. Time latency results in the first (a) and second (b and c) test.

7.5 Final Remarks

The measurement and communication infrastructure represents a key enabler for the realization of the advanced applications encompassed by the concept of smart grid. The main node of this infrastructure is the smart meter, which constitutes not only a device to monitor the power grid, but also the interface that connects active users to all network stakeholders. In this chapter, we provided an introduction to smart metering, with the main related measurement issues and meter requirements. The main research developments and industrial products were examined. Furthermore, the realization and metrological characterization of a custom smart meter implementation and the related AMI with support for demand response programs were described in detail.

Still, the realization of a fully smart and adaptable grid requires that a number of technical challenges be addressed:

- Decision tools for operators are needed to increase visibility and situational awareness, enable planning and forecasting, and provide logic for decision making.
- Communications infrastructure today is inadequate and must be improved to enable interconnections among various components and systems, public networks, and devices, as well as operations and planning functions.
- Adequate metrics are needed, to understand, manage, and control performance, flexibility, and a host of other elements better.
- Today data management and analytics are not sufficient for effectively collecting, storing, and interpreting the massive amounts of data that can potentially be collected.
- Robust operational and business models are needed to enable effective operations and planning and to incorporate diverse generation sources, storage options, and models for flexibility.

References

[1] Hierzinger, R., Albu, M., van Elburg, H. *et al.* (2013). "European Smart Metering: Landscape Report 2012 — update 2013", presented at Intelligent Energy Europe, Vienna, Austria, 2013.

[2] Giordano, V., Meletiou, A., Covrig, C.F. *et al.* (2013). *Smart Grids Projects in Europe: Lessons Learned and Current Developments*, Luxembourg Publications Office of the European Union, Luxembourg.

[3] Pike Research (2011). "Smart Grids in Europe", Pike Research Cleantech Market Intelligence. Available at: http://www.pikeresearch.com/research/smart-grids-in-europe. Accessed February 2011.

[4] Ehanakaye, J., Liyanage, K., Wu, J. *et al.* (2012). *Smart Grid: Technology and Applications*, Wiley Publications, Hoboken, NJ.

[5] OpenMeter Deliverable D1.1 (2010), "Report on the Identification and Specification of Functional, Technical, Economical and General Requirements of Advanced Multi-Metering Infrastructure, Including Security Requirements", OPENMeter, Energy Project No 226369. Funded by EC. Available at: http://www.openmeter.com/files/deliverables/Open%20Meter_D3%201_Architecture_v6_.pdf. Accessed March 2011.

[6] OpenMeter Deliverable D3.1 (2010), "Design of the Overall System Architecture", OPENmeter, Energy Project No 226369. Funded by EC. Available at: http://www.openmeter.com/files/deliverables/Open%20Meter_D3%201_Architecture_v6_.pdf. Accessed April 2011.

[7] Arcauz, N., Goñi, A., Adriansen, M. *et al.* (2012). "Open Meter Overview Of The Market For Smart Metering", open metering deliverables public report 31/1/2012. Available at: http://www.openmeter.com. Accessed January 2012.

[8] Meter ON project. Available at: www.meter-on.eu. Accessed August 2014.

[9] Bollen, M. and Gu, I. (2006). *Signal Processing of Power Quality Disturbances*, IEEE Press, Hoboken, NJ.

[10] IEEE (2010). "IEEE Standard Definitions for the Measurement of Electric Power Quantities Under Sinusoidal, Nonsinusoidal, Balanced, or Unbalanced Conditions", IEEE Std 1459-2010 (Revision of IEEE Std 1459-2000), doi: 10.1109/IEEESTD.2010.5439063.

[11] Echelon (2014). Products Available at: https://www.echelon.com/products/smart-meters/. Accessed September 2014.

[12] GE Digital Energy (2014). Grid IQ AMI P2MP. Available at: http://www.gedigitalenergy.com/smartmetering/catalog/p2mp.htm. Accessed September 2014.

[13] Texas Instruments (2014). Smart E-Meter: AMR/AMI. Available at: http://www.ti.com/solution/docs/appsolution.tsp?appId=407. Accessed September 2014.

[14] Accent (2014). Smart Metering. Available at: http://www.accent-soc.com/applications/smart_metering.php. Accessed August 2014.

[15] Di Leo, G., Landi, M., Paciello, V. *et al.* (2012). Smart metering for demand side management, *Proc. 2012 IEEE International Instrumentation and Measurement Technology Conference Proceedings*, 1798–1803.

[16] Del Prete, G., and Landi, C. (2011). "Energy saving smart meter using low-cost arm processor", presented at 18th IMEKO TC4 Symp. Meas. of Elec. Quantities, Natal, Brazil, 27–30 September 2011.

[17] Landi, C., Del Prete, G. and Gallo, D. (2012). "Real-time smart meters network for energy management", presented at XX IMEKO World Congress, Busan, Republic of Korea, 9–12 September 2012.

[18] Serra, H., Correira, J., Gano, A.J. *et al.* (2005). Domestic power consumption measurement and automatic home appliance detection, *IEEE International Workshop on Intelligent Signal Processing*, 128–132.

[19] Delle Femine, A., Gallo, D., Landi, C. *et al.* (2007). "Broadband voltage transducer with optically insulated output for power quality analyses", presented at IEEE Instr. and Meas. Tech. Conf. IMTC 2007, Warsaw, Poland, 1–3 May 2007.

[20] Gallo, D., Landi, C., Luiso, M. *et al.* (2013). Realization and characterization of an electronic instrument transducer for MV networks with fiber optic insulation, *WSEAS Trans. Pow. Syst.*, **8(1)**, 45–56.

[21] Gallo, D., Landi, C. and Rignano, N. (2006). "Multifunction DSP based real-time power quality analyzer", presented at XVIII IMEKO World Congress, Rio de Janeiro, Brazil, 17–22 September 2006.

[22] Moraes, F., Amory, A., Calazans, N. *et al.* (2001). "Using the CAN protocol and reconfigurable computing technology for web-based smart house automation", presented at 14th Symp. on Integrated Circuits and Systems Design, Pirenopolis, Brazil, 10–15 September 2001.

[23] ISO 11898-1:2003, Road vehicles — Controller area network (CAN) — Part 1: Data link layer and physical signalling.

[24] ST (2014). STM32F107VCT6 datasheet. Available at: http://www.st.com/st-web-ui/static/active/en/resource/technical/document/datasheet/CD00220364.pdf. Accessed September 2014.

[25] Gallo, D., Ianniello, G., Landi, C. *et al.* (2010). An advanced energy/power meter based on ARM microcontroller for smart grid applications, *17th Symp. IMEKO TC4, 3rd Symp. IMEKO TC19 and 15th IWADC*, Kosice, Slovakia, 8–10 September 2010.

[26] Ciancetta, F., Fiorucci, E., D'Apice, B. *et al.* (2007). A peer-to-peer distributed system for multipoint measurement techniques, *IEEE Instr. and Meas. Tech. Conf. IMTC 2007*, Warsaw, Poland, 1–3 May 2007.

[27] IEEE (2009). "IEEE Recommended Practice for Monitoring Electric Power Quality", IEEE Std 1159-2009 (Revision of IEEE Std 1159-1995), 2009, c1–81.

[28] Delle Femine, A., Gallo, D., Landi, C. *et al.* (2009). Power quality monitoring instrument with FPGA transducer compensation, *IEEE T. Instrum. Meas.*, **58(9)**, 3149–3158.

[29] IEC EN 62053-21 — Electricity metering equipment (a.c.) — Particular requirements Part 21: Static meters for active energy (classes 1 and 2). 2003-11.

[30] IEC EN 62053-23 — Electricity metering equipment (a.c.) — Particular requirements Part 23: Static meters for reactive energy (classes 2 and 3). 2003-11

[31] Delle Femine, A., Gallo, D., Landi, C. *et al.* (2009). Advanced instrument for field calibration of electrical energy meters, *IEEE T. Instrum. Meas.*, **58(3)**, 618–625.

[32] IEC EN 50160, Voltage characteristics of electricity supplied by public distribution systems, CENELEC, 1999.

[33] Del Prete, G., Gallo, D., Landi, C. *et al.* (2012). "The use of real-time instruments for smart power systems," presented at IEEE International Energy Conference and Exhibition, Florence, Italy, 9–12 September 2012.

[34] IEC Standard EN 61000-4-7, Testing and measurement techniques — General guide on harmonics and interharmonics measurements and instrumentation, for power supply systems and equipment connected thereto, 2003.
[35] Dridi, S., Gouissem, B., Hasnaoui, S. *et al.* (2006). "Coupling latency time to the throughput performance analysis on wireless CAN networks", presented at 2006 International Multi-Conference on Computing in the Global Information Technology.
[36] Flick, T., and Morehouse, J. (2011). *Securing the Smart Grid: Next Generation Power Grid Security*, Elsevier Inc., Burlington, MA.
[37] IEC EN 61000-4-30: Testing and measuremnent techniques — Power quality measurement methods.

Index

www.ingramcontent.com/pod-product-compliance
Lightning Source LLC
Chambersburg PA
CBHW050552190326
41458CB00007B/2007

* 9 7 8 1 7 8 3 2 6 5 8 7 9 *